Jesus, Interrupted

Also by Bart D. Ehrman

*God's Problem: How the Bible Fails to Answer Our
Most Important Question—Why We Suffer*

Misquoting Jesus: The Story Behind Who Changed the Bible and Why

The Lost Gospel of Judas Iscariot: Betrayer and Betrayed Reconsidered

Studies in the Textual Criticism of the New Testament

*Peter, Paul, and Mary Magdalene:
The Followers of Jesus in History and Legend*

*Truth and Fiction in the DaVinci Code: A Historian Reveals
What We Can Really Know about Jesus, Mary, and Constantine*

A Brief Introduction to the New Testament

Lost Christianities: The Battle for Scripture and the Faiths We Never Knew

Lost Scriptures: Books That Did Not Become the New Testament

The Apostolic Fathers

Jesus: Apocalyptic Prophet of the New Millennium

After the New Testament: A Reader in Early Christianity

The New Testament and Other Early Christian Writings: A Reader

The New Testament: A Historical Introduction to the Early Christian Writings

*The Orthodox Corruption of Scripture: The Effect of
Early Christological Controversies on the Text of the New Testament*

Didymus the Blind and the Text of the Gospels

Jesus, Interrupted

Revealing the

Hidden Contradictions in the Bible

(and Why We Don't Know About Them)

Bart D. Ehrman

HarperOne

An Imprint of HarperCollinsPublishers

HarperOne

HarperCollins Web site: http://www.harpercollins.com
HarperCollins®, 📖®, and HarperOne™ are
trademarks of HarperCollins Publishers

FIRST HARPERCOLLINS PAPERBACK EDITION PUBLISHED IN 2010
Designed by Level C

Library of Congress Cataloging-in-Publication Data
Ehrman, Bart D.
Jesus, interrupted : revealing the hidden contradictions in the Bible
(and why we don't know about them) / Bart D. Ehrman. — 1st ed.
p. cm.
ISBN 978-0-06-117394-3
1. Bible—Criticism, interpretation, etc.
2. Jesus Christ—Historicity. 3. Bible—Controversial literature.
4. Christianity—Controversial literature. I. Title.
BS533.E47   2009
220.6—dc22   2008051961

23 24 25 26 27 LBC 22 21 20 19 18

To Aiya, granddaughter extraordinaire

Contents

Preface

Iarrived at Princeton Theological Seminary in August 1978, fresh out of college and recently married. I had a well-thumbed Greek New Testament, a passion for knowledge, and not much else. I had not always been passionate about learning. No one who knew me five or six years earlier would ever have predicted that I'd be headed for a career in academia. But I had been bitten by the academic bug somewhere along the way in college. I suppose it was first at the Moody Bible Institute, in Chicago, a fundamentalist Bible college I started attending at the ripe young age of seventeen. There my academic drive was fueled not by intellectual curiosity so much as by a religious desire for certainty.

Studying at Moody was an intense experience for me. I had gone there because I had had a "born-again" experience in high school and decided that to be a "serious" Christian I would need serious training in the Bible. And somehow, during my first semester in college, something happened to me: I became passionate—fierce, even—in my quest for knowledge about the Bible. At Moody not only did I take every Bible and theology course that I could, but on my own I also memorized entire books of the Bible by rote. I studied during every free moment. I read books and mastered lecture notes. Just about every week I pulled an all-nighter, preparing for classes.

Three years of that will change a person's life. It will certainly toughen up one's mind. When I graduated from Moody I headed off to Wheaton College to get a degree in English literature, but I kept up my intense focus on the Bible, taking interpretation courses and teaching the Bible every week to kids in my youth group at church. And I learned Greek so that I could study the New Testament in its original language.

As a committed Bible-believing Christian I was certain that the Bible, down to its very words, had been inspired by God. Maybe that's what drove my intense study. These were God's words, the communications of the Creator of the universe and Lord of all, spoken to us, mere mortals. Surely knowing them intimately was the most important thing in life. At least it was for me. Understanding literature more broadly would help me understand this piece of literature in particular (hence my major in English literature); being able to read it in Greek helped me know the actual words given by the Author of the text.

I had decided already in the course of my freshman year at Moody that I wanted to become a professor of the Bible. Then, at Wheaton, I realized that I was pretty good at Greek. And so my next step was virtually chosen for me: I would do a doctorate in New Testament studies, and work especially on some aspect of the Greek language. My beloved professor of Greek at Wheaton, Gerald Hawthorne, introduced me to the work of Bruce Metzger, the most revered scholar of Greek biblical manuscripts in the country, who happened to teach at Princeton Theological Seminary. And so I applied to Princeton, knowing nothing—absolutely nothing—about it, except that Bruce Metzger taught there and that if I wanted to become an expert in Greek manuscripts, Princeton was where I needed to go.

I guess I did know *one* thing about Princeton Seminary: it was not an evangelical institution. And the more I learned about it in the months leading up to my move to New Jersey, the more nervous I became. I learned from friends that Princeton was a "liberal" seminary where they did not hold to the literal truth and verbal inspiration of the Bible. My biggest challenge would not be purely academic, doing well enough in my master's-level classes to earn the right to go on to do a Ph.D. It would be holding on to my faith in the Bible as the inspired and inerrant Word of God.

And so I came to Princeton Theological Seminary young and poor but passionate, and armed to take on all those liberals with their watered-down view of the Bible. As a good evangelical Christian I was ready to fend off any attacks on my biblical faith. I could answer any apparent contradiction and resolve any potential discrepancy in the Word of God, whether in the Old or New Testament. I knew I had a lot to learn, but I was not *about* to learn that my sacred text had any mistakes in it.

Some things don't go as planned. What I actually did learn at Princeton led me to change my mind about the Bible. I did not change my mind willingly—I went down kicking and screaming. I prayed (lots) about it, I wrestled (strenuously) with it, I resisted it with all my might. But at the same time I thought that if I was truly committed to God, I also had to be fully committed to the truth. And it became clear to me over a long period of time that my former views of the Bible as the inerrant revelation from God were flat-out wrong. My choice was either to hold on to views that I had come to realize were in error or to follow where I believed the truth was leading me. In the end, it was no choice. If something was true, it was true; if not, not.

I've known people over the years who have said, "If my beliefs are at odds with the facts, so much the worse for the facts." I've never been one of these people. In the chapters that follow I try to explain why scholarship on the Bible forced me to change my views.

This kind of information is relevant not only to scholars like me, who devote their lives to serious research, but also to everyone who is interested in the Bible—whether they personally consider themselves believers or not. In my opinion this really matters. Whether you are a believer—fundamentalist, evangelical, moderate, liberal—or a nonbeliever, the Bible is the most significant book in the history of our civilization. Coming to understand what it actually is, and is not, is one of the most important intellectual endeavors that anyone in our society can embark upon.

Some people reading this book may be very uncomfortable with the information it presents. All I ask is that, if you're in that boat, you do what I did—approach this information with an open mind and be willing to change if change you must. If, on the other hand, you find nothing shocking or disturbing in the book, all I ask is that you sit back and enjoy.

I owe a mountain of gratitude to a number of careful and insightful readers who have plowed through my manuscript and vigorously insisted—not in vain, I hope—that I change it in places to make it better: Dale Martin of Yale University and Jeff Siker of Loyola Marymount University; my daughter, Kelly Ehrman Katz; my graduate students Jared Anderson and Benjamin White. A special thanks to all those at HarperOne for their hard work: Mark Tauber, Mickey Maudlin, Terri Leonard, Suzanne Stradley, Jan Baumer, Jim Warner, Suzanne Wickham, Julie Burton, Laina Adler, Abby Berendt, and especially to Claudia Boutote, for her unwavering support, and Roger Freet, my very sharp and helpful editor.

Translations of the Hebrew Bible (Old Testament) are taken from the New Revised Standard Version; those of the New Testament are either from the NRSV or are my own; quotations of the Apostolic Fathers are my own.

I have dedicated the book to my two-year-old granddaughter, Aiya—who is perfect in every way.

A Historical Assault on Faith

The Bible is the most widely purchased, extensively read, and deeply revered book in the history of Western Civilization. Arguably it is also the most thoroughly misunderstood, especially by the lay reading public.

Scholars of the Bible have made significant progress in understanding the Bible over the past two hundred years, building on archaeological discoveries, advances in our knowledge of the ancient Hebrew and Greek languages in which the books of Scripture were originally written, and deep and penetrating historical, literary, and textual analyses. This is a massive scholarly endeavor. Thousands of scholars just in North America alone continue to do serious research in the field, and the results of their study are regularly and routinely taught, both to graduate students in universities and to prospective pastors attending seminaries in preparation for the ministry.

Yet such views of the Bible are virtually unknown among the population at large. In no small measure this is because those of us who spend our professional lives studying the Bible have not done a good job communicating this knowledge to the general public and because many pastors who learned this material in seminary have, for a variety of reasons, not shared it with their parishioners once they take up positions in the church. (Churches, of course, are the most obvious place where the Bible is—or, rather, ought to be—taught and

discussed.) As a result, not only are most Americans (increasingly) ignorant of the *contents* of the Bible, but they are also almost completely
in the dark about what scholars have been saying about the Bible for
the past two centuries. This book is meant to help redress that problem. It could be seen as my attempt to let the cat out of the bag.

The perspectives that I present in the following chapters are not
my own idiosyncratic views of the Bible. They are the views that
have held sway for many, many years among the majority of serious
critical scholars teaching in the universities and seminaries of North
America and Europe, even if they have not been effectively com-
municated to the population at large, let alone among people of faith
who revere the Bible and who would be, presumably, the ones most
interested. For all those who aspire to being well educated, knowledgeable, and informed about our civilization's most important book,
that has to change.

A SEMINARIAN'S INTRODUCTION TO THE BIBLE

Most of the people who are trained in Bible scholarship have been
educated in theological institutions. Of course, a wide range of students head off to seminaries every year. Many of them have been
involved with Bible studies through their school years, even dating
back to their childhood Sunday School classes. But they have typically approached the Bible from a devotional point of view, reading it
for what it can tell them about what to believe and how to live their
lives. As a rule, such students have not been interested in or exposed
to what scholars have discovered about the difficulties of the Bible
when it is studied from a more academic, historical perspective.

Other students are serious about doing well academically in
seminary but do not seem to know the Bible very well or to hold
particularly high views of Scripture as the inspired Word of God.
These students are often believers born and raised, who feel called
to ministry—most of them to ministry in the church, but a good
number of them to other kinds of social ministry. For the country's

mainline denominations—Presbyterian, Methodist, Lutheran, Episcopalian, and so on—a good number of these students are already what I would call liberal. They do not believe in the inerrancy of the Bible and are more committed to the church as an institution than to Scripture as a blueprint for what to believe and how to live one's life. And many of them, frankly, don't know very much about the Bible and have only a kind of vague sense of its religious value.

It was not always like this in Protestant seminaries. In earlier decades it could be assumed that a student would arrive at seminary with a vast knowledge of the Bible, and the training for ministry could presuppose that students had at their command the basic contents of both Old and New Testaments. That, sadly, is no longer the case. When I was at Princeton Theological Seminary (a Presbyterian school) in the late 1970s, most of my classmates were required to take remedial work in order to pass an exam that we called the "baby Bible" exam, a test of a student's knowledge about the most basic information about the Bible—What is the "Pentateuch"? In what book is the Sermon on the Mount found? Who is Theophilus?—information that most of us from stronger evangelical backgrounds already had under our belts.

My hunch is that the majority of students coming into their first year of seminary training do not know what to expect from courses on the Bible. These classes are only a small part of the curriculum, of course. There are required courses in church history, systematic theology, Christian education, speech, homiletics (preaching), and church administration. It's a lot to squeeze into three years. But everyone is required to take introductory and advanced courses in biblical studies. Most students expect these courses to be taught from a more or less pious perspective, showing them how, as future pastors, to take the Bible and make it applicable to people's lives in their weekly sermons.

Such students are in for a rude awakening. Mainline Protestant seminaries in this country are notorious for challenging students' cherished beliefs about the Bible—even if these cherished beliefs are simply a warm and fuzzy sense that the Bible is a wonderful guide to faith and practice, to be treated with reverence and piety. These seminaries teach serious, hard-core Bible scholarship. They don't pander to piety. They are taught by scholars who are familiar with what German- and English-speaking scholarship has been saying about the Bible over the past three hundred years. They are keen to make students knowledgeable *about* the Bible, rather than teach what is actually *in* the Bible. Bible classes in seminary are usually taught from a purely academic, historical perspective, unlike anything most first-year students expect and unlike anything they've heard before, at home, at church, or in Sunday School.

The approach taken to the Bible in almost all Protestant (and now Catholic) mainline seminaries is what is called the "historical-critical" method. It is completely different from the "devotional" approach to the Bible one learns in church. The devotional approach to the Bible is concerned about what the Bible has to say—especially what it has to say to me personally or to my society. What does the Bible tell me about God? Christ? The church? My relation to the world? What does it tell me about what to believe? About how to act? About social responsibilities? How can the Bible help make me closer to God? How does it help me to live?

The historical-critical approach has a different set of concerns and therefore poses a different set of questions. At the heart of this approach is the historical question (hence its name) of what the biblical writings meant in their original historical context. Who were the actual authors of the Bible? Is it possible (yes!) that some of the authors of some of the biblical books were not in fact who they claimed, or were claimed, to be—say, that 1 Timothy was not actually written by Paul, or that Genesis was not written by Moses? When did these authors live? What were the circumstances under which they wrote? What issues were they trying to address in their own day? How were they affected by the cultural and historical assumptions of their time? What sources did these authors use? When were these sources produced? Is it possible that the perspectives of these sources differed from one another? Is it possible that the authors who used these sources had different perspectives, both from their sources and from one another? Is it possible that the books of the Bible, based on a variety of sources, have internal contradictions? That there are irreconcilable differences among them? And is it possible that what the books originally meant in their original context is not what they are taken to mean today? That our interpretations of Scripture involve taking its words out of context and thereby distorting its message?

And what if we don't even have the original words? What if, during the centuries in which the Bible—both the Old Testament, in Hebrew, and the New Testament, in Greek—was copied by hand, the words were changed by well-meaning but careless scribes, or by fully alert scribes who wanted to alter the texts in order to make them say what they wanted them to say?

These are among the many, many questions raised by the historical-critical method. No wonder entering seminarians have to prepare for "baby Bible" exams even before they could begin a serious study of the Bible. This kind of study presupposes that you know what you're talking about before you start talking about it.

A very large percentage of seminarians are completely blind-sided by the historical-critical method. They come in with the expectation of learning the pious truths of the Bible so that they can pass them along in their sermons, as their own pastors have done for them. Nothing prepares them for historical criticism. To their surprise they learn, instead of material for sermons, all the results of what historical critics have established on the basis of centuries of research. The Bible is filled with discrepancies, many of them irreconcilable contradictions. Moses did not write the Pentateuch (the first five books of the Old Testament) and Matthew, Mark, Luke, and John did not write the Gospels. There are other books that did not make it into the Bible that at one time or another were considered canonical—other Gospels, for example, allegedly written by Jesus' followers Peter, Thomas, and Mary. The Exodus probably did not happen as described in the Old Testament. The conquest of the

Promised Land is probably based on legend. The Gospels are at odds on numerous points and contain nonhistorical material. It is hard to know whether Moses ever existed and what, exactly, the historical Jesus taught. The historical narratives of the Old Testament are filled with legendary fabrications and the book of Acts in the New Testament contains historically unreliable information about the life and teachings of Paul. Many of the books of the New Testament are pseudonymous—written not by the apostles but by later writers *claiming* to be apostles. The list goes on.

Some students accept these new views from day one. Others—especially among the more conservative students—resist for a long time, secure in their knowledge that God would not allow any falsehoods into his sacred book. But before long, as students see more and more of the evidence, many of them find that their faith in the inerrancy and absolute historical truthfulness of the Bible begins to waver. There simply is too much evidence, and to reconcile all of the hundreds of differences among the biblical sources requires so much speculation and fancy interpretive footwork that eventually it gets to be too much for them.

PROBLEMS WITH THE BIBLE

For students who come into seminary with a view that the Bible is completely, absolutely, one hundred percent without error, the realization that most critical scholars have a very different view can come as a real shock to their systems. And once these students open the floodgates by admitting there might be mistakes in the Bible, their understanding of Scripture takes a radical turn. The more they read the text carefully and intensely, the more mistakes they find, and they begin to see that in fact the Bible makes *better* sense if you acknowledge its inconsistencies instead of staunchly insisting that there aren't any, even when they are staring you in the face.

To be sure, many beginning students are expert at reconciling differences among the Gospels. For example, the Gospel of Mark indicates that it was in the last week of his life that Jesus "cleansed the Temple" by overturning the tables of the money changers and saying, "This is to be a house of prayer . . . but you have made it a den of thieves" (Mark 11), whereas according to John this happened at the very beginning of Jesus' ministry (John 2). Some readers have thought that Jesus must have cleansed the Temple twice, once at the beginning of his ministry and once at the end. But that would mean that neither Mark nor John tells the "true" story, since in both accounts he cleanses the temple only once. Moreover, is this reconciliation of the two accounts historically plausible? If Jesus made a disruption in the temple at the beginning of his ministry, why wasn't he arrested by the authorities then? Once one comes to realize that the Bible might have discrepancies it is possible to see that the Gospels of Mark and John might want to teach something different about the cleansing of the Temple, and so they have located the event to two different times of Jesus' ministry. Historically speaking, then, the accounts are not reconcilable.

The same can be said of Peter's denials of Jesus. In Mark's Gospel, Jesus tells Peter that he will deny him three times "before the cock crows twice." In Matthew's Gospel he tells him that it will be "before the cock crows." Well, which is it—before the cock crows once or twice? When I was in college I purchased a book that was intent on reconciling differences of this kind. It was called *The Life of Christ in Stereo*. The author, Johnston Cheney, took the four Gospel accounts and wove them together into one big mega-Gospel, to show what the *real* Gospel was like. For the inconsistency in the account of the denials of Peter, the author had a very clever solution: Peter actually denied Jesus *six* times, three times before the cock crowed and three more times before it crowed twice. This can also explain why Peter denies Jesus to more than three different people (or groups of people) in the various accounts. But here again, in order to resolve the tension between the Gospels the interpreter has to write his *own* Gospel, which is unlike any of the Gospels found in the New Testament. And isn't it a bit absurd to say that, in effect, only "my" Gospel—the one I create from parts of the four in the New Testament—is the right one, and that the others are only partially right?

The same problem occurs in the accounts of Jesus' resurrection. On the third day after Jesus' death, the women go to the tomb to anoint his body for burial. And whom do they see there? Do they see a man, as Mark says, or two men (Luke), or an angel (Matthew)? This is normally reconciled by saying that the women *actually* saw "two angels." That can explain everything else—why Matthew says they saw *an* angel (he mentions only one of the two angels, but doesn't deny there was a second), why Mark says it was a man (the angels appeared to be men, even though they were angels, and Mark mentions only one of them without denying there was a second), and why Luke says it was two men (since the angels appeared to be men). The problem is that this kind of reconciling again requires one to assert that what really happened is unlike what *any* of the Gospels say—since none of the three accounts states that the women saw "two angels."

As we will see, there are lots of other discrepancies in the New Testament, some of them far more difficult to reconcile (virtually impossible, I would say) than these simple examples. Not only are there discrepancies among different books of the Bible, but there are also inconsistencies *within* some of the books, a problem that historical critics have long ascribed to the fact that Gospel writers used different sources for their accounts, and sometimes these sources, when spliced together, stood at odds with one another. It's amazing how internal problems like these, if you're not alerted to them, are so easily passed by when you read the Gospels, but how when someone points them out they seem so obvious. Students often ask me, "Why didn't I see this before?" For example, in John's Gospel, Jesus performs his first miracle in chapter 2, when he turns the water into wine (a favorite miracle story on college campuses), and we're told that "this was the first sign that Jesus did" (John 2:11). Later in that chapter we're told that Jesus did "many signs" in Jerusalem (John 2:23). And then, in chapter 4, he heals the son of a centurion, and the author says, "This was the second sign that Jesus did" (John 4:54). Huh? One sign, many signs, and then the second sign?[1]

One of my favorite apparent discrepancies—I read John for years without realizing how strange this one is—comes in Jesus' "Farewell Discourse," the last address that Jesus delivers to his disciples, at his last meal with them, which takes up all of chapters 13 to 17 in the Gospel according to John. In John 13:36, Peter says to Jesus, "Lord, where are you going?" A few verses later Thomas says, "Lord, we do not know where you are going" (John 14:5). And then, a few minutes later, at the same meal, Jesus upbraids his disciples, saying, "Now I am going to the one who sent me, yet none of you asks me, 'Where are you going?'" (John 16:5). Either Jesus had a very short attention span or there is something strange going on with the sources for these chapters, creating an odd kind of disconnect.

These kinds of problems turn out to be even more common in the Old Testament, starting at its very beginning. Some people go to great lengths to smooth over all these differences, but when you look at them closely, they are very difficult indeed to reconcile. And why should they be reconciled? Maybe they are simply differences. The creation account in Genesis 1 is very different from the account in Genesis 2. Not only is the wording and writing style different, as is very obvious when you read the text in Hebrew, and not only do the two chapters use different names for God, but the very content of the chapters differs in numerous respects. Just make a list of everything that happens in chapter 1 in the order it occurs, and a separate list for chapter 2, and compare your lists. Are animals created *before* humans, as in chapter 1, or *after*, as in chapter 2? Are plants created before humans or afterward? Is "man" the first living creature to be created or the last? Is woman created at the same time as man or separately? Even within each story there are problems: if "light" was created on the first day of creation in Genesis 1, how is it that the sun, moon, and stars were not created until the fourth day? Where was the light coming from, if not the sun, moon, and stars? And how could there be an "evening and morning" on each of the first three days if there was no sun?

That's just the beginning. When Noah takes the animals on the ark, does he take seven pairs of all the "clean" animals, as Genesis 7:2 states, or just two pairs, as Genesis 7:9–10 indicates?

In the book of Exodus, God tells Moses, "I appeared to Abraham, Isaac, and Jacob as God Almighty, but by my name 'The LORD' [= Yahweh] I did not make myself known to them" (Exodus 6:3). How does this square with what is found earlier, in Genesis, where God *does* make himself known to Abraham as The LORD: "Then he [God] said to him [Abraham], 'I am The LORD [= Yahweh] who brought you from Ur of the Chaldeans'" (Genesis 15:7)?

Or consider one of my all-time favorite passages, the description of the ten plagues that Moses brought down on the heads of the Egyptians in order to compel Pharaoh to "let my people go." The fifth plague was a pestilence that killed "all of the livestock of the Egyptians" (Exodus 9:5). How is it, then, that a few days later the seventh plague, of hail, was to destroy all of the Egyptian livestock in the fields (Exodus 9:21–22)? What livestock?

A close reading of the Bible reveals other problems besides the many discrepancies and contradictions. There are places where the text seems to embrace a view that seems unworthy of God or of his people. Are we really to think of God as someone who orders the wholesale massacre of an entire city? In Joshua 6, God orders the soldiers of Israel to attack the city of Jericho and to slaughter every man, woman, and child in the city. I suppose it makes sense that God would not want bad influences on his people—but does he really think that murdering all the toddlers and infants is necessary to that end? What do they have to do with wickedness?

Or what is one to make of Psalm 137, one of the most beautiful Psalms, which starts with the memorable lines "By the rivers of Babylon—there we sat down and there we wept, when we remembered Zion." Here is a powerful reflection by a faithful Israelite who longs to return to Jerusalem, which had been destroyed by the Babylonians. But his praise of God, and of his holy city, takes a vicious turn at the end, when he plots his revenge on God's enemies: "Happy shall they be who take your [Babylonian] little ones, and dash them against the rock." Knocking the brains out of the Babylonian babies in retaliation for what their father-soldiers did? Is this in the Bible?

The God of vengeance is found not only in the Old Testament, as some Christians have tried to claim. Even the New Testament God is a God of judgment and wrath, as any reader of the book of Revelation knows. The Lake of Fire is stoked up and ready for everyone who is opposed to God. This will involve *eternal* burning—an everlasting punishment, even for those who have sinned against God, intermittently, say, for twenty years. Twenty trillion years of torment in exchange for twenty years of wrong living; and that's only the beginning. Is this really worthy of God?

I should stress that scholars and students who question such passages are not questioning God himself. They are questioning what the Bible has to *say* about God. Some such scholars continue to think that the Bible is in some sense inspired—other scholars, of course, do not. But even if the authors of the Bible were in some sense inspired, they were not completely infallible; in fact, they made mistakes. These mistakes involved discrepancies and contradictions, but they also involved mistaken notions about God, who he really was and what he really wanted. Does he really want his followers to splash the brains of their enemies' infants against the rocks? Does he really plan to torment unbelievers for trillions of years?

These are the questions many seminarians are forced to grapple with as they move away from the devotional commitment to the Bible that they bring with them to seminary and begin to study the Bible in light of scholarship. They are questions raised, in large extent, as a result of being trained in the historical-critical approach to the Bible, the approach that is taught in most mainline Protestant seminaries and that is the more or less "orthodox" view among biblical scholars in America and Europe.

This view insists that each author of the Bible lived in his own time and place—and not in ours. Each author had a set of cultural and religious assumptions that we ourselves may not share. The historical-critical method tries to understand what each of these authors may have meant in his original context. According to this view, each author must be allowed to have his own say. Within the New Testament, the author of Matthew isn't saying the same thing as Luke. Mark is different from John. Paul may not see eye to eye with James. The author of Revelation seems to be different from all the others. And once you throw the Old Testament into the mix, things get completely jumbled. The authors of Job and Ecclesiastes explicitly state that there is no afterlife. The book of Amos insists that the people of God suffer because God is punishing them for their sins; the book of Job insists that the innocent can suffer; and the book of Daniel indicates that the innocent in fact will suffer. All of these books are different, all of them have a message, and all of the messages deserve to be heard.

FROM SEMINARY TO PULPIT

One of the most amazing and perplexing features of mainstream Christianity is that seminarians who learn the historical-critical method in their Bible classes appear to forget all about it when it comes time for them to be pastors. They are taught critical approaches to Scripture, they learn about the discrepancies and contradictions, they discover all sorts of historical errors and mistakes, they come to realize that it is difficult to know whether Moses existed or what Jesus actually said and did, they find that there are other books that were at one time considered canonical but that ultimately did not become part of Scripture (for example, other Gospels and Apocalypses), they come to recognize that a good number of the books of the Bible are pseudonymous (for example, written in the name of an apostle by someone else), that in fact we don't have the original copies of any of the biblical books but only copies made centuries later, all of which have been altered. They learn all this, and yet when they enter church ministry they appear to put it back on the shelf. For reasons I will explore in the conclusion, pastors are, as a rule, reluctant to teach what they learned about the Bible in seminary.[2]

I vividly recall the first time I came to realize this concretely. I had just started teaching at the University of North Carolina at Chapel Hill, and was still a Christian. The pastor of a Presbyterian church in North Carolina asked me to do a four-week series on "the historical Jesus." So I did. In my lectures I talked about why historians have problems using the Gospels as historical sources, in view of their discrepancies and the fact that they were written decades after the life of Jesus by unknown authors who had inherited their accounts about him from the highly malleable oral tradition. I also talked about how scholars have devised methods for reconstructing what probably happened in the life of Jesus, and ended the series by laying out what we can actually know about him. There was nothing at all novel in what I discussed—it was standard scholarly material, the kind of thing that has been taught in seminaries for over fifty years. I learned all this material while I was at Princeton Seminary myself.

Afterward a dear elderly lady came up to me and asked me in frustration, "Why have I never heard this before?" She was not distressed at what I had said; she was distressed that her pastor had never said it. I remember looking across the fellowship hall to the pastor, who was talking to a couple of other parishioners, and wondering the same thing myself: Why had he never told her? He, too, had gone to Princeton Theological Seminary, he too had learned all these things; he taught adult education classes at this church and had been doing so for more than five years. Why had he not told his parishioners what he knew about the Bible and the historical Jesus? Surely they deserved to hear. Was it because he didn't think they were "ready" for it—a patronizing attitude that is disturbingly common? Was he afraid to "make waves"? Was he afraid that historical information might destroy the faith of his congregation? Was he afraid that church leaders might not take kindly to the dissemination of such knowledge? Did church leaders actually put pressure on him to stick to the devotional meaning of the Bible in his preaching and teaching? Was he concerned about job security? I never found out.

I am not saying that churches should be mini-universities where pastors function as professors from the pulpit. But surely the ministry involves more than preaching the "good news" (however that is understood) every week. It also involves teaching. Most churches have adult education classes. Why aren't adults being educated? My experience in this particular church is not an isolated case.

Every year I teach hundreds of students in my "Introduction to the New Testament" course at Chapel Hill. Normally there are three hundred to three hundred fifty students in the class. I teach the class, of course, not from a confessional or devotional point of view—the view that most of these students, having been raised in the church, are accustomed to hearing—but from a historical-critical point of view. The information and perspectives I present in the class are nothing radical. They are the views found among critical scholars who approach the Bible historically—whether the scholars themselves are believers or unbelievers, Protestant, Catholic, Jewish, agnostic, or whatever else. They are the views I learned in seminary and the views that are taught at divinity schools and universities throughout the country. But they are views that my students have never heard before, even though most of these students have spent a good deal of their lives in Sunday School and church.

My students have a range of reactions to these views. Many of my more conservative students are like me at that age—certain of the Bible's absolute truthfulness and wary of anyone who might call it into question. Some of these students refuse to listen—it is almost as if they cover their ears and hum loudly so they don't have to hear anything that might cause them to doubt their cherished beliefs about the Bible. Others are eager to break away from the confines of the church and religion entirely, devouring the information I give as if it provides a license to disbelieve.

I personally don't think either reaction—the radical rejection or the all-too-eager embrace of the new perspective on the Bible—is ideal. What I prefer are students who carefully study the material, consider it thoughtfully, question some of its (and their own) assumptions and conclusions, reflect on how it might affect the way they look at the Bible and the Christian religion on which they were raised, and cautiously consider how it might affect them personally. One of my main goals, of course, is to get them to learn the material for the course. It is, after all, historical information about a historical religion and a historically based set of documents. The class is not meant to be a theological exercise to strengthen or weaken one's faith. But since the documents we consider are, for many students, documents of faith, inevitably the historical-critical method we use in class has some implications for faith. And another ultimate objective that I have—as should every university professor—is to get students to *think*.

ACCEPTING THE HISTORICAL-CRITICAL METHOD

Like lots of other seminary students, once I came to see the potential value of historical criticism at Princeton Seminary, I started adopting this new (for me) approach, very cautiously at first, as I didn't want to concede too much to scholarship. But eventually I saw the powerful logic behind the historical-critical method and threw myself heart and soul into the study of the Bible from this perspective.

It is hard for me to pinpoint the exact moment that I stopped being a fundamentalist who believed in the absolute inerrancy and verbal inspiration of the Bible. As I point out in *Misquoting Jesus,* the key issue for me early on was the historical fact that we don't have the original writings of any of the books of the Bible, but only copies made later—in most instances, many centuries later. For me, it started making less and less sense to think that God had inspired the very words of the text if we didn't actually have these words, if the texts had in fact been changed, in many thousands of places, most of the changes insignificant but many of them of real importance. If God wanted us to have his words, why didn't he preserve his words?

At about the time I started to doubt that God had inspired the words of the Bible, I began to be influenced by Bible courses taught from a historical-critical perspective. I started seeing discrepancies in the text. I saw that some of the books of the Bible were at odds with one another. I became convinced by the arguments that some of the books were not written by the authors for whom they were named. And I began to see that many of the traditional Christian doctrines that I had long held to be beyond question, such as the doctrines of the divinity of Christ and of the Trinity, were not present in the earliest traditions of the New Testament but had developed over time and had moved away from the original teachings of Jesus and his apostles.

These realizations had a profound impact on my faith, as I think they did on that of many of my fellow seminarians at the time and continue to have on many seminarians today. Unlike most of my seminarian friends, though, I did not revert to a devotional approach to the Bible the day after I graduated with my master's of divinity degree. Instead I devoted myself even more wholeheartedly to learning more about the Bible from a historical perspective, and about the Christian faith that I had thought was taught by the Bible. I had started seminary as a born-again fundamentalist; by the time I graduated I was moving toward a liberal form of evangelical Christianity, one that still saw the Bible as conveying important teachings of God to his people, but also as a book filled with human perspectives and mistakes.

As time went on my views continued to evolve. I did not go from being an evangelical to an agnostic overnight. Quite the contrary: for some fifteen years after I had given up on my views of the verbal inspiration of the Bible, I continued to be a faithful Christian—a churchgoing, God-believing, sin-confessing Christian. I did become increasingly liberal in my views. My research led me to question important aspects of my faith. Eventually, not long after I left the seminary, I came to the place where I still believed completely in God, but understood the Bible in a more metaphorical, less literal, sense: the Bible seemed to me to contain inspired literature, in that it could inspire true and useful thinking about God, but it was still the product of human hands and contained all the kinds of mistakes that any human undertaking will bring.

There came a time when I left the faith. This was not because of what I learned through historical criticism, but because I could no longer reconcile my faith in God with the state of the world that I saw all around me. This is the issue I deal with in my book *God's Problem: How the Bible Fails to Answer Our Most Important Question—Why We Suffer*. There is so much senseless pain and misery in the world that I came to find it impossible to believe that there is a good and loving God who is in control, despite my knowing all the standard rejoinders that people give.

That is the subject of another book, but it is of some relevance to the present book because over the fifteen years between the time I gave up my evangelical commitments and the time I became agnostic, I was intimately involved with the historical criticism of the Bible, especially the New Testament. Here I want to stress a point that I will be reiterating, with vigor, in my final chapter. I decidedly do *not* think that historical criticism necessarily leads to a loss of faith.

All of my closest friends (and next-to-closest friends) in the guild of New Testament studies agree with most of my historical views of the New Testament, the historical Jesus, the development of the Christian faith, and other similar issues. We may disagree on this point or that (in fact we do—we are, after all, scholars), but we all agree on the historical methods and the basic conclusions they lead to. All of these friends, however, have remained committed Christians. Some teach in universities, some in seminaries and divinity schools. Some are ordained ministers. Most are active in their churches. Historical-critical approaches to the Bible came to many of them as a shock in seminary, but their faith withstood the shock. In my case, historical criticism led me to question my faith. Not just its superficial aspects but its very heart. Yet it was the problem of suffering, not a historical approach to the Bible, that led me to agnosticism.

This book is not, then, about my loss of faith. It is, however, about how certain kinds of faith—particularly the faith in the Bible as the historically inerrant and inspired Word of God—cannot be sustained in light of what we as historians know about the Bible. The views I set out in this book are standard fare among scholars. I don't know a single Bible scholar who will learn a single thing from this book, although they will disagree with conclusions here and there. In theory, pastors should not learn much from it either, as this material is widely taught in seminaries and divinity schools. But most people in the street, and in the pew, have heard none of this before. That is a real shame, and it is time that something is done to correct the problem.

A World of Contradictions

When students are first introduced to the historical, as opposed to a devotional, study of the Bible, one of the first things they are forced to grapple with is that the biblical text, whether Old Testament or New Testament, is chock full of discrepancies, many of them irreconcilable. Some of these discrepancies are simple details where one book contradicts what another says about a minor point—the number of soldiers in an army, the year a certain king began his reign, the details of an apostle's itinerary. In some cases seemingly trivial points of difference can actually have an enormous significance for the interpretation of a book or the reconstruction of the history of ancient Israel or the life of the historical Jesus. And then there are instances that involve major issues, where one author has one point of view on an important topic (How was the world created? Why do the people of God suffer? What is the significance of Jesus' death?), and another author has another. Sometimes these views are simply different from one another, but at other times they are directly at odds.

In this chapter I will talk about some of the important and interesting discrepancies of the Bible that emerge when it is examined from a historical perspective. Since my specialty is the New Testament, I will be dealing with the kinds of problems that are found there. But you can rest assured that very much the same problems can be found in the Old Testament as well—in fact, even more so. Whereas the New Testament, consisting of twenty-seven books, was written by maybe sixteen or seventeen authors over a period of seventy years, the Old Testament, the Jewish Scriptures, consists of thirty-nine books written by dozens of authors over at least six hundred years. There is a lot of room for differing perspectives, and if you look for them, you will find them in droves.

My point is not simply that the Bible is full of contradictions, as I explain more fully at the end of the chapter. My students sometimes suspect that this is the ultimate point—that the Bible is riddled with problems and therefore "cannot be believed." But this is not the ultimate point—even though the discrepancies in the Bible do create certain problems for people with a certain kind of Christian faith (not for all Christians, however). But there are other reasons for discovering that the Bible contains contradictions. It is best to provide these reasons at the end of the chapter, however, rather than the beginning; one should always know what the data *are* before deciding too quickly what the data *mean*.

My goal is not to point out every discrepancy that can be discovered in the New Testament, but only some of the most interesting or important ones. I will start with the Gospels and then move on to Paul. Throughout this discussion I will not be dealing with the very important question of who the authors of these books really were (disciples of Jesus? companions of the apostles? later Christians?). That is the subject of a later chapter. For now it is enough to note that whoever wrote these books, they sometimes stand at odds with one another.

Why is it that casual, and even avid, readers of the Bible never detect these discrepancies, some of which may seem obvious once they are pointed out? My view is that it has to do with the way people read these books. Most people simply read here and there in the Bible—open it up, choose a passage, read it, and try to figure out what it means. There is little or no effort to make a detailed comparison with other, similar passages, in other books. You read a snippet here, a snippet there, and it all sounds like the Bible. To engage in a historical study of the text, however, requires that you read and compare the texts carefully, down to the minute details.

Yet even careful readers of the Bible often fail to detect differences among its books, again because of the way they read them. Most general readers, unlike those who read the Bible critically from a historical point of view, read the books in sequence. That makes sense—it is, after all, how we read *most* anthologies. And so, if you want to read the New Testament, you start with Matthew and you begin with chapter 1, verse 1, and you read the book from beginning to end, to get a sense of what he is trying to say about the life of Jesus. Then you read Mark, starting at the beginning and reading to the end—and it sounds a lot like Matthew. A lot of the same stories, often in the same words—a few things left out here and there, maybe, but basically the same kind of book. Then you read Luke, beginning to end. Here again: same or similar stories, similar words. When you read John you might notice some differences, but basically it all sounds the same: stories about the things Jesus said and did before he traveled to Jerusalem, was betrayed, arrested, crucified, and raised from the dead.

This is the most natural way of reading any book, from beginning to end. I call this approach "vertical" reading. You start at the top of the page and move to the bottom; start at the beginning of the book and move to the end. There is absolutely nothing wrong with reading the Gospels this way, as this is no doubt how they were written to be read. But there is another way to read them: horizontally. In a horizontal reading you read a story in one of the Gospels, and then read the same story as told by another Gospel, as if they were written in columns next to each other. And you compare the stories carefully, in detail.[1]

Reading the Gospels horizontally reveals all sorts of differences and discrepancies. Sometimes the differences are simply variations on a story, possibly significant for knowing what one or the other Gospel writer wanted to emphasize, but not contradicting one another. For example, in the accounts of Jesus' birth in Matthew and Luke, a horizontal reading shows that Matthew tells the story of the wise men coming to worship Jesus, whereas Luke tells the story of the shepherds coming to worship him. There are no shepherds in Matthew and no wise men in Luke. This is not a contradiction: Matthew wants (for important reasons, as it turns out) to tell the story of the wise men, and Luke (for other reasons) wants to tell the story of the shepherds.

Then there are differences that may not represent flat-out contradictions but that do seem to stand somewhat at odds with each other. I have already mentioned the cleansing of the Temple in Mark 11 and John 2. In Mark it happens a week before Jesus dies; in John it is the first public event of his three-year ministry. Strictly speaking this difference is not a contradiction: if you are creative enough, you can figure out a plausible explanation for both accounts being right. As I mentioned in the previous chapter, maybe Jesus cleansed the Temple twice, once at the beginning and once at the end of his ministry. On the other hand, this does seem a bit far-fetched, as the question suggests itself: Why wasn't he arrested the first time? Moreover, it means that in order to make Mark and John fit together you have had to create your own version of the Gospel, one different from both of the ones you are reading, for in your version there are two cleansings of the Temple, not one.

There are other differences that, in the opinion of a large number of historical critics, simply cannot be reconciled without doing real violence to the text. I'll be dealing with some of these throughout this chapter, and don't want to spoil the fun by giving the most interesting examples here. For now my point is that most readers don't see these differences because they have been trained, or at least are inclined, to read the Bible in only one way, vertically, whereas the historical approach suggests that it is also useful to read it another way, horizontally.

If you are interested in finding discrepancies yourself, it is in fact very easy to do. Pick a story in the Gospels—for example, Jesus' birth, the healing of Jairus's daughter, the crucifixion, the resurrection—most any story will do. Read the account in one Gospel, listing carefully everything that happens in sequence; then read the same story in another Gospel, again taking careful notes. Finally, compare your notes. Sometimes the differences are slight, but sometimes they matter a lot—even if at first glance they seem rather unimportant. That is the case with my first example. The issue at stake is a very simple and basic one, which can be expressed in a seemingly unambiguous question: When did Jesus die? That is, on what day, and at what time of day, was Jesus crucified? It turns out that the answer differs, depending on which Gospel you read.

AN OPENING ILLUSTRATION:
THE DEATH OF JESUS, IN MARK AND JOHN

This is an illustration of discrepancies within the New Testament that I frequently use with my students.[2] It is a "textbook case" because both Mark and John give explicit indications of when Jesus dies. And he dies at different times, depending on which Gospel you read.

Mark was probably the first Gospel to be written. Scholars have long thought that it was produced about thirty-five or forty years after Jesus' death, possibly around 65 or 70 CE.[3] The first ten chapters of Mark are about Jesus' public ministry in Galilee, the northern part of Israel, where he teaches, heals the sick, casts out demons, and confronts his Jewish opponents, the Pharisees. At the end of his life he makes a journey to Jerusalem in order to celebrate the Jewish feast of Passover; while he is there he is arrested and crucified (chapters 11–16).

To make sense of Mark's dating of the crucifixion (and of John's, for that matter), I need to provide some important background information. In the days of Jesus, the Passover, held annually, was the most important Jewish festival. It was instituted to commemorate the events of the Exodus that had occurred centuries earlier, in the time of Moses, as recounted in the Old Testament book of Exodus (Exodus 5–15). According to that account, the children of Israel had been enslaved in Egypt for four hundred years, but God heard their cries and raised up for them a savior, Moses. Moses was sent to the Pharaoh and demanded, speaking for God, that he "let my people go." But the Pharaoh had a hard heart and refused. In order to persuade him, God empowered Moses to send ten horrible plagues against the Egyptians, the last of which was the most awful: every firstborn Egyptian child and animal would be killed by the angel of death.

The Israelites were given instructions to avoid having their own children slain. Each family was to sacrifice a lamb, take some of its blood, and spread it on the doorposts and lintel of the house where they lived. Then, when the angel of death arrived that night, he would see the blood on the door and "pass over" that Israelite house, moving on to houses without the blood, to murder a firstborn child. And so it happened. Pharaoh was struck to the heart, and in anguish he let the Israelites (600,000 men, plus the women and children) leave his land. But after they set out, he had a change of heart, marshaled his army, and chased after them. He tracked them down at the Red Sea—called the "Sea of Reeds" in Hebrew—but God performed yet another miracle, allowing Moses to part the waters of the sea so the Israelites could cross on dry land. When the Egyptian armies followed in chase, God caused the waters to return and drowned the whole lot of them.

And so Israel was saved from its slavery in Egypt. God commanded Moses that from that time onward the Israelites were to commemorate this great event by a special meal, the annual Passover celebration (Exodus 12). In Jesus' day, Jews from around the world would come to Jerusalem to celebrate the event. On the day before the celebratory meal was eaten, Jews would bring a lamb to the Jerusalem Temple, or more likely purchase one there, and have it slaughtered by the priests. They would then take it home to prepare the meal. This happened on the Day of Preparation for the Passover.

Now the only confusing aspect of this celebration involves the way ancient Jews told time—the same way modern Jews do. Even today the "Sabbath" is Saturday, but it begins on Friday night, when it gets dark. That is because in traditional Judaism the new day begins at nightfall, with the evening. (That's why, in the book of Genesis, when God creates the heavens and the earth, we're told that "there was evening and morning, the first day"; a day consisted of night and day, not day and night.) And so the Sabbath begins Friday night—and in fact every day begins with nightfall.

And so, on the Day of Preparation the lamb was slaughtered and the meal was prepared in the afternoon. The meal was eaten that night, which was actually the beginning of the next day: Passover day. The meal consisted of a number of symbolic foods: the lamb, to commemorate the original slaughter of the lambs in Exodus; bitter herbs, to remind the Jews of their bitter slavery in Egypt; unleavened bread (bread made without yeast) to remind them that the Israelites had to flee from Egypt without much warning, so that they could not wait for the bread to rise; and several cups of wine. The Passover day, then, began with the evening meal and lasted approximately twenty-four hours, through the morning and afternoon of the next day, after which would begin the day after Passover.

Now we can return to Mark's account of Jesus' death. Jesus and his disciples have made a pilgrimage to Jerusalem for the Passover feast. In Mark 14:12, the disciples ask Jesus where they are to prepare the Passover meal for that evening. In other words, this is on the Day of Preparation for Passover. Jesus gives them instructions. They make the preparations, and when it is evening—the beginning of Passover day—they have the meal. It is a special meal indeed. Jesus takes the symbolic foods of the Passover and imbues them with yet more symbolic meaning. He takes the unleavened bread, breaks it, and says, "This is my body." By implication, his body must be broken for salvation. Then after supper he takes the cup of wine and says, "This is my blood of the covenant, that is poured out for many" (Mark 14:22–25), meaning that his own blood must be shed.

After the disciples eat the Passover meal they go out to the Garden of Gethsemane to pray. Judas Iscariot brings the troops and performs his act of betrayal. Jesus is taken to stand trial before the Jewish authorities. He spends the night in jail, and the next morning he is put on trial before the Roman governor, Pontius Pilate, who finds him guilty and condemns him to death by crucifixion. We are told that he is crucified that same day, at nine o'clock in the morning (Mark 15:25). Jesus, then, dies on the day of Passover, the morning after the Passover meal was eaten.

All this is clear and straightforward in Mark's Gospel, but despite some basic similarities, it is at odds with the story told in the Gospel of John, which is also clear and straightforward. Here, too, Jesus goes to Jerusalem in the last week of his life to celebrate the Passover feast, and here, too, there is a last meal, a betrayal, a trial before Pilate, and the crucifixion. But it is striking that in John, at the beginning of the account, in contrast to Mark, the disciples do not ask Jesus where they are "to prepare the Passover." Consequently, he gives them no instructions for preparing the meal. They do eat a final supper together, but in John, Jesus says nothing about the bread being his body or the cup representing his blood. Instead he washes the disciples' feet, a story found in none of the other Gospels (John 13:1–20).

After the meal they go out. Jesus is betrayed by Judas, appears before the Jewish authorities, spends the night in jail, and is put on trial before Pontius Pilate, who finds him guilty and condemns him to be crucified. And we are told exactly when Pilate pronounces the sentence: "It was the Day of Preparation for the Passover; and it was about noon" (John 19:14).

Noon? On the Day of Preparation for the Passover? The day the lambs were slaughtered? How can that be? In Mark's Gospel, Jesus lived through that day, had his disciples prepare the Passover meal, and ate it with them before being arrested, taken to jail for the night, tried the next morning, and executed at nine o'clock A.M. on the Passover day. But not in John. In John, Jesus dies a day earlier, on the Day of Preparation for the Passover, sometime after noon.

I do not think this is a difference that can be reconciled. People over the years have tried, of course. Some have pointed out that Mark also indicates that Jesus died on a day that is called "the Day of Preparation" (Mark 15:42). That is absolutely true—but what these readers fail to notice is that Mark tells us what he means by this phrase: it is the Day of Preparation "for the Sabbath" (*not* the Day of Preparation for the Passover). In other words, in Mark, this is not the day before the Passover meal was eaten but the day before Sabbath; it is called the day of "preparation" because one had to prepare the meals for Saturday on Friday afternoon.

And so the contradiction stands: in Mark, Jesus eats the Passover meal (Thursday night) and is crucified the following morning. In John, Jesus does not eat the Passover meal but is crucified on the day before the Passover meal was to be eaten.[4] Moreover, in Mark, Jesus is nailed to the cross at nine in the morning; in John, he is not condemned until noon, and then he is taken out and crucified.

Some scholars have argued that we have this difference between the Gospels because different Jews celebrated Passover on different days of the week. This is one of those explanations that sounds plausible until you dig a bit and think a bit more. It is true that some sectarian groups not connected with the Temple in Jerusalem thought that the Temple authorities followed an incorrect calendar. But in both Mark and John, Jesus is not outside Jerusalem with some sectarian group of Jews: he is in Jerusalem, where the lambs are being slaughtered. And in Jerusalem, there was only one day of Passover a year. The Jerusalem priests did not accommodate the calendrical oddities of a few sectarian fringe groups.

What is one to make of this contradiction? Again, on one level it seems like a rather minor point. I mean, who really cares if it was one day or the next? The point is that Jesus got crucified, right?

Well, that is both right and wrong. Another question to ask is not "Was Jesus crucified?" but also "What does it mean that Jesus was crucified?" And for this, little details like the day and time actually matter. The way I explain the importance of such minutiae to my students is this: When, today, a homicide is committed, and the police detectives come in to the crime scene, they begin searching for little scraps of evidence, looking for the trace of a fingerprint or a strand of hair on the floor. Someone might reasonably look at what they are doing and say, "What's wrong with you? Can't you see that there's a dead body on the floor? Why are you snooping around for a fingerprint?" Yet sometimes the smallest clue can lead to a solution of the case. Why, and by whom, was this person killed? So, too, with the Gospels. Sometimes the smallest piece of evidence can give important clues about what the author thought was really going on.

I can't give a full analysis here, but I will point out a significant feature of John's Gospel—the last of our Gospels to be written, probably some twenty-five years or so after Mark's. John is the only Gospel that indicates that Jesus is "the lamb of God who takes away the sins of the world." This is declared by John the Baptist at the very beginning of the narrative (John 1:29) and again six verses later (John 1:35). Why, then, did John—our latest Gospel—change the day and time when Jesus died? It may be because in John's Gospel, Jesus is the Passover Lamb, whose sacrifice brings salvation from sins. Exactly like the Passover Lamb, Jesus has to die on the day (the Day of Preparation) and the time (sometime after noon), when the Passover lambs were being slaughtered in the Temple.

In other words, John has changed a historical datum in order to make a theological point: Jesus is the sacrificial lamb. And to convey this theological point, John has had to create a discrepancy between his account and the others.[5]

This preliminary study of just one small discrepancy can lead us to several conclusions that I will be stating more forcefully at the end of the chapter.

- There are discrepancies in the books of the New Testament.

- Some of these discrepancies cannot be reconciled.

- It is impossible that both Mark's and John's accounts are historically accurate, since they contradict each other on the question of when Jesus died.

- To understand what each author is trying to say, we have to look at the details of *each* account—and by no means treat one account as if it were saying the same thing as another account. John is different from Mark on a key, if seemingly minor, point. If we want to understand what John is saying about Jesus, we cannot reconcile the discrepancy, or we miss his point.

DISCREPANCIES IN THE ACCOUNTS OF JESUS' BIRTH AND LIFE

We can now consider a number of discrepancies among the Gospel accounts of Jesus' life, starting with the narratives of his birth. I have somewhat arbitrarily divided these into differences that strike me as particularly important and differences that may seem relatively minor or just curious. Again, I should stress that I am not presenting every possible instance of a discrepancy—that would take a book much longer than this one.

The Birth of Jesus

There are only two accounts of Jesus' birth in the New Testament, the opening chapters of Matthew and of Luke. Mark and John say nothing about his birth (the virgin birth, his being born in Bethlehem, and other elements of the Christmas story); in Mark and John, he appears on the scene as an adult. Nor are the details of his birth mentioned by Paul or any of the other New Testament writers. What people know—or think they know—about the Christmas story therefore comes exclusively from Matthew and Luke. And the story that is told every December is in fact a conflation of the accounts of these two Gospels, a combination of the details of one with the details of the other, in order to create one large, harmonious account. In fact, the accounts themselves are not at all harmonious. Not only do they tell completely different stories about how Jesus was born, but some of the differences appear to be irreconcilable (some others do not pass the test of historical plausibility either, but that is a different matter).

The easiest way to point out the differences between the accounts is by summarizing both. Matthew 1:18–2:23 goes like this: Mary and Joseph are espoused to be married, when Mary is found to be pregnant. Joseph, naturally suspecting the worst, plans to divorce her, but is told in a dream that Mary has conceived by the Holy Spirit.[6] They get married and Jesus is born. Wise men then come from the east, following a star that has led them to Jerusalem, where they ask about where the King of the Jews is to be born. King Herod makes inquiries and learns from the Jewish scholars that it is predicted that the king will come from Bethlehem. He informs the wise men, who proceed to Bethlehem—once again led by the star, which stops over the house where the family of Jesus resides. The wise men offer him gifts and then, warned in a dream, do not return to inform Herod, as he had requested, but make their way home by another route. Herod, since he himself is the king, is fearful of this one born to be king and sends his troops to slaughter every male child two years and younger in and around Bethlehem. But Joseph is warned of the danger in a dream. He, Mary, and Jesus flee from town in advance of the slaughter and travel to Egypt. Later, in Egypt, Joseph learns in a dream that Herod has died, and now they can return. But when they discover that Archelaus, Herod's son, is the ruler of Judea, they decide not to go back, but instead go to the northern district of Galilee, to the town of Nazareth. This then is where Jesus is raised.

One feature of Matthew that makes it distinctive from Luke is how the author continually emphasizes that the various events were "to fulfill what the prophet had said" (Matthew 1:22, 2:6, 2:18, 2:23).

That is, Jesus' birth is a fulfillment of the prophecies of Scripture. Luke probably would not have denied this, but he says nothing about it. There are two points on which he does agree with Matthew, however: Jesus' mother was a virgin, and he was born in Bethlehem. But it is striking just how different Luke's narrative is from Matthew's in the way he makes these two points.

Luke's much longer version (Luke 1:4–2:40) begins with a lengthy account of the angel's announcement to a barren woman, Elizabeth, that she will give birth to John (the Baptist), who, according to Luke, is actually Jesus' cousin (Elizabeth and Mary are related; Luke is the only New Testament writer to say this). Luke says that Mary is a virgin espoused to Joseph. Later an angel appears to her to inform her that she, too, will conceive, by the Holy Spirit, and she will give birth to the Son of God. She visits the six-month-pregnant Elizabeth, whose child leaps in the womb in joy at being visited by "the mother of [the] Lord." Mary then bursts into song. John the Baptist is born, and his father, Zechariah, bursts into prophecy. And then we get to the story of Jesus' own birth.

There is a decree from the Roman emperor Augustus that every one in the empire needs to register for a census; we are told that this is the first census, when Quirinius was the governor of Syria. Everyone is to return to their ancestral home to register. Since Joseph's ancestors were from Bethlehem (he is descended from King David, who was born there), he travels there with Mary, his espoused. While there she gives birth to Jesus and wraps him in bands of cloth and lays him in a manger, "for there was no room for them in the inn." Shepherds in the field are visited by an angelic host who tells them that the Messiah has been born in Bethlehem; they go and worship the child. Eight days later, Jesus is circumcised. Jesus is then presented to God in the Temple, and his parents offer the sacrifice prescribed for this occasion by the law of Moses. Jesus is recognized there as the Messiah by a righteous and devout man named Simeon and by an elderly and pious widow, Anna. When Joseph and Mary have finished "everything required by the Law of the Lord" concerning the birth of their firstborn, they return to Nazareth, where Jesus is raised.

The "Law of the Lord" referred to repeatedly throughout this account is Leviticus 12, which specifies that the offerings in the Temple are to be made thirty-three days after the birth of the child.

Before examining the differences between these two accounts, I should point out that the historian finds real difficulties in both of them. In Matthew, for example, what does it mean that there is a star guiding the wise men, that this star stops over Jerusalem, and then starts up again, leads them to Bethlehem, and stops again over the very house where Jesus was born? What kind of star would this be, exactly? A star that moves slowly enough for the wise men to follow on foot or on camel, stops, starts again, and stops again? And how exactly does a star stop over a house? I tell my students to go outside on some starry night, pick one of the brightest stars in the sky, and figure out which house on their block it is standing over. Obviously what is being narrated here is a miraculous event, but it is very hard to understand what the author actually has in mind. It doesn't appear to be a real star, a nova, a comet, or any astronomical phenomenon ever known.

In terms of the historical record, I should also point out that there is no account in any ancient source whatsoever about King Herod slaughtering children in or around Bethlehem, or anyplace else. No other author, biblical or otherwise, mentions the event. Is it, like John's account of Jesus' death, a detail made up by Matthew in order to make some kind of theological point?

The historical problems with Luke are even more pronounced. For one thing, we have relatively good records for the reign of Caesar Augustus, and there is no mention anywhere in any of them of an empire-wide census for which everyone had to register by return-ing to their ancestral home. And how could such a thing even be imagined? Joseph returns to Bethlehem because his ancestor David was born there. But David lived a thousand years before Joseph. Are we to imagine that everyone in the Roman Empire was required to return to the homes of their ancestors from a thousand years earlier? If we had a new worldwide census today and each of us had to return to the towns of our ancestors a thousand years back—where would *you* go? Can you imagine the total disruption of human life that this kind of universal exodus would require? And can you imagine that such a project would never be mentioned in any of the newspapers? There is not a single reference to any such census in any ancient source, apart from Luke. Why then does Luke say there was such a census? The answer may seem obvious to you. He wanted Jesus to be born in Bethlehem, even though he knew he came from Nazareth. Matthew did, too, but he got him born there in a different way.

The differences between the accounts are quite striking. Virtually everything said in Matthew is missing from Luke, and all the stories of Luke are missing from Matthew. Matthew mentions dreams that came to Joseph that are absent in Luke; Luke mentions angelic visitations to Elizabeth and Mary that are absent in Matthew. Matthew has the wise men, the slaughter of the children by Herod, the flight to Egypt, the Holy Family bypassing Judea to return to Nazareth— all missing from Luke. Luke has the birth of John the Baptist, the census of Caesar, the trip to Bethlehem, the manger and the inn, the shepherds, the circumcision, the presentation in the Temple, and the return home immediately afterward—all of them missing from Matthew.

Now it may be that Matthew is simply telling some of the story and Luke is telling the rest of it, so that we are justified every December in combining the two accounts into a Christmas pageant where you get both the shepherds *and* the wise men, both the trip from Nazareth *and* the flight to Egypt. The problem is that when you start looking at the accounts closely, there are not only differences but also discrepancies that appear difficult if not impossible to reconcile.

If the Gospels are right that Jesus' birth occurred during Herod's reign, then Luke cannot also be right that it happened when Quirinius was the governor of Syria. We know from a range of other historical sources, including the Roman historian Tacitus, the Jewish historian Josephus, and several ancient inscriptions, that Quirinius did not become governor of Syria until 6 CE, ten years after the death of Herod.

A careful comparison of the two accounts also shows internal discrepancies. One way to get to the problem is to ask this: According to Matthew, what was Joseph and Mary's hometown? Your natural reaction is to say "Nazareth." But only Luke says this. Matthew says nothing of the sort. He first mentions Joseph and Mary not in connection with Nazareth but in connection with Bethlehem. The wise men, who are following a star (presumably it took some time), come to worship Jesus in his *house* in Bethlehem. Joseph and Mary evidently live there. There is nothing about an inn and a manger in Matthew. Moreover, when Herod slaughters the children, he instructs his soldiers to kill every male two years and under. This must indicate that Jesus had been born some time before the wise men show up. Otherwise the instruction does not make much sense: surely even Roman soldiers could recognize that a toddler walking around the playground was not an infant born some time last week. So Joseph and Mary are still living in Bethlehem months or even a year or more after the birth of Jesus. So how can Luke be right when he says that they are from Nazareth and returned there just a month or so after Jesus' birth? Moreover, according to Matthew, after the family flees to Egypt and then returns upon the death of Herod, they initially plan to return to Judea, where Bethlehem is located. They cannot do so, however, because now Archelaus is the ruler, and so they relocate to Nazareth. In Matthew's account they are not originally from Nazareth but from Bethlehem.

Even more obvious, though, is the discrepancy involved with the events after Jesus' birth. If Matthew is right that the family escaped to Egypt, how can Luke be right that they returned directly to Nazareth?

In short, there are enormous problems with the birth narratives when viewed from a historical perspective. There are historical implausibilities and discrepancies that can scarcely be reconciled. Why such differences? The answer might seem obvious to some readers. What historical critics have long said about these Gospel accounts is that they both are trying to emphasize the same two points: that Jesus' mother was a virgin and that he was born in Bethlehem. And why did he have to be born in Bethlehem? Matthew hits the nail on the head: there is a prophecy in the Old Testament book of Micah that a savior would come from Bethlehem. What were these Gospel writers to do with the fact that it was widely known that Jesus came from Nazareth? They had to come up with a narrative that explained how he came from Nazareth, in Galilee, a little one-horse town that no one had ever heard of, but was born in Bethlehem, the home of King David, royal ancestor of the Messiah. To get Jesus born in Bethlehem but raised in Nazareth, Matthew and Luke independently came up with solutions that no doubt struck each of them as plausible. But the historian can detect the problems with each narrative, and the careful reader can see that when the stories are placed side by side (read horizontally) they are at odds with each other at several key points.

The Genealogy of Jesus

Genealogies are not usually among the favorite passages of readers of the Bible. Sometimes my students complain when I have them read the genealogies of Jesus in Matthew and Luke. If they think this is bad, I tell them they should take a class on the Hebrew Bible and read the genealogy of 1 Chronicles. It covers nine full chapters, name after name. By comparison, the genealogies of Jesus in Matthew and Luke are short and sweet. The problem is that the genealogies are different.

Once again, Matthew and Luke are our only Gospels that give Jesus' family line. Both of them trace his lineage through Joseph to the Jewish ancestors. This in itself creates a puzzling situation. As we have seen, both Matthew and Luke want to insist that Jesus' mother was a virgin: she conceived not by having sex with Joseph but by the

Holy Spirit. Joseph is not Jesus' father. But that creates an obvious problem. If Jesus is not a blood-relation to Joseph, why is it that Matthew and Luke trace Jesus' bloodline precisely through Joseph? This is a question that neither author answers: both accounts give a genealogy that can't be the genealogy of Jesus, since his only bloodline goes through Mary, yet neither author provides her genealogy.

Apart from this general problem, there are several obvious differences between the genealogies of Matthew 1 and Luke 3. Some of them are not discrepancies per se; they are just differences. For example, Matthew gives the genealogy at the very outset of his Gospel, in the opening verses; Luke gives his after the baptism of Jesus in chapter 3 (an odd place for a genealogy, since genealogies have to do with your birth, not your baptism as a thirty-year-old. But Luke may have had his reasons for locating it where he does). Matthew's genealogy traces Joseph's lineage back through King David, the ancestor of the Messiah, all the way to Abraham, the father of the Jews. Luke's genealogy goes back well beyond that, tracing the line to Adam, father of the human race.

I have an aunt who is a genealogist, who is proud to have traced our family back to a passenger on the *Mayflower*. But here is a genealogy that goes back to Adam. As in Adam and Eve—the first humans. It's an amazing genealogy.

One might wonder why the two authors have different end points for their genealogies. Usually it is thought that Matthew, a Gospel concerned to show the Jewishness of Jesus, wants to emphasize Jesus' relation to the greatest king of the Jews, David, and to the father of the Jews, Abraham. Luke, on the other hand, is concerned to show that Jesus is the savior of all people, Jew and gentile, as seen in Luke's second volume, the book of Acts, where the gentiles are brought into the church. And so Luke shows that Jesus is related to all of us through Adam.

One other difference between the two genealogies is that Matthew starts at the beginning, with Abraham, and moves down generation by generation to Joseph; Luke goes the other direction, starting with Joseph and moving generation by generation back to Adam.

These then are simply some of the differences between the two accounts. The real problem they pose, however, is that the two genealogies are actually different. The easiest way to see the difference is to ask the simple question, Who, in each genealogy, is Joseph's father, patrilineal grandfather, and great-grandfather? In Matthew the family line goes from Joseph to Jacob to Matthan to Eleazar to Eliud and on into the past. In Luke it goes from Joseph to Heli to Mathat to Levi to Melchi. The lines become similar once we get all the way back to King David (although there are other problems, as we'll see), but from David to Joseph, the lines are at odds.

How does one solve this problem? One typical suggestion is to say that Matthew's genealogy is of Joseph, since Matthew focuses on Joseph more in the birth narrative, and that Luke's is of Mary, since she is the focus of his birth narrative. It is an attractive solution, but it has a fatal flaw. Luke explicitly indicates that the family line is that of Joseph, not Mary (Luke 1:23; also Matthew 1:16).[7]

There are other problems. In some ways Matthew's genealogy is the more remarkable because he stresses the numerological significance of Jesus' ancestry. From Abraham to David, Israel's greatest king, there were fourteen generations; from David to the destruction of Judah by the Babylonians, Israel's greatest disaster, there were fourteen generations; and from the Babylonian disaster to the birth of Jesus, fourteen generations (1:17). Fourteen, fourteen, and fourteen—it is almost as if God had planned it this way. In fact, for Matthew, he had. After every fourteen generations there occurs an enormously significant event. This must mean that Jesus—the fourteenth generation—is someone of very great importance to God.

The problem is that the fourteen-fourteen-fourteen schema doesn't actually work. If you read through the names carefully, you'll see that in the third set of fourteen there are in fact only thirteen generations. Moreover, it is relatively easy to check Matthew's genealogy against his source, the Hebrew Bible itself, which provides him with the names for his genealogy. It turns out that Matthew left out some names in the fourteen generations from David to the Babylonian disaster. In 1:8 he indicates that Joram is the father of Uzziah. But we know from 1 Chronicles 3:10–12 that Joram was not Uzziah's father, but his great-great-grandfather.[8] In other words, Matthew has dropped three generations from the genealogy. Why? The answer should be obvious. If he included *all* the generations, he would not be able to claim that something significant happened at every fourteenth generation.

But why does he stress the number fourteen in particular? Why not seventeen, or eleven? Scholars have given several explanations over the years. Some have pointed out that in the Bible seven is the perfect number. If so, then what is fourteen? Twice seven. This could be a "doubly perfect" genealogy. Another, possibly more convincing, theory is that the genealogy is designed to stress Jesus' status as the Messiah. The Messiah is to be the "son of David," a descendant of Israel's greatest king. It is important to know that in ancient languages, the letters of the alphabet functioned also as numerals, so that the first letter in the Hebrew alphabet, aleph, was also the numeral 1, the second, beth, was 2, the third, gimel, was 3, and so on. Also, in ancient Hebrew no vowels were used. So the name David was spelled D-V-D. In Hebrew, the letter D (daleth) is the number 4 and the V (waw) is 6. If you add up the letters of David's name, it equals 14. That may be why Matthew wanted there to be three groups of precisely fourteen generations in the genealogy of the son of David, the Messiah, Jesus.

Unfortunately, to make the numbers work he had to leave out some names. I might also point out that if Matthew was right in his fourteen-fourteen-fourteen schema, there would be forty-two names between Abraham and Jesus. Luke's genealogy, however, gives fifty-seven names. These are different genealogies.

And the reason for the discrepancies? Each author had a purpose for including a genealogy—or, more likely, several purposes: to show Jesus' connection to the father of the Jews, Abraham (especially Matthew), and the great king of the Jews, David (Matthew), and to the human race as a whole (Luke). Probably the two authors inherited, or possibly they made up, different genealogies. Of course neither could know that his account would be placed in a "New Testament" and be carefully compared with the other by historical critics living two thousand years later. And they certainly didn't consult with each other to get their facts straight. Each gave his account as well as he could, but their accounts ended up different.

Other Discrepancies from the Life of Jesus

Now that we have looked in some detail at a few of the interesting discrepancies among the Gospel accounts, I can touch on some others more quickly. For the most part you can examine these on your own if you choose. And you can find plenty more, simply by reading the Gospels horizontally, story by story.

We can approach some of the discrepancies by asking some simple questions. I'll limit myself here to five.

What Did the Voice at Jesus' Baptism Say?

It depends on which account you read. The baptism is not narrated in John, but we do have accounts in Matthew, Mark, and Luke, all very similar. This is what one would expect: scholars have long known that Matthew and Luke got a number of their stories from Mark, one of their key sources; that's why there are so many cases of verbatim agreement. But there are differences because Matthew and Luke changed the wording of their sources in certain places. In any event, in all three accounts of Jesus' baptism, when he emerges from the water the heavens open up, the Spirit descends in the form of a dove, and a voice comes from heaven. But what does the voice say? In Matthew it says, "This is my son, in whom I am well pleased." The voice appears to be speaking to the people around Jesus, or possibly to John the Baptist, informing them who Jesus is. In Mark, however, the voice says, "You are my son, in whom I am well pleased." In this case the voice appears to be speaking directly to Jesus, telling him, or confirming to him, who he really is. In Luke we have something different (this is a bit complicated, because different manuscripts of Luke's Gospel give the voice different words. I am taking here the original wording of the verse as found in some older manuscripts of the Bible, even though it is not found in most English translations).[9] Here the voice says, "You are my son, today I have begotten you" (3:22), quoting the words of Psalm 2:7.

Each account is trying to do something different with the voice. That is to say, the different words mean different things and have different functions: in Matthew, the words identify Jesus to John the Baptist and the crowd; in Mark, to confirm Jesus' identity to him directly; in Luke, they declare that the baptism has made (or ratified?) him as God's special son. But there remains the question, What did the voice actually say? Early Christians were confused by this problem, so much so that a later Gospel, called the Gospel of the Ebionites, resolved it by indicating that the voice came from heaven on three occasions. First it said the words as related by Mark, which were addressed to Jesus; then it said the words as related by Matthew, addressed to John the Baptist and the crowd; and finally the words as related by Luke. But unless someone is willing to rewrite all three Gospels, the fact is they indicate that the voice said different things.

Where Was Jesus the Day After He Was Baptized?

In Matthew, Mark, and Luke—the so-called Synoptic Gospels—Jesus, after his baptism, goes off into the wilderness where he will be tempted by the Devil.[10] Mark especially is quite clear about the matter, for he states, after telling of the baptism, that Jesus left "immediately" for the wilderness. What about John? In John there is no account of Jesus being tempted by the Devil in the wilderness. The day after John the Baptist has borne witness to the Spirit descending on Jesus as a dove at baptism (John 1:29–34), he sees Jesus again and declares him to be the Lamb of God (John is explicit, stating that this occurred "the next day"). Jesus then starts gathering his disciples around him (1:35–52) and launches into his public ministry by performing his miracle of turning water into wine (2:1–11). So where was Jesus the next day? It depends on which Gospel you read.

Was Jairus's Daughter Already Dead?

To illustrate my point that minor, irreconcilable differences can be found throughout the Gospels, I have chosen just one simple example from Jesus' healing ministry. In Mark, our earliest account, a leader of the synagogue named Jairus comes up to Jesus and begs him to hasten home with him, because his daughter is very sick and he wants Jesus to heal her. Before they can start on their way, though, Jesus is interrupted by a woman with a hemorrhage, whom he heals. Then servants from Jairus's house arrive to tell him that it is too late—the girl has died. Jesus tells them not to fret; he goes to the house and raises the girl from the dead (Mark 5:21–43). Matthew has the same story (9:18–26), but with a key difference. In Matthew's version Jairus comes to Jesus because his daughter has already died. He wants Jesus to come not to heal her but to raise her from the dead. And Jesus does so. It may seem like a minor difference, but it can be seen as highly significant—a matter of life and death.

Who Is for Jesus and Who Is Against Him?

Some sayings of Jesus are rendered in similar but nevertheless diverging ways. One of my favorite examples of this phenomenon is the pair of sayings related in Matthew 12:30 and Mark 9:40. In Matthew, Jesus declares, "Whoever is not with me is against me." In Mark, he says, "Whoever is not against us is for us." Did he say both things? Could he mean both things? How can both be true at once? Or is it possible that one of the Gospel writers got things switched around?

How Long Did Jesus' Ministry Last?

Our earliest Gospel, Mark, does not give an explicit indication of the length of Jesus' public ministry, but does give some suggestive comments. At the beginning of Jesus' ministry, in chapter 2, his disciples are going through the wheat fields and eating the grain, to the consternation of the Pharisees, who believe they are violating the Sabbath. This must be taking place, then, in the fall, at the time of the harvest. After this point the action moves very quickly: one of Mark's favorite words is *euthus*, "immediately"—"immediately" Jesus did this, "immediately" he did that. By chapter 11, after lots of "immediately's" we come to the last week of Jesus' life, at the Passover feast in Jerusalem. Passover is in the spring, and the distinct impression is that the ministry has lasted a few months, from harvest time to spring.

A few months? Doesn't everyone know that Jesus' ministry lasted three years? Actually, the idea that it lasted three years comes not from the Synoptic Gospels—Mark, Matthew, and Luke—but from the last Gospel, John. On three separate occasions John refers to different Passover celebrations, which since they were a year apart would seem to indicate that the ministry must have lasted at least over two years, rounded up to three. But which is it? I would say this is not technically a discrepancy, but it is hard to know what to make of all of Mark's "immediately's" if he didn't really mean them.

One can find many other discrepancies in the accounts of Jesus' ministry if one were inclined to track them all down. Rather than continue on the same track, though, at this point I'd like to move on and talk about discrepancies found in the Passion Narratives—the accounts of Jesus' death and resurrection. Some of these discrepancies, too, are highly significant.

Discrepancies in the Passion Narratives

We have already talked about a couple of the discrepancies between the Gospels of Mark and John with regard to the Passion Narratives: the date of the Temple cleansing (Mark 11; John 2) and the day and time of his death (Mark 14–15; John 18–19). These are not the only differences in our Gospels' accounts of Jesus' death and resurrection. Here I will talk about three important differences at some length, and then give a short rundown of a few others.

The Trial Before Pilate

We start with a comparison of Mark, our earliest canonical Gospel, and John, our latest. In both accounts Jesus is put on trial before the Roman governor, Pontius Pilate, and condemned to death for calling himself the King of the Jews. But there are some very interesting differences between Mark's and John's narratives of the trial.

Mark's account is short and straightforward. Early in the morning the Jewish leaders bring Jesus to Pilate, who asks him if he is, in fact, the King of the Jews. Jesus replies in just two words, in Greek: *"su legeis."* "You say so." The Jewish priests accuse him of many things, and Pilate expresses surprise that Jesus puts up no defense. We are then told that Pilate had a custom of releasing a prisoner to the Jewish people during Passover, and he asks the gathered crowds whether they want him to release the "King of the Jews." The chief priests intervene to stir up the crowd to ask for a murderer named Barabbas to be released to them instead of Jesus. Pilate asks the crowd what they want done with Jesus. They reply that he should crucify him. And "to satisfy the crowd" he does what they ask: he releases Barabbas, has Jesus flogged, and hands him over to be crucified.

If Mark's were our only account of the event, we would have the impression that the trial was very quick; that Jesus said almost nothing (just two words); and that Pilate, the Jewish leaders accusing

Jesus, the crowds, and Jesus himself were all in one place exchanging their views.

But John (18:28–19:14) has a very different account. In John the Jewish leaders take Jesus to Pilate early in the morning, but they refuse to enter Pilate's headquarters because they want to "avoid ritual defilement" so that they can "eat the Passover" that evening (18:28; remember, though, that in Mark's Gospel they had already eaten the Passover meal the night before). We're not told why they would be defiled by entering the headquarters. Because it was a pagan place? Built on a cemetery? Something else? But the result is that the trial proceeds in a rather peculiar way. Jesus is inside the headquarters with Pilate, the Jewish authorities who accuse him are outside the headquarters, along with the Jewish crowd, and Pilate runs back and forth between accuser and accused, talking first to one, then to the other. Pilate enters and leaves the headquarters six times over the course of the trial and has discussions both with Jesus and with the accusers—reasoning with them, pleading with them, trying to get them to listen to sense.

You can find numerous other differences between the accounts if you read them horizontally. Here I mention just three and point out their potential significance. First, Jesus has a lot more to say in John's account than in Mark. In fact, he has sustained conversations with Pilate, speaking of his "kingdom that is not of this world" (18:36), indicating that he has come into the world to speak the truth (18:37), declaring that Pilate has no ultimate power over him, except what has been given him by God (19:11). These extended dialogues conform well with what you find throughout all of John's Gospel, where Jesus engages in long protracted speeches, quite unlike the series of aphorisms and one-liners that you frequently find in the Synoptic Gospels.

Second, rather than having Jesus flogged after his trial is over and the sentence has been pronounced—which, one might think, would be the sensible time to carry out the sentence—in John, Pilate has Jesus flogged in the middle of the proceedings (19:1). A variety of explanations have been given for John's change of this detail; it may be because of what happens next: Pilate brings Jesus out of the headquarters to present him, beaten, bloodied, and in a purple robe, to the Jewish people, and says to them, "Behold the man." For the author of John, Jesus is much more than a man, but Pilate and the Jewish crowds don't recognize it. Pilate and his soldiers are mocking Jesus by dressing him up in a crown of thorns and giving him a purple robe and declaring, "Hail, King of the Jews." In fact, unbeknownst to them their declaration is true. For John, Jesus really is the King, appearances notwithstanding.

Finally, it is significant that in John's Gospel, on three occasions Pilate expressly declares that Jesus is innocent, does not deserve to be punished, and ought to be released (18:38; 19:6; and by implication in 19:12). In Mark, Pilate never declares Jesus innocent. Why this heightened emphasis in John? Scholars have long noted that John is in many ways the most virulently anti-Jewish of our Gospels (see John 8:42–44, where Jesus declares that the Jews are not children of God but "children of the Devil"). In that context, why narrate the trial in such a way that the Roman governor repeatedly insists that Jesus is innocent? Ask yourself: If the Romans are not responsible for Jesus' death, who is? The Jews. And so they are, for John. In 19:16 we are told that Pilate handed Jesus over to the Jewish chief priests so that they could have him crucified.

The Death of Judas

In all four Gospels Judas Iscariot is said to be the one who betrayed Jesus to the authorities, leading to his arrest. The four accounts differ on why Judas did the foul deed. There is no reason stated in Mark, although we are told that he received money for the act, so maybe it was out of greed (14:10–11). Matthew (26:14) states explicitly that Judas did it for the money. Luke, on the other hand, indicates that Judas did it because "Satan entered into him" (22:3). In other words, the devil made him do it. In John, Judas is himself called "a devil"

(6:70–71), and so presumably he betrayed his master because he had an evil streak.

More interesting yet is the question of what happened to Judas after he performed the act of betrayal. Mark and John say nothing about the matter: Judas simply disappears from the scene. So, too, in the Gospel of Luke, but Luke wrote a second volume to accompany his Gospel, the book of Acts.[11] Acts gives an account of what happened to Judas after the betrayal, as does the Gospel of Matthew, but it is striking that the two accounts stand directly at odds with each other on a number of points.

The commonly held view that Judas went out and "hanged himself" comes from Matthew (27:3–10). After Judas sees that his betrayal has led to Jesus' conviction, he feels remorse and tries to return his pay of thirty pieces of silver to the Jewish chief priests, telling them that he has "sinned by betraying innocent blood." They refuse to accept the money, however, so he throws it down in the Temple and goes out and hangs himself. The chief priests then collect the money, but decide that they cannot put it back into the Temple treasure because it is "blood money"— money that has been tainted with innocent blood. So they decide to put it to good use and purchase a "potter's field," presumably a field from which potters took clay, as a place to bury foreigners who died in Jerusalem. It is because it was purchased with Judas's blood money, we are told, that the place "has been called the Field of Blood to this day."

Luke's account in the book of Acts has some similarities: the death of Judas is connected with the purchase of a field that is called "the Field of Blood." But the details are in stark contrast to—even contradict—the story as told by Matthew. In Acts (1:18–19) we are told that Judas himself, not the Jewish priests, purchased the field with "the reward of his wickedness," the money he earned for his betrayal. And it is not said that he hanged himself. Instead we learn that he fell "headlong" and "burst open in the middle" so that "his bowels gushed out." For Luke the reason the field was called the Field of Blood was because Judas bled all over it.

Over the years readers have tried to reconcile these two accounts of the death of Judas. How could he both hang himself and "fall headlong" so that his stomach split open and his intestines spilled all over the ground? Ingenious interpreters, wanting to splice the two accounts together into one true account, have had a field day here. Maybe Judas hanged himself, the rope broke, and he fell to the ground, head first, bursting in the middle. Or maybe he hanged himself, and that didn't work, so he climbed onto a high rock and did a swan dive onto the field below. Or maybe . . . well, maybe something else.

The point is, though, that the two reports give different accounts of how Judas died. However mysterious it may be to say he fell head-long and burst open, at the least that is not "hanging" oneself. And they are flat out contradictory on two other points: who purchased the field (the priests, as per Matthew, or Judas, as per Acts?) and why the field was called the field of blood (because it was purchased with blood money, as Matthew says, or because Judas bled all over it, as Acts says?).

The Resurrection Narratives

Nowhere are the differences among the Gospels more clear than in the accounts of Jesus' resurrection. I often have my first-year students do a simple comparison exercise in which they list everything said in each of the four Gospels about the events between the time Jesus was buried and the end of the Gospels. There can be no better introduction to the idea of horizontal reading. There are scads of differences among the four accounts, and some of these differences are discrepancies that cannot be readily (or ever) reconciled. Students find this a valuable exercise because I'm not simply telling them there are differences between the accounts: they discover the differences themselves and try to make sense of them.

Here let me stress the point that I made in my book *Misquoting Jesus*: we don't have the originals of any of these Gospels, only copies made later, in most instances many centuries later. These copies all differ from one another, very often in the accounts of Jesus' resurrection. Scholars have to determine what the originals said on the basis of these later manuscripts. In some places the decisions are quite straightforward; in others there is a lot of debate.

In one aspect of the resurrection narratives there is little debate: it appears that the final twelve verses of Mark's Gospel are not original to Mark's Gospel but were added by a scribe in a later generation. Mark ended his Gospel at what is now 16:8, with the women fleeing the tomb and not telling anyone what they had seen. In my discussion I accept the scholarly consensus that verses 16:9–21 were a later addition to the Gospel.[12]

With that detail out of the way, what can we say about the resurrection narratives in the four canonical accounts? All four Gospels agree that on the third day after Jesus' crucifixion and burial, Mary Magdalene went to the tomb and found it empty. But on virtually every detail they disagree.

Who actually went to the tomb? Was it Mary alone (John 20:1)? Mary and another Mary (Matthew 28:1)? Mary Magdalene, Mary the mother of James, and Salome (Mark 16:1)? Or women who had accompanied Jesus from Galilee to Jerusalem—possibly Mary Magdalene, Joanna, Mary the mother of James, and "other women" (Luke 24:1; see 23:55)? Had the stone already been rolled away from the tomb (as in Mark 16:4) or was it rolled away by an angel while the women were there (Matthew 28:2)? Whom or what did they see there? An angel (Matthew 28:5)? A young man (Mark 16:5)? Two men (Luke 24:4)? Or nothing and no one (John)? And what were they told? To tell the disciples to "go to Galilee," where Jesus will meet them (Mark 16:7)? Or to remember what Jesus had told them "while he was in Galilee," that he had to die and rise again (Luke 24:7)? Then, do the women tell the disciples what they saw and heard (Matthew 28:8), or do they not tell anyone (Mark 16:8)? If they tell someone, whom do they tell? The eleven disciples (Matthew 28:8)? The eleven disciples and other people (Luke 24:8)? Simon

Peter and another unnamed disciple (John 20:2)? What do the disciples do in response? Do they have no response because Jesus himself immediately appears to them (Matthew 20:9)? Do they not believe the women because it seems to be "an idle tale" (Luke 24:11)? Or do they go to the tomb to see for themselves (John 20:3)?

The questions multiply. You can read horizontally to do a cross-Gospel comparison yourself of what happens next: to whom Jesus appears (if anyone) and when, what he says to them, and what they say in response. On virtually every issue at least one Gospel is out of step.

One point in particular seems to be irreconcilable. In Mark's account the women are instructed to tell the disciples to go meet Jesus in Galilee, but out of fear they don't say a word to anyone about it. In Matthew's version the disciples are told to go to Galilee to meet Jesus, and they immediately do so. He appears to them there and gives them their final instruction. But in Luke the disciples are not told to go to Galilee. They are told that Jesus had foretold his resurrection while *he* was in Galilee (during his public ministry). And they never leave Jerusalem—in the southern part of the Israel, a different region from Galilee, in the north. On the day of the resurrection Jesus appears to two disciples on the "road to Emmaus" (24:13–35); later that day these disciples tell the others what they have seen, and Jesus appears to all of them (24:36–49); and then Jesus takes them to Bethany on the outskirts of Jerusalem and gives them their instructions and ascends to heaven. In Luke's next volume, Acts, we're told that the disciples are in fact explicitly told by Jesus after his resurrection *not* to leave Jerusalem (Acts 1:4), but to stay there until they receive the Holy Spirit on the Day of Pentecost, fifty days after Passover. After giving his instructions, Jesus then ascends to heaven. The disciples do stay in Jerusalem until the Holy Spirit comes (Acts 2). And so the discrepancy: If Matthew is right, that the disciples immediately go to Galilee and see Jesus ascend from there, how can Luke be right that the disciples stay in Jerusalem the whole time, see Jesus ascend from there, and stay on until the day of Pentecost?

Other Differences in the Passion Narratives

These then are just some of the key discrepancies in the accounts of Jesus' last week of life, his death, and his resurrection. They are by no means the only differences, but instead of listing them all I point out here a few of the more interesting ones that you would find if you were to do a complete analysis. I can give these in rapid-fire succession by asking just five simple questions.

1. *When Jesus entered Jerusalem during the Triumphal Entry, how many animals did he ride?* It seems like there should be an obvious answer: he rode one animal, a donkey or a colt. And that in fact is what is said in three of the Gospels, including Mark 11:7. In Matthew's Gospel, however, this triumphal act is said to fulfill prophecy; as we have seen, Matthew sets great store on the fulfillment of Scripture, and in 21:5 he states, quoting Zechariah 9:9:

Behold, your king is coming to you,
humble, and mounted on a donkey,
and on a colt, the foal of a donkey

Scholars of the Hebrew Bible recognize this kind of poetic prophecy: the third line of the text restates what is said in the second line. This is called "synonymous parallelism"—where two lines of poetry say basically the same thing in different words. But Matthew evidently did not understand this poetic convention in this place, leading to some rather bizarre results. In Matthew, Jesus' disciples procure *two* animals for him, a donkey and a colt; they spread their garments over the two of them, and Jesus rode into town straddling them both (Matthew 21:7). It's an odd image, but Matthew made Jesus fulfill the prophecy of Scripture quite literally.

2. *What did Jesus tell the high priest when questioned at his trial?* My sense is that historically, this is something we could never know. Jesus was there, and the Jewish leaders were there, but there were no followers of Jesus there, taking notes for posterity. Nevertheless,

Mark gives us a clear account. The high priest asks Jesus if he is the "Messiah, the Son of the Blessed One" (14:61), and Jesus gives a straightforward reply, "I am. And you will see the Son of Man seated at the right hand of Power and coming with the clouds of heaven" (Mark 14:62). In other words, in the near future God would be sending a cosmic judge of the earth, in fulfillment of the predictions of the Old Testament (Daniel 7:13–14). In fact, it was so near that the high priest himself would see it happen.

What if it doesn't happen? What if the high priest were to die before the Son of Man arrived? Wouldn't that invalidate Jesus' claim? Maybe. And that may be why Luke, writing some fifteen or twenty years after Mark—presumably after the high priest has died—changes Jesus' answer. Now when he replies he says nothing about the high priest being alive when the Son of Man arrives in judgment: "I am, and from now on the Son of Man will be seated at the right hand of the power of God" (Luke 22:69).

3. *Why does Matthew quote the wrong prophet?* When Matthew indicates that Judas betrayed Jesus for thirty pieces of silver, he notes (as by now we expect of him) that this was in fulfillment of Scripture: "Then was fulfilled what had been spoken through the prophet Jeremiah, 'And they took the thirty pieces of silver . . . and they gave them for the potter's field' " (Mathew 27:9–10). The problem is that this prophecy is not found in Jeremiah. It appears to be a loose quotation of Zechariah 11:3.

4. *When was the curtain in the Temple ripped?* The curtain in the Temple separated the holiest place, called the "holy of holies," from the rest of the 'Temple precincts. It was in the holy of holies that God was thought to dwell here on earth (he obviously is reigning in heaven as well). No one could enter that room behind the curtain except once a year, on the Day of Atonement (Yom Kippur), when the high priest could go in to offer a sacrifice, first for his own sins and then for the sins of the people. According to Mark's Gospel, after Jesus breathes his last, the curtain of the Temple is torn in half (15:38). This has long been recognized as a symbolic statement,

for there is no historical evidence to suggest the curtain was ever destroyed before the Temple itself was burned to the ground forty years later in the war with the Romans. For Mark, Jesus' death means the end of the need for Temple sacrifices. In his son's death God is now available to all people; he is no longer separated from them by a thick curtain. Jesus' death makes people one with God: it is an atonement (at-one-ment) for sin.

Luke's Gospel also indicates that the curtain in the Temple was ripped in half. Oddly enough, it does not rip after Jesus dies but is explicitly said to rip while Jesus is still alive and hanging on the cross (23:45–46). I will speak about the significance of this discrepancy in the next chapter, as this change is directly tied to Luke's understanding of Jesus' death.

5. *What did the centurion say when Jesus died?* Again the answer may seem obvious, especially to those who remember the great biblical epic on the silver screen, *The Greatest Story Ever Told*, and the immortal words of the centurion played by John Wayne: "Truly this man was the Son of God." And that is, in fact, what the centurion says in the Gospel of Mark (15:39). But it is worth noting that Luke has changed the words. In his account the centurion says, "Truly this man was innocent" (23:47). There have always been interpreters who have wanted to insist that this comes to the same thing: of course if he's the Son of God he's innocent. But the words are different and have different meanings. If a potential criminal is declared "not guilty" by the court, that is certainly not the same thing as being declared the Son of God. Did the centurion say both things? One could say yes if one's goal were to reconcile the Gospels, and thereby create yet a third version of the scene, unlike either Mark or Luke. But it is probably better to consider why the later Luke might have changed the words. For Luke it was important to stress that Jesus was completely innocent of the charges against him. In John, for example, as in Luke, three times Pilate tries to release Jesus by declaring him innocent (unlike in Mark). And at the end, so, too, does the centurion. The Romans all agree on Jesus' innocence. Who

then is guilty for his death? Not the Romans, but the Jewish authorities, or the Jewish people themselves.

DISCREPANCIES INVOLVING THE LIFE AND WRITINGS OF PAUL

So far in this chapter I have considered just the four canonical Gospels, emphasizing the need to read these horizontally if we want to gain new insights into them, insights unavailable to us if we read them only vertically, in sequence. I do not claim that a horizontal reading is the best or only way to approach these books. Obviously the Gospels were meant to be read like other books, from beginning to end, and historical critics have long recognized the value of doing so and have devised a number of interesting methods that can assist readers who choose to read them in this way.[13]

I am also not claiming that the Gospels are the only books in the New Testament that contain discrepancies. As we have already seen, the book of Acts appears to be at odds with what the Gospels say with respect to the death of Judas (in contrast with Matthew), for example, or with respect to whether the disciples journeyed north to Galilee soon after Jesus' death and resurrection (again, in contrast to Matthew).

The book of Acts as a whole is a narrative of what happened to and among his followers after Jesus' ascension to heaven. Briefly, the apostles spread the Christian faith, first among the Jews who lived in Jerusalem and then elsewhere, taking their message to Jews in other parts of the empire and then, most significantly, to non-Jews, gentiles, living in urban centers dotted around the Mediterranean. Of the many converts to this new religion none was more significant than Saul of Tarsus, who came to be known as the apostle Paul. About two thirds of the narrative of Acts is concerned with Paul, his conversion to Christianity after being a violent opponent of the new faith, his missionary journeys converting others to faith in Christ, his arrest, trials, and eventual imprisonment in the city of Rome.

Paul was not only the hero of Acts but also an author in his own right. Of the twenty-seven books of the New Testament, thirteen claim to be written by Paul. One other book, the letter to the Hebrews, was admitted into the canon because early church fathers believed it was written by Paul, even though it doesn't claim to be. Scholars today are reasonably certain that Paul did not in fact write it. And among the thirteen letters that bear Paul's name, there are reasons for doubting that he actually wrote six of them. This will be the subject of a later chapter, when we discuss the big question "Who Wrote the Bible?" For now it is enough to know that Paul is the subject of Acts and the author of at least some of the writings of the New Testament. The seven letters that virtually all scholars agree Paul wrote—the so-called undisputed Pauline epistles—are Romans, 1 and 2 Corinthians, Galatians, Philippians, 1 Thessalonians, and Philemon.

It is thus possible to do a kind of horizontal reading of Acts, comparing it with the letters of Paul. Sometimes Acts discusses an event in Paul's life that Paul himself mentions in his letters. This allows us to see how the two square up. Historical critics have long disagreed among themselves concerning just how reliable the book of Acts is for understanding the life and writings of Paul. My personal view is that Acts is about as accurate for Paul as Luke's first volume, the Gospel of Luke, is for Jesus: much of the basic information is probably reliable, but a lot of the details managed to get changed.

Most critical scholars think Acts was written sometime after the Gospel of Luke, possibly around 85 or 90 CE—about twenty or twenty-five years after Paul died. If so, it would be no surprise to see that information about him in Acts may not be historically accurate. But the only way to know for sure is to compare what Acts says about Paul with what Paul says about himself, to see if they are basically in agreement or whether there are discrepancies. Here are five examples that strike me as interesting. Some of these are important for understanding the life and teachings of Paul; others of them, frankly, are rather unimportant discrepancies. But together they show that Acts cannot be completely reliable when it comes to reporting on Paul's life.

1. *After his conversion, did Paul go directly to Jerusalem in order to confer with those who were apostles before him?* As noted, Paul was a persecutor of the Christians prior to becoming a Christian himself, so he was not a follower of Jesus during his ministry and he probably never even knew him. Paul lived outside Palestine, and his native language was Greek, not Aramaic. But at some point, for some reason, he "saw the light" (literally, according to Acts 9:3) and converted from an enemy of the Christian faith to one of its greatest proponents. And what did he do then? Paul himself recounts, in Galatians 1:16–20, what happened after his conversion:

> I did not confer with any human being, nor did I go up to Jerusalem to those who were apostles before me, but I went away off to Arabia, and afterwards I returned to Damascus. Then after three years I went up to Jerusalem to visit Cephas and I stayed with him fifteen days; but I did not see any of the other apostles, except James the Lord's brother. In what I am writing to you, before God, I am not lying!

This emphatic statement that Paul is not lying should give us pause. He is completely clear. He did not consult with others after his conversion, did not see any of the apostles for three years, and even then he did not see any except Cephas (Peter) and Jesus' brother James.

This makes the account found in the book of Acts very interesting indeed. For according to Acts 9, immediately after Paul converted he spent some time in Damascus "with the disciples," and when he left the city, he headed directly to Jerusalem, where he met with the apostles of Jesus (Acts 9:19–30). On all counts Acts seems to be at odds with Paul. Did he spend time with other Christians immediately (Acts) or not (Paul)? Did he go straight to Jerusalem (Acts) or not (Paul)? Did he meet with the group of apostles (Acts) or just with Peter and James (Paul)?

For those familiar with Paul's own writings and the book of Acts, it is not difficult to understand why this discrepancy exists. In Paul's letter to the Galatians he wants to insist that his Gospel message came directly from God himself, through Jesus. He didn't get it from anyone else—not even the other apostles—so anyone who disagrees with him about the Gospel is really disagreeing not with him but with God.

The writer of the book of Acts, on the other hand, wants to insist that there was complete continuity in every way among all the genuine apostles of Jesus, both the original disciples and Paul. They met, they talked, they agreed—time and again this is stated in Acts. For Paul himself, however, the issue is his authority, given straight from God. He did *not* confer with others or meet with the apostles. The two authors have different agendas and so have recounted the events differently—creating an interesting but important discrepancy. Whom are we to believe? In this case my vote would go with Paul, who not only should know what he was doing but also swears an oath before God that he's not lying. It's a bit hard to believe that he would be lying.

2. *Did the churches in Judea know Paul?* Here again Paul is quite clear. Sometime after he converted he went around to various churches in the regions of Syria and Cilicia, but he "was still unknown by sight to the churches of Judea" (Galatians 1:21–22). This has struck some scholars as odd. According to the book of Acts, when Paul was earlier persecuting the churches in Christ, it was specifically the Christian churches in "Judea and Samaria" (Acts 8:1–3; 9:1–2). Why is it that Christians in the churches he had formerly persecuted didn't know what he looked like? Wasn't he physically present among them as their enemy earlier? According to Acts, yes; according to Paul, no.

3. *Did Paul go to Athens alone?* When he was making his missionary journeys, and went to Athens to evangelize the pagans there, did Paul go alone? Here again there appears to be a discrepancy. It

may not be one that matters all that much, except that Luke again appears to have gotten some details wrong. When Paul writes his very first letter to the Thessalonians, he indicates that after he had brought them to faith and started a church among them, he traveled to Athens. But he felt concerned about the fledgling new church and so sent his companion Timothy back to see how the Thessalonians were doing. In other words, Timothy accompanied Paul to Athens and then returned to Thessalonica to help build them up in the faith (1 Thessalonians 3:1–2). The book of Acts, however, is equally clear. There we are told that after Paul established the church in Thessalonica, he and Silas and Timothy founded a church in the city of Boroea; the Christians there then "sent Paul away to the coast, but Silas and Timothy remained behind" (17:14–15). Paul proceeded to send instructions that Silas and Timothy should meet up with him when they could. He traveled to Athens alone and met up with his two companions only after leaving the city for Corinth (17:16–8:5). This is another discrepancy hard to resolve: either Timothy went to Athens with Paul (1 Thessalonians), or not (Acts).

4. *How many trips did Paul make to Jerusalem?* In Galatians Paul is intent to show that he did not confer with the apostles in Jerusalem in order to "learn" the Gospel. He already knew what the Gospel was: he had heard it directly from Christ in a divine revelation. He especially wants the Galatians to understand that when there was some dispute about his message, there was a special meeting in Jerusalem to discuss it. The question was this: if a non-Jew converted to become a follower of Jesus, did he or she first have to become a Jew? Paul said, emphatically, no. In particular, gentile men were not to be circumcised, the sign of the covenant for Jews, if they became followers of Christ. Other Christian missionaries took the opposite point of view, and there was a meeting in Jerusalem to consider the issue. According to Paul's account, this was only the second time he had been to Jerusalem (Galatians 1:18; 2:1). According to Acts, it was his third, prolonged, trip there (Acts 9, 11, 15). Once again, it appears

that the author of Acts has confused some of Paul's itinerary—possibly intentionally, for his own purposes.

5. *Were the congregations that Paul established made up of both Jews and gentiles?* According to the book of Acts, the answer is a clear yes. When Paul preaches in Thessalonica, Jews in the synagogue come to faith in Christ, as do non-Jewish Greeks (Acts 17:4). Paul indicates just the opposite. When he writes to this church in Thessalonica, he recalls how he converted them to faith in Christ and speaks of how they "turned to God from idols" (1 Thessalonians 1:9). Only pagans worshiped idols. Paul's converts in both Thessalonica and Corinth (1 Corinthians 12:2) were former pagans. That is why he calls himself the "apostle to the gentiles." There were other missionaries, in particular Peter, who were in charge of taking the message to Jews (Galatians 2:8). The Thessalonian and Corinthian churches were made up of gentiles (Paul), not Jews and gentiles (Acts).

These are just a few of the discrepancies that one can find when one reads Acts horizontally against Paul's letters. Many more can be discovered. What they show is that Acts cannot be relied upon for completely accurate detail when it describes the mission of early apostles such as Paul.

One reason it matters whether Acts is reliable in its historical details is that a lot of the information that people "know" about Paul comes from Acts and only from Acts, since these are pieces of information that Paul doesn't mention in his letters. Some historical critics have raised doubts about these items, including the following: that Paul came from Tarsus (Acts 21:39), that he had studied with the Jewish rabbi Gamaliel in Jerusalem (22:3), that he was a Roman citizen (22:27), that he was a "tent-maker" (18:3), that when he entered a city to evangelize it, he first went into a synagogue to try to convert Jews (for example, 14:1), that he was arrested in Jerusalem and spent years in prison (chapters 21–28), that he appealed to Caesar for his trial, and that's why he ended up in Rome (25:11).

CONCLUSION

We have seen lots of discrepancies in the New Testament in this chapter, some small and relatively inconsequential, others important for understanding what the different authors wanted to say. Some of the discrepancies could probably be reconciled if sufficient interpretive ingenuity were brought to bear; others appear to be flat-out contradictions. This is not an exhaustive treatment of the discrepancies, just a representative example. I picked some that I find to be the most interesting.

What conclusions can we draw from these discrepancies? Three points strike me as the most significant.

1. On one level the discrepancies are significant because they show that the view of the Bible as completely inerrant appears not to be true. There are errors, if the Bible is looked at historically. If two descriptions of an event (for example, Jesus' death) are contradictory in their details, both accounts cannot be historically correct. One of them is historically wrong, or both of them are wrong, but both cannot be right, at least with regard to what actually happened. Does this mean that the Bible should be tossed aside, jettisoned as just another piece of old and basically worthless literature? Not in the least. I argue in my final chapter that we should continue to read, study, and cherish the Bible—but not as an inerrant historical account.

Does this mean that it is impossible any longer for a person to be a Christian? Only Christians of a certain persuasion—such as many of those among whom I live, in the American South—would ever think to ask such a question. But the answer, again, is decidedly no. A Christianity dependent on the inerrancy of the Bible probably cannot survive the reality of the discrepancies. But there are lots of other forms of the Christian faith, many of them unscathed by the fact that the Bible is not a completely perfect book. I will deal with this at greater length in my final chapter

2. Since there are discrepancies between what different authors want to say—sometimes small, insignificant contradictions and

sometimes significant—it is important to let each author speak for himself and not pretend that he is saying the same thing as another. The discrepancies should teach us that Mark's view is not John's, John's is not Matthew's, Matthew's is not Paul's, and so on. Each author has to be read for his own message, so that when you read Mark, you do not import the teachings of Matthew. Read Mark for Mark and Matthew for Matthew. This is an issue we will take up at greater length in the next chapter.

3. The discrepancies that involve historical narratives—what did Jesus or Paul actually say, do, and experience?—make it difficult to establish what really happened in the life of Jesus or the history of the early church. You can't read these books as disinterested historical accounts. None of them is that. What would you do as a judge in a court trial in which you have conflicting testimony from eye witnesses? One thing you would certainly not do is assume that each witness is 100 percent correct. Someone—or everyone—is getting some information wrong. The trick would be to figure out who is wrong and who is right—if anyone is right. The same applies to ancient documents like those in the New Testament. If there is conflicting testimony about historical events, all the witnesses cannot be (historically) right, and we have to figure out ways to decide what most probably really happened. We take up this task in chapter 5.

A Mass of Variant Views

In the mid-nineties I was asked by Oxford University Press to write a college-level textbook on the New Testament. I wasn't sure this would be the best career move for me: I didn't have tenure yet, and sometimes university tenure committees look askance on textbooks as not involving real research. And I wondered what the pitfalls would be in trying to communicate historical-critical scholarship to nineteen-year-olds for whom all this would be news. I decided to call a number of my friends in the field to see what they thought about it. Should I do it? And if so, what kinds of problems would I have in trying to digest hard-core biblical scholarship basically for kids just out of high school?

I received lots of good tips and advice, but I think the wisest comment came from my friend Charlie Cosgrove, who years earlier had helped get me through graduate school (he was a couple of years ahead of me at Princeton Seminary and taught me the ropes). About the textbook Charlie said, "The hardest thing will be deciding what to leave out."

I ended up writing the book, and Charlie was absolutely right. It is very easy to decide what to include in a book on the New Testament because there is so much to include. But to keep the book manageable and affordable, a number of important and beloved topics simply have to be left out. And leaving out topics that are near and dear to your heart is painful.

I had the same experience with this book. When talking about discrepancies in the Bible, I want to go on and on—there are so many of them that are both interesting and important. But I've managed to restrain myself and have kept my discussion to one chapter—the previous one. Yet I have the same problem with the present chapter. I—or any other historical critic—could easily devote an entire book to its topic, but I've restricted myself to a single chapter.

As we saw in the previous chapter, the discrepancies in the Bible are important in part because they force us to take each author seriously. What Mark is saying may not be at all what Luke is saying; Matthew may stand at odds with John, and they both may conflict with what is said in Paul. But when we look at the contrasting messages of the different biblical authors, there is more involved than the kinds of detail and minutiae that we dealt with in chapter 2. There are much larger differences among these authors and books— differences not simply in a detail here or there, a date, a travel itinerary, or who did what with whom. Many of the differences among the biblical authors have to do with the very heart of their message. Sometimes one author's understanding of a major issue is at odds with another author's, on such vital matters as who Christ is, how salvation is attained, and how the followers of Jesus are to live.

Differences of this magnitude do not involve a simple contradiction here or there, but alternative portrayals of major importance. It is impossible to see these alternative portrayals if we do not allow each author to speak for himself. Most people do not read the Bible this way. They assume that since all the books in the Bible are found between the same hard covers, every author is basically saying the same thing. They think that Matthew can be used to help understand John, John provides insights into Paul, Paul can help interpret the book of James, and so on. This harmonizing approach to the Bible, which is foundational to much devotional reading, has the advantage of helping readers see the unifying themes of the Bible, but it also has very serious drawbacks, often creating unity of thought and belief where originally there was none. The biblical authors did not agree on everything they discussed; sometimes they had deeply rooted and significant disagreements.

The historical-critical approach to the Bible does not assume that each author has the same message. It allows for the possibility that each author has his own perspective, his own views, his own understandings of what the Christian faith is and should be. The discrepancies we have already considered are crucial for showing us that there are differences among the biblical writers. The major differences we are about to discuss should force us to recognize that the discrepancies are not merely a matter of minutiae but are issues of great importance.

I am not insisting that the historical-critical approach is the only way to read the Bible. Sophisticated theologians who are fully aware of historical-critical problems with the Bible have devised ways of treating the Bible as Scripture even though it is full of discrepancies. I will have more to say about this later, in chapter 8. For now, though, it is important to come to grips with what the historical-critical approach is and how it can affect the way the Bible is understood.

The approach is predicated, to some extent, on the idea that the "canon" of Scripture—that is the collection of the books into one book considered in some sense to be authoritative for believers—was not the original form in which the biblical books appeared. When Paul wrote his letters to the churches he founded, he did not think that he was writing the Bible. He thought he was writing letters, addressing individual needs as they came up, based on what he thought, believed, and preached at the time. Only later did someone put these letters together and consider them inspired. So, too, with the Gospels. Mark, whatever his real name was, had no idea that his book would be put into a collection with three other books and called Scripture; and he certainly did not think that his book should be interpreted in light of what some other Christian would write some thirty years later in a different country and a different context. Mark no doubt wanted his book to be read and understood on its own, as did Matthew, Luke, John, and all the other writers of the New Testament.

The historical-critical method maintains that we are in danger of misreading a book if we fail to let its author speak for himself, if we force his message to be exactly the same as another author's message, if we insist on reading all the books of the New Testament as one book instead of as twenty-seven books. These books were written in different times and places, under different circumstances, to address different issues; they were written by different authors with different perspectives, beliefs, assumptions, traditions, and sources. And they sometimes present different points of view on major issues.[1]

AN OPENING ILLUSTRATION:
THE DEATH OF JESUS IN MARK AND LUKE

I can begin my comparison of texts by discussing an example that strikes me as particularly clear and gripping. As with the detailed discrepancies we discussed in chapter 2, this kind of difference can be seen only by doing a careful horizontal reading of passages; this time, rather than looking for minute disagreements here or there, we are looking for broader themes, major differences in the way a story is told. One story told very differently in the Gospels is the key story in them all: the crucifixion of Jesus. You might think that all the Gospels have exactly the same message about the crucifixion, and that their differences might simply reflect minor changes of perspective, with one author emphasizing one thing and another something else. But in fact the differences are much larger and more fundamental than that. Nowhere can this be seen more clearly than in the accounts of Jesus' death in Mark and Luke.

Since the nineteenth century, scholars have recognized that Mark was the first Gospel to be written, around 65–70 CE. Both Matthew and Luke, writing fifteen or twenty years later, used Mark as one of their sources for much of their own accounts. That is why almost all of Mark's stories can be found in Matthew or Luke, and it is also why sometimes all three of these Gospels agree word for word in the way they tell the stories. Sometimes just two agree and the third doesn't, because occasionally only one of the later Gospels changed Mark. This means that if we have the same story in Mark and Luke, say, and there are differences, these differences exist precisely because Luke has actually modified the words of his source, sometimes deleting words and phrases, sometimes adding material, even entire episodes, and sometimes altering the way a sentence is worded. It is probably safe to assume that if Luke modified what Mark had to say, it was because he wanted to say it differently. Sometimes these differences are just minor changes in wording, but sometimes they affect in highly significant ways the way the entire story is told. This appears to be true for the portrayal of Jesus going to his death.

Jesus' Death in Mark

In Mark's version of the story (Mark 15:16–39), Jesus is condemned to death by Pontius Pilate, mocked and beaten by the Roman soldiers, and taken off to be crucified. Simon of Cyrene carries his cross. Jesus says nothing the entire time. The soldiers crucify Jesus, and he still says nothing. Both of the robbers being crucified with him mock him. Those passing by mock him. The Jewish leaders mock him. Jesus is silent until the very end, when he utters the wretched cry, "Eloi, Eloi, lama sabachthani," which Mark translates from the Aramaic for his readers as, "My God, my God, why have you forsaken me?" Someone gives Jesus a sponge with sour wine to drink. He breathes his last and dies. Immediately two things happen: the curtain in the Temple is ripped in half, and the centurion looking on acknowledges, "Truly this man was the Son of God."

This is a powerful and moving scene, filled with emotion and pathos. Jesus is silent the entire time, as if in shock, until his cry at the end, echoing Psalm 22. I take his question to God to be a genuine one. He genuinely wants to know why God has left him like this. A very popular interpretation of the passage is that since Jesus quotes Psalm 22:1, he is actually thinking of the ending of the Psalm, where God intervenes and vindicates the suffering psalmist. I think this is reading way too much into the passage and robs the "cry of dereliction," as it is called, of all its power. The point is that Jesus has been rejected by everyone: betrayed by one of his own, denied three times by his closest follower, abandoned by all his disciples, rejected by the Jewish leaders, condemned by the Roman authorities, mocked by the priests, the passersby, and even by the two others being crucified with him. At the end he even feels forsaken by God Himself. Jesus is absolutely in the depths of despair and heart-wrenching anguish, and that's how he dies. Mark is trying to say something by this portrayal. He doesn't want his readers to take solace in the fact that God was really there providing Jesus with physical comfort. He dies in agony, unsure of the reason he must die.

But the reader knows the reason. Right after Jesus dies the curtain rips in half and the centurion makes his confession. The curtain ripping in half shows that with the death of Jesus, God is made available to his people directly and not through the Jewish priests' sacrifices in the Temple. Jesus' death has brought an atonement (see Mark 10:45). And someone realizes it right off the bat: not Jesus' closest followers or the Jewish onlookers but the pagan soldier who has just crucified him. Jesus' death brings salvation, and it is gentiles who are going to recognize it. This is not a disinterested account of what "really" happened when Jesus died. It is theology put in the form of a narrative.

Historical scholars have long thought that Mark is not only explaining the significance of Jesus' death in this account but also quite possibly writing with a particular audience in mind, an audience of later followers of Jesus who also have experienced persecution and suffering at the hands of authorities who are opposed to God. Like Jesus, his followers may not know why they are experiencing such pain and misery. But Mark tells these Christians they can rest assured: even though they may not see why they are suffering, God knows, and God is working behind the scenes to make suffering redemptive. God's purposes are worked precisely through suffering, not by avoiding it, even when those purposes are not obvious at the moment. Mark's version of the death of Jesus thus provides a model for understanding the persecution of the Christians.

Jesus' Death in Luke

Luke's account is also very interesting, thoughtful, and moving, but it is very different indeed (Luke 23:26–49). It is not just that there are discrepancies in some of their details; the differences are bigger than that. They affect the very way the story is told and, as a result, the way the story is to be interpreted.

In Luke as in Mark, Jesus is betrayed by Judas, denied by Peter, rejected by the Jewish leaders, and condemned by Pontius Pilate, but he is not mocked and beaten by Pilate's soldiers. Only Luke tells the story of Pilate trying to get King Herod of Galilee—the son of the King Herod from the birth stories—to deal with Jesus, and it is Herod's soldiers who mock Jesus before Pilate finds him guilty. This is a discrepancy, but it doesn't affect the overall reading of the difference between the two accounts that I'm highlighting here.

In Luke, Jesus is taken off to be executed, and Simon of Cyrene is compelled to carry his cross. But Jesus is not silent on the way to his crucifixion. En route he sees a number of women wailing over what is happening to him, and he turns to them and says, "Daughters of Jerusalem, do not weep for me, but weep for yourselves and for your children" (Luke 23:28). He goes on to prophesy the coming destruction that they will face. Jesus does not appear to be in shock over what is happening to him. He is more concerned with others around him than with his own fate.

Moreover, Jesus is not silent while being nailed to the cross, as in Mark. Instead he prays, "Father, forgive them, for they don't know what they are doing" (Luke 23:34).[2] Jesus appears to have close communion with God and is concerned more for those who are doing this to him than for himself. Jesus is mocked by the Jewish leaders and the Roman soldiers, but explicitly not by both men being crucified with him, unlike in Mark. Instead, one of them mocks Jesus but the other rebukes the first for doing so, insisting that whereas they deserve what they are getting, Jesus has done nothing wrong (remember that Luke stresses Jesus' complete innocence). He then asks of Jesus, "Remember me when you come into your kingdom." And Jesus gives the compelling reply, "Truly I tell you, today you will be with me in Paradise" (23:42–43). In this account Jesus is not at all confused about what is happening to him or why. He is completely calm and in control of the situation; he knows what is about to occur, and he knows what will happen afterward: he will wake up in God's paradise, and this criminal will be there with him. This is a far cry from the Jesus of Mark, who felt forsaken to the end.

Darkness comes over the land and the Temple curtain is ripped while Jesus is still alive, in contrast to Mark. Here the torn curtain must not indicate that Jesus' death brings atonement—since he has not died yet. Instead it shows that his death is "the hour of darkness," as he says earlier in the Gospel (23:53), and it marks the judgment of God against the Jewish people. The ripped curtain here appears to indicate that God is rejecting the Jewish system of worship, symbolized by the Temple.

Most significant of all, rather than uttering a cry expressing his sense of total abandonment at the end ("Why have you forsaken me?"), in Luke, Jesus prays to God in a loud voice, saying, "Father into your hands I commend my spirit." He then breathes his last and dies (23:46). This is not a Jesus who feels forsaken by God and wonders why he is going through this pain of desertion and death. It is a Jesus who feels God's presence with him and is comforted by the fact that God is on his side. He is fully cognizant of what is happening to him and why, and he commits himself to the loving care of his heavenly Father, confident of what is to happen next. The centurion then confirms what Jesus himself knew full well, "Surely this man was innocent."

It is hard to stress strongly enough the differences between these two portrayals of Jesus' death. Earlier I pointed out that scholars have sometimes suggested that Mark's account was written in part to provide hope for those suffering persecution, to let them know that, appearances notwithstanding, God was at work behind suffering to achieve his redemptive purposes. What might Luke's purpose have been in modifying Mark's account, so that Jesus no longer dies in agony and despair?

Some critical interpreters have suggested that Luke may also be writing for Christians experiencing persecution, but his message to those suffering for the faith is different from Mark's. Rather than stressing that God is at work behind the scenes, even though it doesn't seem like it, Luke may be showing Christians a model of how they, too, can suffer—like Jesus, the perfect martyr, who goes to his death confident of his own innocence, assured of God's palpable presence in his life, calm and in control of the situation, knowing that suffering is necessary for the rewards of Paradise and that it will soon be over, leading to a blessed existence in the life to come. The two authors may be addressing similar situations, but they are conveying very different messages, both about how Jesus died and about how his followers can face persecution.

The Payoff

The problem comes when readers take these two accounts and combine them into one overarching account, in which Jesus says, does, and experiences everything narrated in both Gospels. When that is done, the messages of both Mark and Luke get completely lost and glossed over. Jesus is no longer in deep agony, as in Mark (since he is confident as in Luke), and he is no longer calm and in control as in Luke (since he is in despair as in Mark). He is somehow all things at once. Also, his words mean something different now, since he utters the sayings of both. When readers then throw both Matthew and John into the mix, they get an even more confused and conflated portrayal of Jesus, imagining wrongly that they have constructed the events as they *really* happened. To approach the stories in this way is to rob each author of his own integrity as an author and to deprive him of the meaning that he conveys in his story.

This is how readers over the years have come up with the famous "seven last words of the dying Jesus"—by taking what he says at his death in all four Gospels, mixing them together, and imagining that in their combination they now have the full story. This interpretive move does not give the full story. It gives a fifth story, a story that is completely unlike any of the canonical four, a fifth story that in effect rewrites the Gospels, producing a fifth Gospel. This is perfectly fine to do if that's what you want—it's a free country, and no one can stop you. But for historical critics, this is not the best way to approach the Gospels.

My overarching point is that the Gospels, and all the books of the Bible, are distinct and should not be read as if they are all saying the same thing. They are decidedly not saying the same thing—even when talking about the same subject (say, Jesus' death). Mark is different from Luke, and Matthew is different from John, as you can see by doing your own horizontal reading of their respective stories of the crucifixion. The historical approach to the Gospels allows each author's voice to be heard and refuses to conflate them into some kind of mega-Gospel that flattens the emphases of each one.

SOME KEY DIFFERENCES BETWEEN JOHN AND THE SYNOPTIC GOSPELS

Clearly the Synoptic Gospels don't tell the same version of all their stories. But there are strong similarities among them that set them apart from John. It has long been known that the reason they agree on so much is that they all shared the same sources. Both Matthew and Luke, for example, used Mark, reproducing it verbatim in places and changing it—sometimes changing it a lot—when they wanted to tell the stories in different ways.

Although many casual readers of the New Testament have not noticed it, the Gospel of John is a different kettle of fish altogether. With the exception of the Passion Narratives, most of the stories found in John are not found in the Synoptics, and most of the stories in the Synoptic Gospels are not found in John. And when they do cover similar territory, John's stories are strikingly different from the others. This can be seen by doing a kind of global comparison of John and the Synoptics.

Differences in Content

If you were to go through the Synoptic Gospels and make an outline of their key passages—the stories that make up the skeleton of their narratives, so to say—what would it be like? Luke and Mark begin with Jesus being born in Bethlehem to a virgin. The first major event mentioned in all three is Jesus' baptism by John, after which he goes out into the wilderness to be tempted by the Devil. He comes back from the wilderness and begins preaching his message that the "kingdom of God" is soon to appear. The characteristic form of his teaching is through parables. In fact, in Mark's Gospel Jesus is said to have taught the crowds only in parables (Mark 4:11). Jesus also performs miracles. One of his distinctive miracles—the first one in Mark—is casting demons out of those who are possessed. And so he goes through his ministry in Galilee, preaching parables and performing exorcisms, until half way through the accounts, when he takes three of his followers, Peter, James, and John, up onto a mountain, and in their presence experiences his transfiguration, in which he is gloriously transformed in appearance and begins to speak with Moses and Elijah, who have appeared from heaven. After the Transfiguration, Jesus continues his ministry until he goes to Jerusalem in the last week of his life. He cleanses the Temple, has the Last Supper, in which he institutes the Lord's supper by talking about the bread as his body and the cup as his blood. He is put on trial before the Jewish authorities and condemned for blasphemy. Then comes the familiar end, told in different ways, of his death and resurrection.

It is striking that virtually none of these stories that form the skeleton of the narratives of the Synoptics can be found in John. There is no reference to Jesus' birth in Bethlehem and no mention of his mother being a virgin. He is not explicitly said to be baptized and does not undergo his temptations in the wilderness. Jesus does not preach the coming kingdom of God, and he never tells a parable. He never casts out a demon. There is no account of the Transfiguration. He does not cleanse the Temple when coming to Jerusalem (he did that already in John 2). He does not institute the Lord's supper (instead he washes the disciples feet), and he does not have any kind of official trial before the Jewish council.

If John doesn't have any of these accounts that seem fairly essential to the story of Jesus, what does it contain? It has a lot of stories not found in the Synoptics. John starts with a prologue that mysteriously describes the Word of God that was in the very beginning with God, that was itself God, and through which God created the universe. This Word, we are told, became a human being, and that's who Jesus Christ is: the Word of God made flesh. There is nothing like that in the Synoptics.

John does tell of Jesus performing miracles during his public ministry, but the miracles are never called miracles, which literally means "works of power." Instead, they are called signs. Signs of what? Signs of who Jesus is, the one who has come down from heaven to provide eternal life to all who believe in him. Seven signs are narrated in the Gospel of John, most of them not found among the miracles of the Synoptics (two exceptions are walking on the water and feeding the multitudes). The signs narrated in John include some of the favorite miracles known to Bible readers over the ages: turning the water into wine, healing the man born blind, and raising Lazarus from the dead. Jesus also preaches in this Gospel, not about the coming kingdom of God but about himself: who he is, where he has come from, where he is going, and how he can bring eternal life. Unique to John are the various "I am" sayings, in which Jesus identifies himself and what he can provide for people. These "I am" sayings are usually backed up by a sign, to show that what Jesus says about himself is true. And so he says "I am the bread of life" and proves it by multiplying the loaves to feed the multitudes; he says "I am the light of the world" and proves it by healing the man born blind; he says "I am the resurrection and the life" and proves it by raising Lazarus from the dead.

In John, Jesus usually speaks in long discourses rather than in memorable aphoristic sayings as in the other Gospels. There is the long speech to Nicodemus in chapter 3, the speech to the Samaritan woman in chapter 4, and the very long speech to his disciples that covers four entire chapters (13–16), before he launches into a prayer that takes the entire next chapter. None of these discourses or any of the "I am" sayings can be found in the Synoptics.

Differences in Emphasis

Much more could be said about the unique features of John; my point is not simply that there are discrepancies between John and the Synoptics but that the portrayals of Jesus are very different. Certainly the three Synoptics are not identical, but the differences between any one of the Synoptics and John are especially striking, as can be seen by considering some of their various thematic emphases.

The Virgin Birth and the Incarnation

The orthodox Christian doctrine about Christ's coming into the world that has been accepted for centuries is that he was a preexistent divine being, equal with but not identical to God the Father, and that he became "incarnate," became a human being, through the Virgin Mary. But this doctrine is not set forth in any of the Gospels of the

New Testament. The idea that Jesus preexisted his birth and that he was a divine being who became human is found only in the Gospel of John; the idea that he was born of a virgin is found only in Matthew and Luke. It is only by conflating the two views that one could come up with the view that became the traditional, orthodox doctrine. For the writers of the Gospels, the idea of a virgin birth and the idea of an incarnation were very different indeed.

Mark's Gospel doesn't say anything about either. The story starts with Jesus as an adult, and Mark gives no indication of the circumstances of his birth. If your only Gospel was Mark—and in the early church, for some Christians it *was* the only Gospel—you would have no idea that Jesus' birth was unusual in any way, that his mother was a virgin, or that he existed before appearing on earth.

Matthew's Gospel is quite explicit that Jesus' mother was a virgin, but is also quite restrained in any kind of speculation about what that means theologically. We have seen that Matthew is particularly keen to show that everything in Jesus birth, life, and death was a fulfillment of Scriptural prophecy. So why was he born of a virgin? It was because the Hebrew prophet Isaiah indicated that "a virgin shall conceive and bear a son, and they shall call him Immanuel" (Matthew 1:23, quoting Isaiah 7:14). Actually, that's not exactly what Isaiah said. In the Hebrew Bible, Isaiah indicates that a "young woman" will conceive and bear a son, a prediction not of a future Messiah but of an event that was soon to take place in Isaiah's own day.[3] When the Hebrew Bible was translated into Greek, however, Isaiah's "young woman" (Hebrew *alma*; there is a different Hebrew word for "virgin") came to be rendered by the Greek word for "virgin" (*parthenos*), and that is the form of the Bible that Matthew read. And so he thought that Isaiah was predicting something not about his own day but about the future Messiah (though the term "Messiah" does not occur in Isaiah 7). So Matthew wrote that Jesus was born of a virgin because that's what he thought Scripture predicted.

Luke has a different view. He, too, thinks Jesus was born of a virgin, but he does not cite a prophecy of Scripture to explain it.

Instead, he has a more direct explanation: Jesus was literally the Son of God. God caused Mary to conceive, so that her son was also God's son. As Mary learns from the angel Gabriel (recounted only in Luke): "The Holy Spirit will come upon you, and the power of the Most High will overshadow you; therefore the child to be born will be holy; he will be called the Son of God" (Luke 1:35). Impregnated not by her espoused or any other human, but by God, Mary gives birth to a being who is in some sense divine.

So Matthew and Luke appear to have different interpretations of why Jesus was born of a virgin, but, more important, in neither Matthew nor Luke is there any sense that this one born to the virgin existed prior to his birth. For these authors, Jesus came into existence when he was born. There is not a word in either Gospel about the preexistence of Jesus. That idea comes from John, and only from John.

John does not make any reference to Jesus' mother being a virgin, instead explaining his coming into the world as an incarnation of a preexistent divine being. The prologue to John's Gospel (1:1–18) is one of the most elevated and powerful passages of the entire Bible. It is also one of the most discussed, controverted, and differently interpreted. John begins (1:1–3) with an elevated view of the "Word of God," a being that is independent of God (he was "with God") but that is in some sense equal with God (he "was God"). This being existed in the beginning with God and is the one through whom the entire universe was created ("all things came into being through him, and apart from him not one thing came into being").

Scholars have wrangled over details of this passage for centuries.[4] My personal view is that the author is harking back to the story of creation in Genesis 1, where God spoke and creation resulted: "And God said, 'Let there be light,' and there was light." It was by speaking a word that God created all that there was. The author of the Fourth Gospel, like some others in the Jewish tradition, imagined that the word that God spoke was some kind of independent entity in and of itself. It was "with" God, because once spoken, it was apart from God; and it "was" God in the sense that what God spoke was a part of his being. His speaking only made external what was already internal, within his mind. The Word of God, then, was the outward manifestation of the internal divine reality. It both was with God, and was God, and was the means by which all things came into being.

In John's Gospel, this preexistent divine Word of God became a human being: "And the Word became flesh and dwelt among us, and we beheld his glory" (1:14). It comes as no surprise who this human being was: Jesus Christ. Jesus, here, is not simply a Jewish prophet who suddenly bursts onto the scene, as in Mark; and he is not a divine-human who has come into existence at the point of his conception (or birth) by a woman who was impregnated by God. He is God's very word, who was with God in the beginning, who has temporarily come to dwell on earth, bringing the possibility of eternal life.

John does not say how this Word came into the world. He does not have a birth narrative and says nothing about Joseph and Mary, about Bethlehem, or about a virginal conception. And he varies from Luke on this very key point: whereas Luke portrays Jesus as having come into being at some historical point (conception or birth), John portrays him as the human manifestation of a divine being who transcends history.

What happens when the two views are combined? The distinctive emphases of both are lost. The message of each author is swallowed up into the orthodox doctrine of the incarnation through the virgin Mary. Readers of the New Testament who conflate the two texts have created their own story, one that bypasses the teaching of both Luke and John and proffers a teaching that is found in neither one.

Differences in the Teachings of Jesus

The Gospel of John also presents a different view of what Jesus talked about in his public ministry. Here I will use as a point of contrast our earliest Synoptic Gospel, Mark.

Jesus' Teaching in Mark

In many ways the teaching of Jesus in Mark is summarized in the first words he speaks: "The time has been fulfilled; the kingdom of God is near. Repent and believe the good news!" (Mark 1:15). Anyone familiar with ancient Judaism can recognize the apocalyptic nature of this message. Jewish apocalypticism was a worldview that came into existence about a century and a half before Jesus' birth and was widely held among Jews in his day. The Greek word apocalypsis means a "revealing" or an "unveiling." Scholars have called this view apocalyptic because its proponents believed that God had revealed or unveiled to them the heavenly secrets that could make sense of the realities they were experiencing—many of them nasty and ugly—here on earth. One of the questions apocalypticists were intent on answering was why there was so much pain and suffering in the world, especially among the people of God. It might make sense that wicked people suffer: they are simply getting their due. But why do the righteous suffer? In fact, why do the righteous suffer more than the wicked, at the hands of the wicked? Why does God allow that?

Jewish apocalypticists believed that God had revealed to them the secrets that made sense of it all. There are cosmic forces in the world aligned against God and his people, powers like the Devil and his demons. These forces are in control of the world and the political powers that run it. For some mysterious reason God has allowed these forces to thrive in the present evil age. But a new age is coming in which God would overthrow the forces of evil and bring in a good kingdom, a kingdom of God, in which there will be no more pain, misery, or suffering. God will rule supreme, and the Devil and his demons, along with all the other nasty powers causing such suffering (hurricanes, earthquakes, famine, disease, war), will be done away with.

Jesus' teaching in Mark is apocalyptic: "The time has been fulfilled" implies that this current evil age, seen on a time line, is almost over. The end is almost within sight. "The Kingdom of God is near" means that God will soon intervene in this age and overthrow its wicked powers and the kingdoms they support, such as Rome, and establish his own kingdom, a kingdom of truth, peace, and justice. "Repent and believe the good news" means that people need to prepare for this coming kingdom by changing their lives, beginning to align themselves with the forces of good instead of the forces of evil, and by accepting Jesus' teaching that it was soon to happen.

For Mark's Jesus, this kingdom is soon to come. As he tells his disciples at one point, "Truly I tell you, some of those standing here will not taste death before they see the Kingdom of God having come in power" (Mark 9:1); later he tells them, after describing the cosmic upheavals that would transpire at the end of the age, "Truly I tell you, this generation will not pass away before all these things take place" (Mark 13:30).

How will that kingdom arrive? For Mark it will be brought about by "the Son of Man," a cosmic judge of the earth who will judge people according to whether they accept the teachings of Jesus: "For whoever is ashamed of me and my words in this adulterous and sinful generation, of that one will the Son of Man also be ashamed, when he comes in the glory of his Father with the holy angels" (Mark 8:38). And who is this Son of Man? For Mark it is Jesus himself, who must be rejected by his people and their leaders, executed, and then raised from the dead (Mark 8:31). Jesus will die, he will be raised, and then he will return in judgment, bringing with him the kingdom of God.

But since Jesus is the one who will bring the kingdom, for Mark the kingdom is already being manifest in the earthly life and ministry of Jesus in an anticipatory way. In the kingdom there will be no demons, and so Jesus casts out demons; in the kingdom there will be no disease, and so Jesus heals the sick; in the kingdom there will be no more death, and so Jesus raises the dead. The kingdom of God could already be seen in Jesus' own ministry and that of his followers (6:7–13). That is the point of many of Jesus' parables in Mark:

the kingdom has a small, even hidden, appearance in the activities of Jesus, but it will appear in a big way at the end. It is like a small mustard seed that when put in the ground becomes an enormous shrub (4:30–32). Most of Jesus' listeners rejected his message, but a judgment day was coming, and God's kingdom would arrive in power, and then this world will be remade (Mark 13).

Jesus does not actually teach much about himself in the Gospel of Mark. He talks mainly about God and the coming kingdom, and how people need to prepare for it. When he does refer to himself as the Son of Man, it is always obliquely: he never says, "I am the Son of Man." And he does not state that he is the Messiah, the anointed ruler of the future kingdom, until the very end, when he is placed under oath by the high priest (Mark 14:61–62).

Although Jesus is acknowledged as the Son of God in this Gospel (see 1:11; 9:7; 15:39), that is not his preferred title for himself, and he only acknowledges it reluctantly (14:62). It is important to know that for ancient Jews the term "son of God" could mean a wide range of things. In the Hebrew Bible the "son of God" could refer to the nation of Israel (Hosea 11:1), or to the king of Israel (1 Samuel 7:14). In these cases the son of God was someone specially chosen by God to perform his work and mediate his will on earth. And for Mark, Jesus was certainly all that—he was the one who performed the ultimate will of God, going to his death on the cross. It is striking, though, in the Gospel of Mark, that Jesus never refers to himself as a divine being, as someone who preexisted, as someone who was in any sense equal with God. In Mark, he is not God and he does not claim to be.

Jesus' Teaching in John

Things are quite different in the Gospel of John. In Mark, Jesus teaches principally about God and the coming kingdom, hardly ever talking directly about himself, except to say that he must go to Jerusalem to be executed, whereas in John, that is practically all that

Jesus talks about: who he is, where he has come from, where he is going, and how he is the one who can provide eternal life.

Jesus does not preach about the future kingdom of God in John. The emphasis is on his own identity, as seen in the "I am" sayings. He is the one who can bring life-giving sustenance ("I am the bread of life" 6:35); he is the one who brings enlightenment ("I am the light of the world" 9:5); he is the only way to God ("I am the way, the truth, and the life. No one comes to the Father but by me" 14:6). Belief in Jesus is the way to have eternal salvation: "whoever believes in him may have eternal life" (3:36). He in fact is equal with God: "I and the Father are one" (10:30). His Jewish listeners appear to have known full well what he was saying: they immediately pick up stones to execute him for blasphemy.

In one place in John, Jesus claims the name of God for himself, saying to his Jewish interlocutors, "Before Abraham was, I am" (John 8:58). Abraham, who lived 1,800 years earlier, was the father of the Jews, and Jesus is claiming to have existed before him. But he is claiming more than that. He is referring to a passage in the Hebrew Scriptures where God appears to Moses at the burning bush and commissions him to go to Pharaoh and seek the release of his people. Moses asks God what God's name is, so that he can inform his fellow Israelites which divinity has sent him. God replies, "I Am Who I Am . . . say to the Israelites, 'I Am has sent me to you' (Exodus 3:14). So when Jesus says "I Am," in John 8:58, he is claiming the divine name for himself. Here again his Jewish hearers had no trouble understanding his meaning. Once more, out come the stones.

The difference between Mark and John is not only that Jesus speaks about himself in John and identifies himself as divine but also that Jesus does *not* teach what he teaches in Mark, about the coming kingdom of God. The idea that there would be a future kingdom on earth in which God would rule supreme and all the forces of evil would be destroyed is no part of Jesus' proclamation in John. Instead he teaches that people need to have eternal life, in heaven above, by achieving a heavenly birth (3:3–5). That's what the "kingdom of God" means in John, the very few times it occurs: it means life in heaven, above, with God—not a new heaven and new earth down here below. Faith in Jesus is what gives eternal life. Those who believe in Jesus will live with God forever; those who do not will be condemned (3:36).

For many historical critics it makes sense that John, the Gospel that was written last, no longer speaks about the imminent appearance on earth of the Son of Man to sit in judgment on the earth, to usher in the utopian kingdom. In Mark, Jesus predicts that the end will come right away, during his own generation, while his disciples are still alive (Mark 9:1; 13:30). By the time John was written, probably from 90 to 95 CE, that earlier generation had died out and most if not all the disciples were already dead. That is, they died before the coming of the kingdom. What does one do with the teaching about an eternal kingdom here on earth if it never comes? One reinterprets the teaching. The way John reinterprets it is by altering the basic conceptualization.

An apocalyptic worldview like that found in Mark involves a kind of historical dualism in which there is the present evil age and the future kingdom of God. This age, and the age to come: they can be drawn almost like a time line, horizontally across the page. The Gospel of John rotates the horizontal dualism of apocalyptic thinking so that it becomes a vertical dualism. It is no longer a dualism of this age on earth and the one that has yet to come, also on earth; instead, it is a dualism of life down here and the life above. We are down here, God is above. Jesus as God's Word comes down from above, precisely so we can ourselves experience a birth "from above" (the literal meaning of John 3:3—not that "you must be born a second time," but that "you must be born from above").[5] When we experience this new birth by believing in Christ, the one who comes from above, then we, too, will have eternal life (John 3:16). And when we die, we will then ascend to the heavenly realm to live with God (John 14:1–6).

No longer is the kingdom coming to earth. The kingdom is in heaven. And we can get there by believing in the one who came from there to teach us the way. This is a very different teaching from what you find in Mark.

The Miracles of Jesus

Why did Jesus perform miracles? Most people would probably say that it was because he felt compassion for people and wanted to relieve their suffering. And that answer holds true for the Synoptic Gospels. But even more than that, the miracles in the Synoptics indicate that in Jesus the long-awaited kingdom has already begun to arrive:

> The Spirit of the Lord is upon me,
> Because he has anointed me to bring good news to the poor.
> He has sent me to proclaim release to the captives
> And recovery of sight to the blind. . . .
> Today [says Jesus] this scripture has been fulfilled in your hearing.
> (Luke 4:18–21)

In another passage the followers of John the Baptist come to Jesus wanting to know if he is the one to appear at the end of the age, or if they are to expect someone else. Jesus tells them, "Go and tell John what you hear and see: the blind receive their sight, the lame walk, the lepers are cleansed, the deaf hear, the dead are raised, and the poor have good news brought to them. And blessed is anyone who takes no offense at me" (Matthew 11:2–6). In the Synoptic Gospels, Jesus is the long-expected one who will usher in the kingdom.

And yet in these earlier Gospels, Jesus quite explicitly refuses to perform miracles in order to prove who he is to people who do not believe. In Matthew some of the Jewish leaders ask Jesus, "Teacher, we wish to see a sign from you" (Matthew 12:38). They want proof that his authority comes from God. Instead of complying, Jesus states forcefully, "An evil and adulterous generation asks for a sign, but no sign will be given to it except the sign of the prophet Jonah" (Matthew 12:38). He goes on to explain that just as Jonah was in effect dead for three days and nights in the belly of the great fish, so, too, would "the Son of Man" be "in the heart of the earth" for three days and nights.

This is a reference to the Hebrew Bible book of Jonah, which recounts how God sent the prophet Jonah to the dreaded enemies of Israel, the Assyrians in the city of Nineveh, in order to get them to repent. Jonah refused and set sail in the other direction. God raised a storm that swamped the boat; the sailors found that it was because of Jonah's disobedience, and threw him overboard. He was swallowed by a great fish, but after three days he was vomited up on the land. Rather than incur further wrath, Jonah went to Nineveh, preached his message, and converted the city.

Jesus contrasts his own situation with that of Jonah. He, Jesus, is preaching to a recalcitrant people, but they don't repent. He refuses, however, to perform a miracle to establish his divine credentials. The only proof the people will be given will be the "sign of Jonah," which in the context of Matthew's Gospel means the sign of the resurrection. Jesus will be dead for three days and will then reappear. This event, not something he does in his public ministry, will need to convince people of the truth he proclaims.

This is Matthew's view throughout his Gospel, and it helps us makes sense of one of his most puzzling stories. Before Jesus begins his public ministry he goes out into the wilderness and is tempted by the Devil (Matthew 4:1–11). Matthew mentions three specific temptations, but only two of them make obvious sense. For the first, after Jesus goes without food for forty days, the Devil tempts him to turn the stones into bread. Jesus refuses: his miracles are not meant for himself but for others. The third temptation is for Jesus to worship Satan and be given, as a reward, the kingdoms of earth. The temptation is obvious—who wouldn't want to rule the world? But it has a particular twist for Matthew, who knows that Jesus *will* rule the world eventually. First, though, Jesus has to die on the cross. This temptation is to bypass the Passion. Jesus again refuses: God alone is to be worshipped.

But what is the second temptation about? The Devil takes Jesus to the top of the Jewish Temple and urges him to jump off: if he does, the angels of God will swoop down and catch him before he scrapes a toe. What exactly is tempting about taking a plunge from a building ten stories high? One needs to understand where this is taking place: in Jerusalem, the heart of Judaism, in the Temple, the center for the worship of God. Lots of Jews would be milling around the place. Jesus is tempted to jump off, in full view, so that the angels will appear and catch him. In other words, this is a temptation for Jesus to provide a public, miraculous proof to the crowds that he really is the Son of God. Jesus spurns this as a Satanic temptation: "You shall not put the Lord your God to the test."

In Matthew, Jesus will perform no sign to prove himself. That is why his miracles are called miracles, not signs in this Gospel. They are demonstrations of power meant to help those in need and to show that the kingdom of God is soon to appear.

What about John? In John's Gospel, Jesus' spectacular deeds are called signs, not miracles. And they are performed precisely to prove who Jesus is, to convince people to believe in him. Claiming to be the "Bread of Life," he performs the sign of the loaves to feed the crowds (John 6); claiming to be the "Light of the World," he does the sign of healing the man born blind (John 9); claiming to be the "Resurrection and the Life," he does the sign of raising Lazarus from the dead (John 11).

It is striking that Matthew's story of Jesus refusing to give the Jewish leaders a sign, except for the sign of Jonah, cannot be found in John. But why would it be? For John, Jesus spends his ministry giving signs. John also does not tell the story of the three temptations in the wilderness. Again, how could he? For him, Jesus' proving his identity through miraculous signs is not a satanic temptation; it is his divine calling.

These signs in John are meant to promote faith in Jesus. As Jesus himself tells a royal official who has asked Jesus to heal his son: "Unless you see signs and wonders, you will not believe" (John 4:48). Jesus heals the boy, and the man comes to believe (4:53). So, too, the author of John thought that it was the signs that proved Jesus' identity and led people to faith: "Jesus did many other signs in the presence of his disciples, which are not written in this book. But these are written so that you may believe that Jesus is the Messiah, the Son of God, and that through believing you may have life in his name" (20:30–31). Whereas supernatural proofs of Jesus' identity were strictly off limits in Matthew, in John they are the principal reason for Jesus' miraculous acts.

SOME KEY DIFFERENCES BETWEEN PAUL AND THE GOSPEL WRITERS

Major differences among the New Testament writers can be found not only in the four Gospels but also among many of the other books of the New Testament, such as the writings of the apostle Paul.

Paul was writing before any of the Gospels were written. Most of his letters were composed in the fifties of the Christian Era, about ten or fifteen years before our earliest Gospel, Mark. Paul and the Gospel writers all were writing after Jesus' death, and the Gospel writers were not simply recording for all posterity the things Jesus "really" said and did. They told the stories of Jesus' words and deeds in light of their own theological understandings, as we have seen time and again. Paul also wrote from his own theological perspective. But many of the views that one finds in Paul are at odds with what one can find in the Gospels, as well as in the book of Acts, written by the author of the Gospel of Luke.

Paul and Matthew on Salvation and the Law

One important aspect of Paul's teaching is the question of how a person can have a right standing before God. At least since the

Reformation, some theologians have argued that this was Paul's main concern. Today most Pauline scholars recognize that this is an oversimplification that bypasses a good deal of what comes to us in the seven undisputed Pauline letters mentioned in chapter 2. But certainly Paul was concerned with how persons—those he was trying to convert, for example—could be put into a right relationship with God, and he was convinced this could happen only through trusting in the death and resurrection of Jesus, not by following the requirements of the Jewish law.

This teaching stands somewhat at odds with other views in the New Testament, including those set forth in the Gospel of Matthew. Do followers of Jesus need to keep the Jewish law if they are to be saved? It depends on which author you ask. Does a right standing before God depend completely on faith in Jesus' death and resurrection? At least one key story in Matthew's Gospel differs from Paul on this point.

Paul's View of "Justification"

Paul uses the word "justification" to refer to a person's having a right standing before God. Paul's view of justification can be found principally in his letters to the Galatians and the Romans. In these letters he had various ways of explaining how a person could have a right standing before God. His best-known and arguably most pervasive view (which is found in his other letters as well) is that a person is "justified by faith" in Christ's death and resurrection, not by observing the works of the Jewish law.

One way to make sense of Paul's theology of justification is to try to think through his logic. This requires starting at the beginning, when Paul was not yet a follower of Jesus, but rather someone who saw faith in Christ as a blasphemy deserving of violent opposition. Writing some twenty years after his persecuting days, Paul never tells us what he had originally found to be so reprehensible about the Christians' belief, but there are some suggestions scattered throughout his letters. It may well be that he was offended by the very claim that Jesus was the Messiah.

As a religious Jew, prior to believing in Jesus, Paul no doubt had ideas what the Messiah would be like. Before Christianity appeared, there weren't any Jews who believed that the Messiah would suffer and die. Quite the contrary, whatever different Jews thought about the matter, they all agreed that the Messiah would be a figure of grandeur and power who would implement God's purposes on earth in a forceful way. Jews did not understand the passages of Scripture that refer to the suffering of God's righteous one as a reference to the Messiah. And none of these passages (Isaiah 53; Psalm 22) mentions the Messiah.

The Messiah stood under God's special favor and was his forceful and powerful presence on earth. And who was Jesus? A little-known itinerant preacher who got on the wrong side of the law and was crucified for insurrection against the state. For most first-century Jews, to call Jesus the Messiah was ludicrous at best, blasphemous at worst. Nothing could be crazier, no one could be less messianic, than a crucified criminal (see 1 Corinthians 1:23). Evidently Paul thought so, too. But then something happened to Paul. Later he claimed that he had a vision of Jesus after Jesus' death (1 Corinthians 15:8). This vision convinced him that Jesus was not dead. But how could he not be dead?

As an apocalyptic Jew before coming to faith in Jesus, Paul already believed in the idea that at the end of this evil age there would be a resurrection of the dead, that when God overthrew the forces of evil he would raise every human from the dead and all would face judgment, the good being given an eternal reward and the wicked eternal punishment. If Jesus was no longer dead, as Paul "knew," because he had seen him alive (say, a year or two later), then it must be because God had raised him from the dead. But if God raised him from the dead, it must mean that he *was* the one who stood under God's special favor. He must be the Messiah, not in the way any Jew previously thought but in some other way.

But if he was God's chosen one, the Messiah, why did he die? This is where we start thinking with Paul—in reverse, as it were, starting from the end, the resurrection of Jesus, and moving back toward Jesus' death and life. Paul reasoned that Jesus must not have died for anything wrong that he did if he was the Messiah, who stood under God's special favor. He must not have died for his own sins. For what, then? Evidently for the sins of others. Like the sacrifices in the Jerusalem Temple, Jesus was a sacrifice for the sins that other people committed.

Why would God have Jesus die for others? Evidently because a human sacrifice was the only way a perfect sacrifice could be made. The Jewish sacrificial system must not be adequate to deal with sins. But does that mean God has changed his mind about how people are to be right with him? Didn't he call the Jews to be his special people and give them the law so that they would be set apart from all other people as his chosen ones? Yes, reasoned Paul, he did. The law and the prophets must be pointing toward Christ, God's ultimate solution to the human problem.

But what is the human problem? It appears to be that everyone—not just gentiles, but also Jews—has violated God's laws and needs the perfect sacrifice for their sins. But this would mean that everyone—not just Jews, but also gentiles—must accept this sacrifice of God's Messiah in order for their sins to be covered over, or atoned for, before God. Can't people be right with God by doing what God instructed in the law? Evidently not. If they could be, there would have been no reason for the Messiah to be crucified. By being crucified, Jesus shed his blood for others and brought about an atoning sacrifice for sins. Those who believe in his death (and his resurrection, which demonstrated that Jesus' death was part of God's plan) will be right with God—justified. Those who don't, cannot be justified.

All of this means that keeping the Jewish law can have no place in salvation. Even Jews who keep the law to the nth degree cannot be right with God through the law. What about gentiles: should they become Jews and try to keep the law once they have faith in Christ? For Paul the answer was absolutely not. Trying to keep the law would show that a person thought that it was possible to *earn* God's favor—have boasting rights, as it were. Anyone who tries to be justified by keeping the law will still be caught up in sin, and so it will be to no avail.

The only way to be justified is by having faith in the death and resurrection of Jesus. In Galatians 2:15, Paul says, "We have come to believe in Christ Jesus, so that we might be justified by faith in Christ, and not by doing the works of the law, because no one will be justified by the works of the law."

This is Paul's teaching throughout both Romans (1–3) and Galatians (1–3). Followers of Jesus are not to try to keep the law, except insofar as "loving your neighbor as yourself" and living a good ethical life is something that God still expects of his people. But following the precepts and requirements of the law—getting circumcised, keeping kosher, observing Sabbath and other Jewish festivals—none of this was necessary for salvation, and if you thought (and acted) otherwise, you were in danger of losing your salvation (Galatians 5:4).[6]

Paul's and Matthew's Views on the Law

I have often wondered what would have happened if Paul and Matthew had been locked up in a room together and told they could not come out until they had hammered out a consensus statement on how followers of Jesus were to deal with the Jewish law. Would they ever have emerged, or would they still be there, two skeletons locked in a death grip?

If Matthew, who wrote some twenty-five or thirty years after Paul, ever read any of Paul's letters, he certainly did not find them inspiring, let alone inspired. Matthew has a different view of the law from Paul. Matthew thinks that the followers of Jesus need to keep the law. In fact, they need to keep it better even than the most religious Jews, the scribes, and the Pharisees. In Matthew, Jesus is recorded as saying:

> Do not think that I have come to abolish the law or the prophets; I have not come to abolish but to fulfill. For truly I tell you, until heaven and earth pass away, not one letter, not one stroke of a letter, will pass from the law until all is accomplished. Therefore whoever breaks one of the least of these commandments, and teaches others to do the same, will be called least in the kingdom of heaven, but whoever does them and teaches them will be called great in the kingdom of heaven. For I tell you, unless your righteousness exceeds that of the scribes and Pharisees, you will never enter the Kingdom of heaven. (Matthew 5:17–20)

Paul thought that followers of Jesus who tried to keep the law were in danger of losing their salvation. Matthew thought that followers of Jesus who did not keep the law, and do so even better than the most religious Jews, would never attain salvation. Theologians and interpreters over the years have tried to reconcile these two views, which is perfectly understandable, since both of them are in the canon. But anyone who reads the Gospel of Matthew and then reads the letter to the Galatians would never suspect that there was a reason, or a way, to reconcile these two statements. For Matthew, to be great in the kingdom requires keeping the very least of the commandments; just getting into the kingdom requires keeping them better than the scribes and Pharisees. For Paul, getting into the kingdom (a different way of saying being justified) is made possible only by the death and resurrection of Jesus; for gentiles, keeping the Jewish law (for example, circumcision) is strictly forbidden.

Of course, Matthew also knows all about the death and resurrection of Jesus. He spends a good part of his Gospel narrating it. And he, too, thinks that apart from Jesus' death there can be no salvation. But salvation also requires keeping God's laws. He did give these laws, after all. Presumably he meant them the first time and didn't change his mind later.

One passage in Matthew suggests, in fact, that salvation is not just a matter of belief but also of action, an idea completely alien to the thinking of Paul. In one of the great discourses of Jesus, found only in Matthew, he describes the Day of Judgment that will come at the end of time. The Son of Man comes in glory, with his angels, and people from all the nations of earth are gathered before him (Matthew 25:31–45). He separates them into two groups "as a shepherd separates the sheep from the goats." The sheep are on his right and the goats on his left. He welcomes the sheep into the Kingdom of God "prepared for you from the foundation of the world." Why are these people brought into the kingdom?

> Because I was hungry and you gave me food, I was thirsty and you gave me something to drink, I was a stranger and you welcomed me, I was naked and you clothed me, I was sick and you took care of me, I was in prison and you visited me.

The "sheep" are perplexed, though. They don't remember ever meeting Jesus, the Son of Man, let alone doing these things for him. But he tells them, "Just as you did it to one of the least of these, my brothers and sisters, so you did it to me." In other words, it is by caring for the hungry, thirsty, naked, sick, and imprisoned that one inherits God's kingdom.

The goats, on the other hand, are sent away to the "eternal fire that is prepared for the devil and his angels." And why? Unlike the sheep, they did not take care of the Son of Man when he was in need. They, too, are perplexed, for they don't recall ever seeing him. But they saw others in need and turned their backs on them: "Just as you did not do it to one of the least of these, my brothers and sisters, so you did not do it to me." Matthew concludes his story with this stark statement: "And these will go away into eternal punishment, but the righteous into eternal life." These are Jesus' final public words in the Gospel of Matthew.

How do these words stack up against Paul? Not so well. Paul believed eternal life comes to those who believe in the death and resurrection of Jesus. In Matthew's account of the sheep and the goats, salvation comes to those who have never even heard of Jesus. It comes to those who treat others in a humane and caring way in their hour of deepest need. This is a completely different view of salvation.[7]

There is another striking story in Matthew. A rich man comes up to Jesus and asks him, "Teacher, what good deed must I do to have eternal life?" Jesus tells him, "If you wish to enter into life, keep the commandments." When asked, "Which ones?" Jesus lists as examples some of the Ten Commandments. The man insists he has already done all these—what else is needed? Jesus replies that he should give up everything he owns, "and you will have treasure in heaven" (Matthew 19:16–22). Jesus then says, "And come, follow me"—but note: following Jesus comes only after the man will have inherited heavenly treasure by giving all away.

I wonder what would have happened if the same man had come up to Paul, twenty years later. If Paul were asked how someone could have eternal life, would he have said, "Keep the commandments"? Not Paul. The commandments have nothing to do with it. Jesus' death and resurrection do. Would Paul have said that giving away all he owned would earn him treasure in heaven? No way. Only faith in Jesus could bring eternal life.

One can't argue that Jesus was talking about salvation before his death, and Paul about salvation afterward, because Matthew was writing after Paul. Moreover, in Matthew, Jesus is talking about the last judgment, which obviously would take place after his death and resurrection. And so the problem is this: if Matthew's Jesus was right, that keeping the law and loving others as yourself could bring salvation, how could Paul be right that doing these things were irrelevant for attaining salvation?

SEVERAL OTHER DIFFERENT PERSPECTIVES IN THE NEW TESTAMENT

There are other large and small differences in the books of the New Testament. The best way to cite a few examples is by asking pointed questions.

Why Did Jesus Die?

The death of Jesus is central to both Paul and to each of the Gospel writers. But *why* did he die? And what relation did his death have to salvation? The answer depends on which author you read.

Mark is clear that Jesus' death brought about an atonement for sin. As Jesus himself states in an early chapter of Mark: "The Son of Man came not to be served but to serve, and to give his life as a ransom for many" (Mark 10:45). The death of Jesus ransoms others from the debt they owe to God because of sin; it is an atoning sacrifice.

Luke used Mark's Gospel as a source for his own, adding, deleting, and altering Mark's words as he saw fit. And what did he do with this current verse? He completely deleted it. Why would Luke delete the verse? Possibly he has a different understanding of Jesus' death.

In this connection it is striking that in Mark, the "evidence" that Jesus' death brought an atonement is found immediately after Jesus dies, when the curtain in the Temple is ripped in half, showing that in Jesus' death people have access to God. But Luke changes the timing: the ripping of the curtain occurs while Jesus is still living. Many scholars think this is significant: the ripping of the curtain no longer signifies the atoning significance of Jesus' death but the judgment of God on the Temple of the Jews, a symbolic statement that it will be destroyed.

So what is the reason for Jesus' death in Luke? The matter becomes clearer in Luke's second volume, the book of Acts, where the apostles preach about the salvation that has come in Christ in order to convert others to the faith. In none of these missionary sermons is there a single word about Jesus' death being an atonement. Instead, the constant message is that people are guilty for rejecting the one sent from God and having him killed. The death of the innocent one (Jesus) should make people repent of their sins and turn to God, so he can forgive them (see Acts 2:36–38; 3:17–19). Luke's view is that salvation comes not through an atoning sacrifice but by forgiveness that comes from repentance.[8]

But aren't atonement and forgiveness the same thing? Not at all. It's like this. Suppose you owe me a hundred dollars but can't pay. There are a couple of ways the problem could be solved. Someone else (a friend, your brother, your parents) could pay the hundred dollars for you. That would be like atonement: someone else pays your penalty. Or, instead of that, I could simply say, "Never mind, I don't need the money." That would be like forgiveness, in which no one pays and God simply forgives the debt.

The death of Jesus is important to both Mark and Luke. But for Mark, his death is an atonement; for Luke, it is the reason people realize they are sinful and need to turn to God for forgiveness. The reason for Jesus' death, then, is quite different, depending on which author you read.

When Did Jesus Become the Son of God, the Lord, and the Messiah?

The missionary speeches of Acts deal not only with issues of salvation; they also make bold statements about Christ and how God exalted him after his death. In Paul's speech to potential converts in Antioch of Pisidia, he speaks of God's raising of Jesus in fulfillment of Scripture:

What God promised to our ancestors he has fulfilled for us, their children, by raising Jesus; as also it is written in the second psalm, 'You are my Son, today I have begotten you.' (Acts 13:32–33)

In this text the "day" Jesus became begotten as God's son was the day of the resurrection. But how does that square with what Luke says elsewhere? In Luke's Gospel, the voice utters the same words, "You are my Son, *today* I have begotten you" (Luke 3:22), when Jesus is baptized.[9] But even earlier, the angel Gabriel announced to Mary prior to Jesus' conception and birth that "the Holy Spirit will come upon you, and the power of the Most High will overshadow you; therefore the child to be born will be holy; he will be called the Son of God" (Luke 1:35). In this instance it appears that Jesus is the Son of God because of the virginal conception: he is physically God's son. How can Luke say all three things? I'm not sure it's possible to reconcile these accounts; it may be that Luke got these different traditions from different sources that disagreed with one another on the issue.

The same type of problem occurs with some of the other things Luke says about Jesus. For example, in Peter's speech on the day of Pentecost, he speaks of the death of Jesus and affirms that God raised him up and exalted him to heaven: "Therefore let the entire house of Israel know with certainty that God has made him both Lord and Messiah, this Jesus whom you crucified" (Acts 2:36). Here, again, it appears that Jesus receives this exalted status at the resurrection—that is when God "made him" Lord and Messiah. But what then is one to think of the birth narrative in Luke, where the angel informs the shepherds who are "watching over their flock by night" that "to you is born this day in the city of David a Savior, who is the Messiah, the Lord" (2:11). In this instance, Jesus is Messiah and Lord already at his birth. How did Jesus become both Messiah and Lord at both points in time? Here again there appears to be an internal discrepancy within Luke's own writings, possibly because different sources were used to create his accounts.

Has God Overlooked the Ignorance of Idolaters?

We have seen that the book of Acts occasionally presents discrepancies not only with the Gospels but also with the writings of the hero of its narratives, Paul. One particularly interesting instance occurs in one of the few instances in Acts in which Paul is said to deliver a message to a pagan audience, his sermon to the philosophers in Athens while standing on the Areopagus (Acts 17:22–31). Paul begins this sermon by complimenting his hearers on their great religiosity, but he goes on to indicate that they have committed a great error in thinking that they could worship God by worshipping idols, for God "does not live in shrines made by human hands." Instead he is the Lord of the earth, the creator of all. But "God has overlooked the times of human ignorance, and now commands all people everywhere to repent." This is a key verse. According to Paul, the pagans have worshipped pagan gods out of ignorance. They simply didn't know any better. God has overlooked all that and given them a chance now to face the truth and to come to believe in him through Christ, who has been raised from the dead.

What makes this point of view so interesting is that Paul himself speaks about pagan religions in one of his letters and makes it ever so plain that he does not at all think that pagans worship idols out of ignorance, or that God has overlooked their actions in hopes that they will repent. In Romans 1:18–32, Paul indicates quite the contrary, that the "wrath of God" is poured out upon pagans because they willfully and consciously rejected the knowledge of God that was innate within them. "For what can be known about God is plain to them, because God has shown it to them" (Romans 1:19). They have not pursued their religious fantasies out of ignorance but in full knowledge of the truth: "Though they knew God, they did not honor him as God or give thanks to him . . . and they exchanged the glory of the immortal God for images resembling a mortal human being or birds or four-footed animals or reptiles."

Has God overlooked their sin? By no means: "They are without excuse." And God punishes them, not only in some undisclosed time in the future but also in the present, by making them, or allowing them to become, increasingly corrupt, wicked, and immoral.

And so we have two contrasting portrayals of Paul's view of the pagans and their worship of idols. Do they worship idols out of ignorance? The "Paul" of Acts says yes, Paul in his own writings says no. Does God overlook what they've done? Acts says yes, Paul says no. Are they responsible for their idolatrous activities? Acts says no, Paul says yes. Does God inflict his wrathful judgment on them in the present as a result? Acts says no, Paul says yes.

Scholars have often tried to reconcile these contrary views. Most often it is claimed that since in Acts Paul is talking to the idolaters themselves, wanting to convert them, he doesn't tell them what he really thinks, so as not to give offense. I frankly have always found this hard to believe. It would mean that Paul, in order to gain some converts, would straight out lie about what he thought was God's view of their religious activities. Paul was a lot of things, but I don't think a dissembler was one of them. The real Paul would more likely have preached some fire and brimstone to get these people to realize the error of their ways; tact is another characteristic rarely attached to the historical Paul. It appears that the Paul of Acts is not the same as the real Paul, at least when it comes to this very fundamental issue of the divine reaction to pagan idolatry.

Is the Roman State a Force of Good or Evil?

My final question regarding a major discrepancy of perspective is one asked by many of the early Christians: What is to be the appropriate Christian attitude toward the state? Different authors answered that question differently; sometimes these answers were at odds with one another. The apostle Paul represents one end of the spectrum:

Let every person be subject to the governing authorities; for there is no authority except from God, and those authorities that exist have been instituted by God. Therefore whoever resists authority resists what God has appointed . . . for it is God's servant for your good. (Romans 13:1–2, 4)

The governing authorities are from God, He has instituted them for the good, and no one should resist them because to resist them is to resist God.

The polar opposite view is represented in the book of Revelation, which sees the governing powers as wicked, instituted, and controlled by the forces of evil, and subject in the end to the overwhelming wrath of God. Here are such "ruling authorities" as the Anti-Christ and his minions. Here the city of Rome is described as "the great whore" and the "mother of whores and of earth's abominations," "drunk with the blood of the saints and the blood of the witnesses to Jesus." Why should this "whore of Babylon" of Revelation 17 be thought of as referring to the Roman authorities, the ones Paul had such praise for? Because an angel gives us an interpretation of the meaning of this vision of the "whore of Babylon." The beast on which she sits has seven heads, which represent the "seven mountains on which the woman is seated"; she herself is "the great city that rules over the kings of the earth" (Revelation 17:18). What is the great ruling city of the first century, seated on seven mountains? Of course it is Rome, the city "built on seven hills."

In the book of Revelation, Rome is not the kindly disposed institution working to bring about the good, not God's servant appointed for the well-being of God's people that it is in Paul. In Revelation, Rome is a heinous, wretched, blasphemous, flagrantly immoral, violently oppressive authority, not appointed by God but established by God's enemies. But its day is coming; God will soon overthrow the Roman state in order to bring in his good kingdom and wipe the whore of Babylon off the face of the earth.

CONCLUSION

For nearly twenty-five years now I have taught courses on the New Testament in universities, mainly Rutgers and the University of North Carolina at Chapel Hill. In all this time, the lesson that I have found most difficult to convey to students—the lesson that is the hardest to convince them of—is the historical-critical claim that each author of the Bible needs to be allowed to have his own say, since in many instances what one author has to say on a subject is not what another says. Sometimes the differences are a matter of stress and emphasis; sometimes they are discrepancies in different narratives or between different writers' thoughts; and sometimes these discrepancies are quite large, affecting not only the small details of the text but the very big issues that these authors were addressing.

I've tried to cover some of the interesting "large" discrepancies in this chapter: Who was Jesus? How did he come into the world? What did he teach? Why did he perform miracles? What was his attitude toward his own death? Why did he have to die? How are people made right with God? What is God's attitude toward "false" religions? How should Christians relate to the ruling authorities? These are, by all counts, major issues. And different New Testament authors answers them in different ways.

Who were these authors, exactly, that they should disagree with one another so much of the time on such fundamental issues? That is the topic we take up next in our historical-critical examination of the New Testament writings: Who, really, wrote the Bible?

Who Wrote the Bible?

Students taking a college-level Bible course for the first time often find it surprising that we don't know who wrote most of the books of the New Testament. How could that be? Don't these books all have the authors' names attached to them? Matthew, Mark, Luke, John, the letters of Paul, 1 and 2 Peter, and 1, 2 and 3 John? How could the wrong names be attached to books of Scripture? Isn't this the Word of God? If someone wrote a book claiming to be Paul while knowing full well that he wasn't Paul—isn't that lying? Can Scripture contain lies?

When I arrived at seminary I was fully armed and ready for the onslaught on my faith by liberal biblical scholars who were going to insist on such crazy ideas. Having been trained in conservative circles, I knew that these views were standard fare at places like Princeton Theological Seminary. But what did *they* know? Bunch of liberals.

What came as a shock to me over time was just how little actual evidence there is for the traditional ascriptions of authorship that I had always taken for granted, and how much real evidence there was that many of these ascriptions are wrong. It turned out the liberals actually had something to say and had evidence to back it up; they weren't simply involved in destructive wishful thinking. There were some books, such as the Gospels, that had been written anonymously, only later to be ascribed to certain authors who probably did not write them (apostles and friends of the apostles). Other books were written by authors who flat out claimed to be someone they weren't.

In this chapter I'd like to explain what that evidence is.

WHO WROTE THE GOSPELS?

Though it is evidently not the sort of thing pastors normally tell their congregations, for over a century there has been a broad consensus among scholars that many of the books of the New Testament were not written by the people whose names are attached to them. So if that is the case, who *did* write them?

Preliminary Observations: The Gospels as Eyewitness Accounts

As we have just seen, the Gospels are filled with discrepancies large and small. Why are there so many differences among the four Gospels? These books are called Matthew, Mark, Luke, and John because they were traditionally thought to have been written by Matthew, a disciple who was a tax collector; John, the "Beloved Disciple" mentioned in the Fourth Gospel; Mark, the secretary of the disciple Peter; and Luke, the traveling companion of Paul. These traditions can be traced back to about a century after the books were written.

But if Matthew and John were both written by earthly disciples of Jesus, why are they so very different, on all sorts of levels? Why do they contain so many contradictions? Why do they have such fundamentally different views of who Jesus was? In Matthew, Jesus comes into being when he is conceived, or born, of a virgin; in John, Jesus is the incarnate Word of God who was with God in the beginning and through whom the universe was made. In Matthew, there is not a word about Jesus being God; in John, that's precisely who he is. In Matthew, Jesus teaches about the coming kingdom of God and almost never about himself (and never that he is divine); in

John, Jesus teaches almost exclusively about himself, especially his divinity. In Matthew, Jesus refuses to perform miracles in order to prove his identity; in John, that is practically the only reason he does miracles.

Did two of the earthly followers of Jesus really have such radically different understandings of who he was? It is possible. Two people who served in the administration of George W. Bush may well have radically different views about him (although I doubt anyone would call him divine). This raises an important methodological point that I want to stress before discussing the evidence for the authorship of the Gospels.

Why did the tradition eventually arise that these books were written by apostles and companions of the apostles? In part it was in order to assure readers that they were written by eyewitnesses and companions of eyewitnesses. An eyewitness could be trusted to relate the truth of what actually happened in Jesus' life. But the reality is that eyewitnesses cannot be trusted to give historically accurate accounts. They never could be trusted and can't be trusted still. If eyewitnesses always gave historically accurate accounts, we would have no need for law courts. If we needed to find out what actually happened when a crime was committed, we could just ask someone. Real-life legal cases require multiple eyewitnesses, because eyewitnesses' testimonies differ. If two eyewitnesses in a court of law were to differ as much as Matthew and John, imagine how hard it would be to reach a judgment.

A further reality is that all the Gospels were written anonymously, and none of the writers claims to be an eyewitness. Names are attached to the titles of the Gospels ("the Gospel according to Matthew"), but these titles are later additions to the Gospels, provided by editors and scribes to inform readers who the editors thought were the authorities behind the different versions. That the titles are not original to the Gospels themselves should be clear upon some simple reflection. Whoever wrote Matthew did not call it "The Gospel according to Matthew." The persons who gave it that title are telling you who, in their opinion, wrote it. Authors never title their books "according to."[1]

Moreover, Matthew's Gospel is written completely in the third person, about what "they"—Jesus and the disciples—were doing, never about what "we"—Jesus and the rest of us—were doing. Even when this Gospel narrates the event of Matthew being called to become a disciple, it talks about "him," not about "me." Read the account for yourself (Matthew 9:9). There's not a thing in it that would make you suspect the author is talking about himself.

With John it is even more clear. At the end of the Gospel the author says of the "Beloved Disciple": "This is the disciple who is testifying to these things and has written them, and we know that his testimony is true" (John 21:24). Note how the author differentiates between his source of information, "the disciple who testifies," and *himself*: "*we* know that his testimony is true." He/we: this author is not the disciple. He claims to have gotten some of his information from the disciple.

As for the other Gospels, Mark was said to be not a disciple but a companion of Peter, and Luke was a companion of Paul, who also was not a disciple. Even if they had been disciples, it would not guarantee the objectivity or truthfulness of their stories. But in fact none of the writers was an eyewitness, and none of them claims to be.

Who, then, wrote these books?

The Authors of the Gospels

A good place to start is with a basic question: What do we know about the followers of Jesus? Our earliest and best information about them comes from the Gospels themselves, along with the book of Acts. The other books of the New Testament, such as the writings of Paul, make only passing reference to the twelve disciples, and these references tend to confirm what we can ferret out of the Gospels themselves. Outside the New Testament, all we have are legends that were produced many decades and centuries later—for example, the famous Acts of John, which narrates the miraculous missionary endeavors of John after the resurrection. No historian thinks that these Acts are historically reliable.[2]

From the Gospels we learn that the disciples of Jesus, like him, were lower-class peasants from rural Galilee. Most of them—certainly Simon Peter, Andrew, James, and John—were day laborers (fishermen and the like); Matthew is said to be a tax collector, but it is not clear how high up he was in the tax collecting organization, whether he was a kind of general contractor who worked directly with the ruling authorities to secure tax revenues or, and possibly more likely, the kind of person who came banging on your door to make you pay up. If the latter, there is nothing to suggest that he would have required much of an education.

The same can certainly be said of the others. We have some information about what it meant to be a lower-class peasant in rural areas of Palestine in the first century. One thing it meant is that you were almost certainly illiterate. Jesus himself was highly exceptional, in that he could evidently read (Luke 4:16–20), but there is nothing to indicate that he could write. In antiquity these were two separate skills, and many people who could read were unable to write.

How many could read? Illiteracy was widespread throughout the Roman Empire. At the best of times maybe 10 percent of the population was roughly literate. And that 10 percent would be the leisured classes—upper-class people who had the time and money to get an education (and their slaves and servants taught to read for the benefit of such services to their masters). Everyone else worked from an early age and was unable to afford the time or expense of an education.[3]

Nothing in the Gospels or Acts indicates that Jesus' followers could read, let alone write. In fact there is an account in Acts in which Peter and John are said to be "unlettered" (Acts 4:13)—the ancient word for illiterate. As Galilean Jews, Jesus' followers, like Jesus himself, would have been speakers of Aramaic. As rural folk they probably would not have any knowledge of Greek; if they did, it would have been extremely rough, since they spent their time with other illiterate Aramaic-speaking peasants trying to eke out a hand-to-mouth existence.

In short, who were Jesus' disciples? Lower-class, illiterate, Aramaic-speaking peasants from Galilee.

And who were the authors of the Gospels? Even though they all kept their identities anonymous, we can learn a few things about them from the books they wrote. What we learn stands completely at odds with what we know about the disciples of Jesus. The authors of the Gospels were highly educated, Greek-speaking Christians who probably lived outside Palestine.

That they were highly educated Greek speakers goes virtually without saying. Although there have been scholars from time to time who thought that the Gospels may originally have been written in Aramaic, the overwhelming consensus today, for lots of technical linguistic reasons, is that the Gospels were all written in Greek. As I've indicated, only about 10 percent of the people in the Roman Empire, at best, could read, even fewer could write out sentences, far fewer still could actually compose narratives on a rudimentary level, and very few indeed could compose extended literary works like the Gospels. To be sure, the Gospels are not the most refined books to appear in the empire—far from it. Still, they are coherent narratives written by highly trained authors who knew how to construct a story and carry out their literary aims with finesse.

Whoever these authors were, they were unusually gifted Christians of a later generation. Scholars debate where they lived and worked, but their ignorance of Palestinian geography and Jewish customs suggests they composed their works somewhere else in the empire—presumably in a large urban area where they could have received a decent education and where there would have been a relatively large community of Christians.[4]

These authors were not lower-class, illiterate, Aramaic-speaking peasants from Galilee. But isn't it possible that, say, John wrote the Gospel as an old man? That as a young man he was an illiterate,

Aramaic-speaking day laborer—a fisherman from the time he was old enough to help haul in a net—but that as an old man he wrote a Gospel?

I suppose it's *possible*. It would mean that after Jesus' resurrection John decided to go to school and become literate. He learned the basics of reading, picked up the rudiments of writing, and learned Greek, well enough to become completely fluent. By the time he was an old man he had mastered composition and was able to write a Gospel. Is this likely? It hardly seems so. John and the other followers of Jesus had other things on their minds after experiencing Jesus' resurrection. For one thing, they thought they had to convert the world and run the church.

The Witness of Papias

In spite of the evidence that none of the disciples wrote a Gospel, we need to deal with the early church tradition that indicates that some of them did so. How is one to deal with this tradition?

The earliest source of this tradition, an early Christian church father named Papias, deals with only two early Christian Gospels, Mark and Matthew. Papias is an enigmatic figure who wrote a five-volume work called *Expositions of the Sayings of the Lord*. Scholars have plausibly dated the work to a point somewhere between 110 and 140 CE, forty to seventy years after the first Gospel was written.[5] Papias's work no longer survives: a number of later Christian authorities found Papias's views either offensive or insufficiently sophisticated, and so the work was not copied extensively for posterity.[6] Everything we know about the work comes from quotations of it by later church fathers.

Papias has nonetheless often been portrayed as a useful source for establishing early church tradition, in part because of how he indicates he received his information. In some of the quotations of the *Expositions* that survive, he states that he personally talked with Christians who had known a group of people he calls "the elders," that they had known some of the disciples, and that he has passed along information that he received from them. So in reading Papias we have access to third- or fourth-hand information from people who knew companions of the disciples.

A much-quoted passage by Papias (recorded by Eusebius) describes this kind of third- or fourth-hand information, concerning Mark and Matthew as authors of Gospels.

> This is what the elder used to say, "when Mark was the interpreter [translator?] of Peter he wrote down accurately everything that he recalled of the Lord's words and deeds—but not in order. For he neither heard the Lord nor accompanied him; but later, as I indicated, he accompanied Peter, who used to adapt his teachings for the needs at hand, not arranging, as it were, an orderly composition of the Lord's sayings. And so Mark did nothing wrong by writing some of the matters as he remembered them. For he was intent on just one purpose: not to leave out anything that he heard or to include any falsehood among them."

He goes on to say about Matthew:

> And so Matthew composed the sayings in the Hebrew tongue, and each one interpreted [translated?] them to the best of his ability. (Eusebius, *Church History* 3. 39)

Isn't this evidence that Matthew really wrote Matthew, and Mark really wrote Mark?

There are some very serious complications in trying to assess the historical value of Papias's remarks. Let's begin with Matthew. For one thing, with Matthew—unlike with Mark—we don't learn what the source of Papias's information is, or if he even has a source. Is it third-hand? Fourth-hand? Fifth-hand? If Papias was writing, say, in 120 or 130, it was something like forty or fifty years after Matthew was anonymously written. The Gospel had been in anonymous circulation for decades. Isn't it possible that the tradition that Papias relates had been made up in the meantime?

In this connection it is worth noting that the two pieces of solid information that Papias gives us about Matthew are not true of "our" Matthew. Our Matthew is not just a collection of Jesus' sayings, and the Gospel was certainly written in Greek, not Hebrew.[7] Has Papias simply gotten his information wrong? Or is he talking about some other book written by Matthew—for example, a collection of Jesus' sayings—that we no longer possess?

If Papias is not reliable about Matthew, is he reliable about Mark? In this instance he indicates that we are receiving third- or fourth-hand information.[8] And again, one of the points that he emphatically makes is certainly wrong: he claims that one of Mark's two primary goals was to tell *everything* that he had heard from Peter about Jesus. There is simply no way that can be true. The Gospel of Mark takes about two hours to read out loud. After Peter had spent all those months, or years, with Jesus, and after Mark listened to Peter preach about Jesus day and night, are we to imagine that all Mark heard was two hours' worth of information?

In any event, Papias does not seem to provide us with the kind of information we can place a lot of confidence in. I should point out, in this connection, that scholars have almost uniformly rejected just about everything else that Papias is recorded to have said in the surviving references to his work. Consider another piece of fourth-hand information:

Thus the elders who saw John, the disciple of the Lord, remembered hearing him say how the Lord used to teach about those times, saying:

"The days are coming when vines will come forth, each with ten thousand boughs; and on a single bough will be ten thousand branches. And indeed, on a single branch will be ten thousand shoots and on every shoot ten thousand clusters; and in every cluster will be ten thousand grapes, and every grape, when pressed, will yield twenty-five measures of wine. And when any of the saints grabs hold of a cluster, another will cry out, 'I am better, take me, bless the lord through me.'" (Eusebius, *Church History* 3.39.1)

No one thinks that Jesus really said this. Or that John the disciple of Jesus said that Jesus said this. Did the elders who knew John really say this?[9]

If scholars are inclined to discount what Papias says in virtually every other instance, why is it that they sometimes appeal to his witness in order to show that we have an early tradition that links Matthew to one of our Gospels, and Mark to another? Why do these scholars accept some of what Papias said but not all of what he said? I suspect it is because they want to have support for their own points of view (Matthew really wrote Matthew) and have decided to trust Papias when he confirms their views, and not trust him when he does not.

The result of this quick examination of Papias is, I think, that he passes on stories that he has heard, and he attributes them to people who knew other people who said so. But when he can be checked, he appears to be wrong. Can he be trusted in the places that he cannot be checked? If you have a friend who is consistently wrong when he gives directions to places you are familiar with, do you trust him when he gives directions for someplace you've never been?

Papias is not recorded as having said anything about either Luke or John. I'm not sure why. But the bottom line is this: we do not have any solid reference to the authors of our four Gospels in which we can trust (for example, that the author is actually referring to our Matthew and our Mark) until closer to the end of the second century—nearly a full hundred years after these books had been anonymously placed in circulation.

The Witness of Irenaeus and Others

The first certain reference to the four Gospels is in the writings of the church father Irenaeus. In a five-volume attack on Christian heresies he names as the four Gospels of the church Matthew, Mark, Luke, and John. By the time of Irenaeus (180 CE), it is not surprising that church fathers would want to know who wrote these anonymous books. As we will see in a later chapter, there were lots of other Gospels floating around in the early church—most of them actually claiming to have been written by disciples of Jesus, for example, Peter, Thomas, and Philip. How was one to decide which Gospels were to be trusted as apostolic? This was a thorny problem, since most of these "other" Gospels represented theological perspectives branded heretical by the likes of Irenaeus. How can one know the true teachings of Jesus? Only by accepting Gospels that actually were written by his followers, or close companions of his followers.

But the Gospels that were widely accepted as authoritative in Irenaeus's circles were originally anonymous. The solution to the problem of validating these texts was obvious: they needed to be attributed to real, established authorities. Traditions had been floating around for decades that Matthew had written a Gospel, and so what is now our first Gospel came to be accepted as that book. Mark was thought to be a companion of Peter: our second Gospel came to be associated with him, giving Peter's view of Jesus' life. The author of our third Gospel wrote two volumes, the second of which, Acts, portrayed Paul as a hero. Church leaders insisted that it must have been written by a companion of Paul, and so assigned it to Luke.[10] And to round it all out, the fourth Gospel, which explicitly claims not to be written by an eyewitness, was nonetheless attributed to one, John, one of Jesus' closest disciples (he is never actually named in the Fourth Gospel).

None of these attributions goes back to the authors themselves. And none of the Gospels was written by a follower of Jesus, all of whom were lower-class Aramaic speakers from Galilee, not highly educated Greek-speaking Christians of a later generation.

And so we have an answer to our ultimate question of why these Gospels are so different from one another. They were not written by Jesus' companions or by companions of his companions. They were written decades later by people who didn't know Jesus, who lived in a different country or different countries from Jesus, and who spoke a different language from Jesus. They are different from each other in part because they also didn't know each other, to some extent they had different sources of information (although Matthew and Luke drew on Mark), and they modified their stories on the basis of their own understandings of who Jesus was.

The fact that the Gospels were not actually written by apostles does not make them unusual in the New Testament. Quite the contrary, it makes them typical. Most of the books of the New Testament go under the names of people who didn't actually write them. This has been well known among scholars for the greater part of the past century, and it is taught widely in mainline seminaries and divinity schools throughout the country. As a result, most pastors know it as well. But for many people on the street and in the pews, this is "news."

ARE THERE FORGERIES IN THE NEW TESTAMENT?

Of the twenty-seven books of the New Testament, only eight almost certainly go back to the author whose name they bear: the seven undisputed letters of Paul (Romans, 1 and 2 Corinthians, Galatians, Philippians, 1 Thessalonians, and Philemon) and the Revelation of John (although we aren't sure who this John was).

The other nineteen books fall into three groups.

- *Misattributed writings.* As we have already seen, the Gospels are probably misattributed. John the disciple did not write John, and Matthew did not write Matthew. Other anonymous books have been wrongly attributed to someone famous. The book of Hebrews does not name Paul as its author, and it almost certainly was not written by Paul.[11] But it was eventually admitted into the canon of Scripture (see chapter 7) because church fathers came to think it was written by Paul.

- *Homonymous writings.* The term "homonymy" means "having the same name." A "homonymous writing" is one that is written by someone who has the same name as someone who is famous. For example, the book of James was no doubt written by someone named James, but the author does not claim to be any particular James. It was an extraordinarily common name. Later church fathers accepted the book as part of Scripture because they claimed that this James was James the brother of Jesus. In the book itself there is no such claim.

- *Pseudepigraphic writings.* Some books of the New Testament were written in the names of people who did not actually write them. Scholars have known this for well over a century. The term for this phenomenon is "pseudepigraphy"—literally, "writing that goes under a false name." Scholars have not been overly precise in their use of this term and tend to use it because it avoids the negative connotations associated with the term "forgery." Whichever term they use, biblical scholars have argued for a long time that there are New Testament books whose authors knowingly claimed to be someone other than who they were.

Pseudepigraphy in the Ancient World

To make sense of this situation we need to learn more about authorship and false authorship in the ancient world.

Definitions

To begin with, it is important to be precise in our terminology. The term "pseudepigraphy" can refer to any writing that has a false name attached to it. They may be false attributions, and they may be writings whose authors falsely claim to be someone else.

There are two kinds of falsely attributed writings. Some are books written anonymously that later readers, editors, or scribes wrongly claim to have been written by someone famous; others are books written homonymously, by someone who happens to share the name of someone else who was famous. In the ancient world, most people didn't have last names, so "John" could refer to any one of hundreds or thousands of people. If an author named John wrote a book and someone later claimed that this John was in fact John the son of Zebedee (as some people claimed for the book of Revelation), then it would be a false attribution based on homonymity.[12]

There are also two kinds of "pseudonymous" writings, writings written under a "false name." A pen name is a simple pseudonym. When Samuel Clemens wrote *The Adventures of Huckleberry Finn* and signed off as Mark Twain, he didn't intend to deceive anyone; he simply was choosing a different name to publish under. There are very few instances of this kind of pseudonymity in the ancient world, although it did happen on occasion. The Greek historian Xenophon wrote his famous work, *The Anabasis*, under a pen name, "Themistogenes." More frequently in antiquity we find the other kind of pseudonymous writing, where the author uses the name of someone else who is well known in order to deceive his audience into thinking that he really is that person. This kind of pseudonymous writing is literary forgery.

Prevalence of Forgery in the Ancient World

Literary forgery was a common phenomenon in the ancient world. We know this because ancient authors themselves talk about it, a lot. Discussions of forgery can be found in the writings of some of the best-known authors from antiquity. Among the Greeks and Romans you can find references to and discussions of forgery in such far-flung authors as Herodotus, Cicero, Quintillian, Martial, Suetonius,

Galen, Plutarch, Philastratus, and Diogenes Laertius. Among Christian authors there are discussions in the writings of such well-known figures as Irenaeus, Tertullian, Origen, Eusebius, Jerome, Rufinus, and Augustine.

It is sometimes argued by scholars of the New Testament that forgery was so common in the ancient world that no one took it seriously: since the deceit could normally be easily detected, it was never really meant to fool anyone.[13] I have spent the past couple of years examining the ancient discussions of forgery and have come to the conclusion that the only people who make this argument are people who haven't actually read the ancient sources.

Ancient sources took forgery seriously. They almost universally condemn it, often in strong terms. How widely was it condemned? Odd as it might seem, the practice of forgery is sometimes condemned even in documents that are forged. Furthermore, the claim that no one was ever fooled is completely wrong. People were fooled all the time. That's why people wrote forgeries—to fool people.

I don't need to give a detailed account of the ancient discussions of forgery here; there is plenty of scholarship on the problem, although unfortunately the most exhaustive works are in German.[14] But I can illustrate the point by giving one particularly telling anecdote.

In second-century Rome there was a famous physician and author named Galen. Galen tells the story that one day, as he was walking through the streets of Rome, he passed by a bookseller's stall. There he saw two men arguing over a certain book for sale, written in the name of . . . Galen! One man was insisting that the book really was Galen's, and the other was equally vociferous in claiming that it could not be, since the writing style was completely different from Galen's. This, needless to say, warmed the cockles of Galen's heart, since he had not in fact written the book. But he was more than a little perturbed that someone was trying to sell a book under his name. And so he went home and composed a small book called "How to Recognize the Books of Galen." We still have the book today.

Forgery was widely practiced, it was meant to deceive, and it often worked. That it was not an accepted practice is clear from the terms that ancient authors used for it. Two of the most common terms for a forgery in Greek are *pseudon*, a lie, and *nothon*, a bastard child. This latter term is as harsh and unsavory in Greek as it is in English. It is often juxtaposed with the term *gnesion*, which means something like legitimate or authentic.

Motivations for Producing Forgeries

From a wide range of ancient sources it is clear that the intention of a literary forgery was to deceive readers into thinking that someone other than the actual author had written the book. But what motivated authors to do this? Why didn't they just write books using their own names?

There were many motivations for pagan, Jewish, and Christian authors to forge literary texts. Here are ten:

1. *To make a profit.* The two greatest libraries in the ancient world were located in the cities of Alexandria and Pergamum. Acquiring books for a library collection in antiquity was very different from today. Since books were copied by hand, different copies of the same book might differ, sometimes sizably, from one another, so the most important libraries preferred to have an original of a book, rather than a later copy that might have mistakes in it. According to Galen, this led entrepreneurial types to create "original" copies of the classics to sell to the libraries of Alexandria and Pergamum. If librarians were paying cash on the head for original copies of treatises of the philosopher Aristotle, you'd be amazed how many original copies of treatises of Aristotle would start to turn up. So far as I can tell, the profit motive did not have any effect on early Christian writings, since these were not sold in the marketplace until much later times.

2. *To oppose an enemy.* Sometimes a literary work would be forged in order to make a personal enemy look bad. A Greek historian of philosophy, Diogenes Laertius, indicates that a philosopher named

Diotemus forged and then circulated fifty obscene letters in the name of his philosophical nemesis Epicurus. This obviously did not do wonders for Epicurus's reputation. I have sometimes wondered if something of the sort is happening in one of the more peculiar forgeries of early Christianity. The fourth-century heresy hunter Epiphanius indicated that he had read a book allegedly used by a group of highly immoral Christian heretics known as the Phibionites. This book, *The Greater Questions of Mary*, allegedly contained a bizarre account of Jesus and Mary Magdalene, in which Jesus takes Mary up to a high mountain and in her presence pulls a woman out of his side (much as God made Eve from the rib of Adam) and begins having sexual intercourse with her. When he comes to climax, however, he pulls out of her, collects his semen in his hand, and eats it, telling Mary, "Thus must we do, to live." Mary, understandably enough, faints on the spot (Epiphanius, *The Panarion*, book 26). This strange tale is found nowhere outside of Epiphanius, who is famous for making up a lot of his "information" about heretics. I've often wondered whether he made this whole account up, claimed to have found it in one of the Phibionites' books, but fabricated it himself out of whole cloth. If so, in a sense he forged a Phibionite book in the name of Mary in order to make his heretical opponents look very bad indeed.

3. *To oppose a particular point of view.* If I'm right about Epiphanius and *The Greater Questions of Mary*, then part of his motivation would have been to oppose a view, the Phibionite heresy, that he found noxious. Similar motivations can be found in the cases of a large number of other Christian forgeries. In addition to 1 and 2 Corinthians in the New Testament, we have from outside the New Testament a 3 Corinthians.[15] This book was clearly written in the second century, as it opposes certain heretical views known from that time, which propose that Jesus was not a real flesh-and-blood human being and that his followers would not actually be resurrected in the flesh. According to this author, they would be resurrected, as he states in no uncertain terms—while claiming to be the apostle Paul.

It may seem odd to try to counteract a false teaching by assuming a false identity, but there it is. It happened a lot in the forgeries of the early Christian tradition.

4. *To defend one's own tradition as divinely inspired.* There is an ancient collection of writings known as the Sibylline oracles.[16] The Sibyl was reputed to be an ancient pagan prophetess, inspired by the Greek god Apollo. Our surviving oracles, however, are mostly written by Jews. In them the prophetess, allegedly living long before the events she predicts, discusses the future events of history—and she is always right, since the actual author is living after these events—and confirms the validity of important Jewish beliefs and practices. Not to be outdone, later Christians took some of these oracles and inserted references to the coming of Christ in them, so that now this pagan prophetess accurately foresees the coming of the Messiah. What better testimony to the divine truthfulness of one's religion than the prophecies allegedly delivered by the inspired spokesperson of one's enemies?

5. *Out of humility?* It is commonly argued by scholars of the New Testament that members of certain philosophical schools would write treatises in the name of their master-teacher and sign his name to their own work as a gesture of humility, since one's own thoughts are simply the extension of what the master himself said. This is said to be particularly true of a group of philosophers known as the Pythagoreans, named after the great Greek philosopher Pythagoras. There is, however, serious dispute as to whether the Pythagorean philosophers who claimed to be Pythagoras actually did it out of humility: no statements to that effect can be found in their own writings, only in the writings of authors writing centuries later.[17] These Pythagoreans may have been inspired by other motives.

6. *Out of love for an authority figure.* In a similar vein, we do have one author from antiquity who claimed to have forged his work as an act of love and reverence. This is a most unusual situation, one in which a forger was caught red-handed. The story is told by the early-third-century church father Tertullian, who indicates that the well-

known stories of Paul and his female disciple Thecla, famous as a model disciple throughout the Middle Ages, were forged by a leader of a church in Asia Minor, and that he was discovered in the act and deposed from his church office as a result. In his self-defense the forger claimed that he had written his work "out of love for Paul."[18] It is not clear exactly what he meant by that, but it may mean that his devotion to Paul led him to invent a tale in Paul's name to capture some of what he took to be the apostle's most important teachings and views. Actually, the teachings and views found in the surviving Acts of Paul and Thecla are not at all what Paul taught: among other things, we learn from this narrative that Paul proclaimed that eternal life would come not to those who believed in Jesus' death and resurrection, as Paul himself proclaimed, but to those who followed Jesus in remaining sexually abstinent—even if they were married.

7. *To see if you could get away with it.* There were some ancient forgers who created their work simply in order to see if they could pull the wool over other peoples' eyes. The technical term for this is "mystification." The most famous instance, told by Diogenes Laertius, is of an author named Dionysius who set out to fool one of his sworn enemies, Heraclides of Pontus, by forging a play in the name of the famous tragedian Sophocles. Heraclides was fooled and quoted the play as authentic. Dionysius then uncovered his deceit—but Heraclides refused to believe him. And so Dionysius pointed out that if you took the first letters of several lines of the text and wrote them out as words (an acrostic), they spelled the name of Dionysius's boyfriend. Heraclides claimed that it was just a coincidence, until Dionysius showed that later in the text were two other acrostics, one that spelled the message "an old monkey isn't caught in a trap; oh yes, he is caught at last, but it takes time," and another that said, "Heraclides is ignorant of letters and is not ashamed of his ignorance."[19] I don't know of any certain instances of mystification among early Christian forgers.

8. *To supplement the tradition.* Especially in early Christianity there were lots of instances in which forgers would provide

"authoritative" writings that would supplement what was thought to be lacking in the tradition. For example, the author of Colossians 4:17 (Paul?) tells his readers that they are also to read the letter sent to the Christians in the town of Laodicea. We don't have an authentic letter of Paul to the Laodiceans, however. No surprise, then, that in the second century a couple of such letters turned up, forged in Paul's name to supply the lack.[20] Another example: it is well known that the Gospels of the New Testament say virtually nothing about Jesus' early life. This had some early Christians puzzled, and in the second century, accounts of Jesus as a boy started cropping up. The most famous of these was claimed to have been written by someone named Thomas, a name that means "the twin." This may be a reference to the tradition known from Syrian Christians that Jesus' own brother, Jude, was in fact his twin brother, "Judas Thomas." In any event, it is an intriguing narrative of the adventures of the young Jesus, starting when he was a five-year-old.[21]

9. *To counter other forgeries.* One of the least studied phenomena of early Christian forgery is the production of forged texts designed to counter the positions staked out in other forgeries. In the early fourth century, according to the church father Eusebius, an anti-Christian pagan forgery was produced called the Acts of Pilate. Apparently this narrative told the story of Jesus' trial and execution from a Roman point of view, to show that Jesus fully deserved what he got. This was a widely read document: the Roman emperor Maximin Daia issued a decree that it was to be read by schoolboys learning their letters (Eusebius, *Church History* 9.5). Soon afterward, however, a Christian document that was also known as the Acts of Pilate made its appearance. In this account Pilate is in complete sympathy with Jesus and fervently tries to release him as innocent of all charges.[22] The Christian version appears to have been written to counter the pagan one. This phenomenon of Christian counterforgery appears to have been fairly widespread. There was a text written in the fourth century called the Apostolic Constitutions. It claims to have been written by the twelve apostles after the death of Jesus, even though the apostles

had been dead for three hundred years by the time it was written. Among the many remarkable features of this book is its insistence that Christians not read books that falsely claim to be written by apostles (Apostolic Constitutions 6.16). There is something similar even within the New Testament: the author of the book of 2 Thessalonians warns his readers not to be upset by a letter allegedly by Paul (that is, a letter forged in Paul's name; 2 Thessalonians 2:2). But as we will see in a moment, there are good reasons for thinking that 2 Thessalonians itself is a pseudepigraphic book, putatively by Paul but not actually written by him.

10. *To provide authority for one's own views.* This is the motivation that I think is by far the most common in early Christian forgeries. There were lots of Christians in the early centuries of the church who claimed numerous points of view, most of which came to be branded as heresies. Yet all of these Christians claimed to represent the views of Jesus and his disciples. How could you demonstrate that your views were apostolic, in order to, say, convince potential converts? The easiest way was to write a book, claim that it had been written by an apostle, and to put it in circulation. Every group of early Christians had access to writings allegedly written by the apostles. Most of these writings were forgeries.

Early Christian Forgeries

No one can reasonably doubt that a lot of the early Christian literature was forged. From outside the New Testament, for example, we have a large range of other Gospels allegedly (but not really) written by well-known early Christian leaders: Peter, Philip, Thomas, James the brother of Jesus, and Nicodemus, among others; we have a variety of apostolic Acts, such as the Acts of John and of Paul and Thecla; we have epistles, such as the letter to the Laodiceans, 3 Corinthians, an exchange of letters between Paul and the Roman philosopher Seneca, and a letter allegedly written by Peter to James in order to oppose Paul; and we have a number of apocalypses, for example, an Apocalypse of Peter (which very nearly made it into the canon) and an Apocalypse of Paul. We will examine some of these other writings in chapter 6.

Early Christian writers were busy, and one of their common activities was to forge documents in the names of the apostles. This leads us now to the big question: Did any of these forgeries make it into the New Testament?

From a historical perspective, there is no reason to doubt that some forgeries very well could have made it into the canon. We have numerous forgeries outside the New Testament. Why not inside? I don't think one can argue that the church fathers, starting at the end of the second century, would have known which books really were written by apostles and which ones were not. How would they know? Or perhaps more to the point, how can we ourselves know?

This might sound a little strange, but it is easier for us today to detect ancient forgeries than it was for people in the ancient world. The methods we use are the same as theirs. Like Galen, we consider the style in which a letter is written. Is it the same writing style that the author uses elsewhere? If it is different, just how different is it? Slightly different or extremely different? Is it possible that an author wrote in different styles? Or are there some features of the style that are completely unlike what the author uses elsewhere, especially in those aspects of style that we don't think much about when we write (which kinds of conjunctions we use, how we construct complex sentences, how we use participles and infinitives)? We also consider the word choice: is there a set vocabulary that an author uses that is missing from this writing? Or is some of the vocabulary used in this book not attested until later periods of ancient Greek? Most important are the theological ideas, views, and perspectives of the book. Are they the same in this book as in the author's other writings, or at least roughly similar? Or are they strikingly different?

The reason we are better equipped than the ancients to make judgments of this sort now is that we are better equipped! Ancient critics who attempted to detect forgeries obviously didn't have data banks, data retrieval systems, and computers to crunch out detailed evaluations of vocabulary and style. They had to rely a lot on common sense and intuition. We have that, plus lots of data.

Still, even with our improved technologies there remains room for doubt in many instances. There isn't space here for a detailed discussion of every piece of New Testament writing that is in question. Instead I will explain the most compelling reasons for thinking that Paul was not the author of six of the canonical letters that go under his name. I believe all of these books were forged. Their authors may have been well-meaning. They may have thought they were doing the right thing. They may have felt perfectly justified. But in every case, they claimed to be someone other than who they were, presumably in order to get their views heard.

The Pseudepigraphic (Forged) Letters of Paul

In none of the instances that I cover here will I be able to provide in-depth coverage of all the arguments back and forth regarding the authorship of these letters.[25] For my purposes it is enough to explain some of the chief reasons scholars have long argued that these letters were not written by Paul, even though they are claimed to be by him.

Since I have already mentioned 2 Thessalonians, I will start there—a good place to begin, in any event, since it is the most hotly disputed of the six letters of Paul whose authorship is questioned. There are lots of good scholars on both sides of the debate (as opposed to, say, the Pastoral Epistles or 2 Peter, where the vast majority of critical scholars think the letters are pseudonymous). Nonetheless, there are strong reasons for thinking Paul did not write the letter.

2 Thessalonians

One of the reasons the authorship of 2 Thessalonians is heavily debated is that in terms of writing style and vocabulary, it sounds a lot like the letter Paul almost certainly did write, 1 Thessalonians. In fact, it is so much like 1 Thessalonians that some scholars have argued that its pseudonymous author used 1 Thessalonians as a model for constructing the letter, but then added his own content, which differs significantly from that of his model. The similarity of the two letters reveals one of the problems scholars have with establishing whether or not an ancient document is forged. Anyone who is skilled in committing a forgery will naturally do his best to make his work sound like the work of the person he is imitating. Some forgers will be better at this than others. But if someone is particularly good, it is hard to show what he has done, at least on the basis of style.

But why would someone imitate Paul's style yet take a theological position that is different from his? One can think of a lot of possible reasons: maybe the situation in the churches had changed, and the author wanted to address new problems by calling Paul back from the grave, so to speak; maybe the author didn't have a full understanding of Paul and mistook some of his key points (Paul himself indicates this happened in his own lifetime, for example, in his letter to the Romans; see Romans 3:8); maybe the author sincerely thought that his readers had misunderstood Paul's real message and wanted to correct their misunderstanding, not knowing that all along the readers had it right.

My methodological point is this: one would expect a good imitator of Paul to sound like Paul. But one would *not* expect Paul not to sound like Paul. The key to seeing 2 Thessalonians as non-Pauline is that its main thesis seems to contradict what Paul himself said in 1 Thessalonians.

2 Thessalonians is written to counter the view, possibly based on an earlier now-lost letter forged in Paul's name, that "the day of the Lord is already here" (2:2). The Christians being addressed appear to think that the end of the age—Jesus' return in glory—is right around the corner. This author writes to correct that misimpression. And so in chapter 2, the heart of the letter, the author indicates that

there is a sequence of events that must transpire before the end will come. First there will be some kind of general rebellion against God, and then an anti-Christ figure will appear who will take his seat in the Jewish Temple, declaring himself to be God. This lawless one will do all kinds of deceptive miracles and wonders to lead people astray (2:1–12). Only after these things have taken place will the end finally come. The end is not yet here and is not coming right away; it will be preceded by clear and obvious signs, so that the Christians in the know will not be caught unawares.

This is a powerful and intriguing message. The problem is that it doesn't coincide well with what Paul himself said in 1 Thessalonians.

That letter was also written to address the question of what would happen at the end, when Jesus returns from heaven in glory (1 Thessalonians 4:13–18). The reason Paul wrote the letter was that the members of the Thessalonian congregation had been taught by Paul that the end was imminent. They were puzzled and distraught because some of the members of their church had already died before Jesus returned. Had these lost out on the reward to be brought with Jesus at his second coming? Paul writes to assure those who were still alive that the dead will be the first to be raised at Jesus' second coming, and that they, too, would be certain to receive the blessings that were their due.

Paul goes on to reiterate what he had told them when he was among them (1 Thessalonians 5:1–2), that Jesus' coming would be sudden and unexpected, "like a thief in the night" (1 Thessalonians 5:2). It would bring "sudden destruction" (1 Thessalonians 5:3), and so the Thessalonians had to be constantly prepared so that it would not overtake them unexpectedly.

If Paul meant what he said in 1 Thessalonians, that Jesus' return would be sudden and unexpected, it is hard to believe that he could have written what is said in 2 Thessalonians—that the end is *not* coming right away and that there will be clear-cut signs to indicate that the end is near, signs that had not yet appeared. The author of 2 Thessalonians writes, "I told you these things when I was still with you" (2:5). If that were true, why would the Thessalonians have been upset when some members of their community died (1 Thessalonians)? They would have known that the end was not coming right away, but was to be preceded by the appearance of the anti-Christ figure and other signs.

It looks as though Paul did not write both letters. It may be that the heightened expectations of Christians toward the end of the first century led some unknown author in Paul's churches to write 2 Thessalonians in order to calm them down a bit, to let them know that yes, the end was going to come, but it was not coming right away. Some things had to happen first.

Colossians and Ephesians

The arguments against Paul having written Colossians and Ephesians are similar. They and 2 Thessalonians are called "Deutero-Pauline" epistles by scholars, since they are believed not to have been written by Paul, making their standing in the Pauline corpus secondary—the root meaning of "deutero."

In the judgment of most scholars, the argument for the pseudonymity of Colossians and especially of Ephesians is even stronger than in the case of 2 Thessalonians. First, the writing style of both letters is uncharacteristic of Paul's. This is the kind of argument that can't be demonstrated without going into detail about the way the Greek sentences are constructed. The basic idea, though, is that the authors of both Colossians and Ephesians tend to write long and complex sentences, whereas Paul does not. Colossians 1:3–8 is all one sentence in Greek; it's a whopper, and quite unlike the kind of sentence Paul typically wrote. Ephesians 1:3–14 is even longer, twelve verses—not like Paul at all. Nearly 10 percent of the sentences in Ephesians are over fifty words in length; this is uncharacteristic of Paul's undisputed letters. Philippians, about the same length, has only one sentence that long; Galatians is much longer, and also has only one.[24]

There is also a lot of material in Colossians (for example, Colossians 1:15–20) and Ephesians that sounds more theologically advanced and developed than what you find in Paul's letters. More important than that, though, is the fact that there are particular points on which these two authors, assuming they are different authors, and Paul appear to disagree. Both of these authors and Paul want to talk about how things have changed for believers in Jesus who have been baptized. But what they say about the matter differs significantly.

In the early church, baptism was not performed on infants, only on adults after they had come to faith in Christ. For Paul, baptism was an important ceremonial event, not merely a symbolic act. Something actually *happened* when a person was baptized. The person was mystically united with Christ in his death.

Paul works out this idea most carefully in his letter to the Romans. The basic idea is an apocalyptic one. There are powers of evil in the world that have enslaved people and alienated them from God, including the power of sin. Sin is a demonic force, not simply something you do wrong. Everyone is enslaved to this force, which means that everyone is hopelessly alienated from God. The only way to escape the power of sin is to die. That is why Christ died, to release people from this power of sin. To escape the power of sin, then, requires a person to die with Christ. That happens when the person is baptized. By being placed under the water (Paul's churches practiced full immersion), a believer is united with Christ in his death, as he was put in the grave, and so also has died to the powers in control of this world. People who have been baptized are no longer enslaved by the power of sin but have "died with Christ" (Romans 6:1–6).

Paul was quite insistent, however, that even though people had died with Christ, they had not yet been "raised with him." Followers of Jesus would be raised with Christ only when Christ returned from heaven in glory. Then there would be a physical resurrection. Those who had already died in Christ would be raised and those who were still living at the time would experience a glorious transformation of their bodies in which this mortal shell would become immortal, not subject to the pains of life or the possibility of death.

Whenever Paul talked about being raised with Christ, it was always as a future event (see, for example, Romans 6 and 1 Corinthians 15). Within Paul's churches, some of his converts had a different opinion, thinking that they had already experienced a kind of spiritual resurrection with Christ and were already "ruling" with Christ in heaven. This is the view that Paul quite vociferously opposes in his first letter to the Corinthians, the key and climax of which comes at the end of the letter, where Paul stresses that the resurrection is not something already experienced but something yet to come, a real, future, physical resurrection of the body, not a past spiritual resurrection (1 Corinthians 15). Paul is quite emphatic in Romans 6:5 and 8 that those who were baptized had died with Christ, but that they had not yet been raised with him (note his use of the future tense "will"):

> For if we have been united with him in a death like his, we *will* certainly be united with him in a resurrection like his; . . . If we have died with Christ, we believe that we *will* also be raised with him. (*Emphasis added*)

Both Colossians and especially Ephesians disagree. Here is what the author of Colossians says about the very same point:

> When you were buried with him in baptism you *were also raised* with him through faith in the power of God, who raised him from the dead. (Colossians 2:13)

Casual readers might not detect much of a difference between these positions—after all, in both the author speaks of dying and rising with Christ. But precision was very important for Paul. The death with Christ was past, but the resurrection was absolutely not past. It was future. Paul devoted a good chunk of 1 Corinthians to arguing this point, precisely because some of his converts had gotten it dead wrong and he was extremely upset about it. Colossians, though, takes exactly the position that Paul wrote his letter of 1 Corinthians to oppose.

Ephesians is even more emphatic than Colossians. In speaking about the past spiritual resurrection, the author says, in contrast to Paul, "God . . . made us alive together with Christ . . . and raised us up with him and seated us with him in the heavenly places in Christ Jesus" (2:5–6). All this has already happened. Believers are already ruling with Christ. This is what some of the converts of Paul in Corinth and the authors of Colossians and Ephesians—also members of Paul's churches—got wrong.

There are other key points on which Colossians and Ephesians vary from the historical Paul, including differences in vocabulary and differences in how certain terms common to Paul get used in these letters. But my intent is to give at least a sense of why most critical scholars doubt that Paul wrote either of these books. Like 2 Thessalonians, they appear to have been written after Paul's death—maybe a decade or two later, by authors in Paul's churches who wanted to address the Christian community and the problems that had arisen in it since the Paul's death. They did so by claiming to be the apostle himself to fool their readers.

The Pastoral Epistles

Regarding the Pastoral Epistles of 1 and 2 Timothy and Titus, there is even less scholarly debate than in the cases of Colossians and Ephesians. Among critical scholars teaching in North America, the United Kingdom, and western Europe—the leading areas of biblical research—the consensus of opinion for many years has been that Paul did not write these books.

The books are called the Pastoral Epistles because in them "Paul" gives advice to Timothy and Titus, allegedly pastors in Ephesus and on the Island of Crete, about how they should conduct their pastoral duties in their churches. The books are full of pastoral advice on such topics as how these followers of Paul should run a tight ship, get false teachers under control, and choose appropriate church leaders.

Could Paul have written these letters? Of course it is theoretically possible that he did, but the arguments against it seem overwhelmingly convincing to most scholars.

It is generally agreed that the three letters all come from the same person. When you read 1 Timothy and Titus, that will be fairly clear: they deal with many of the same themes, often using the same or similar language. The book of 2 Timothy is different in many ways, but if you compare the opening lines with the opening of 1 Timothy, it, too, looks almost identical.

That this author was not Paul is clear to some scholars on the basis of the letters' vocabulary and writing style. There are 848 different Greek words used in these letters, of which 306 do not occur anywhere else in the letters allegedly written by Paul in the New Testament (even including 2 Thessalonians, Ephesians, and Colossians). This means that over a third of the words are not Pauline. Something like two thirds of these non-Pauline words are words used by Christian writers of the second century. That is to say, the vocabulary of these letters appears to be more developed, more characteristic of Christianity as it developed in later times.

Some of the significant words that this author uses are the same as Paul's, but he uses them in very different ways. Take the word "faith." For Paul, faith meant having a trusting acceptance of Christ's death in order to be put into a right standing with God. It is a relational term, meaning something like "trust." In the Pastoral Epistles the word means something else: the set of beliefs and ideas that make up the Christian religion (Titus 1:13). It is not a relational term but a term that specifies a set of Christian teachings, the content of what has to be believed—which is how the term comes to be used in later Christian contexts. Thus, this is an example of how the Pastoral Epistles appear to stem from a later, non-Pauline setting.

Arguments from vocabulary are notoriously tricky when one is trying to establish whether a particular author wrote a particular book: people use different vocabularies in different circumstances. But in this case the differences do seem pretty stark. An even more compelling argument, though, is the fact that the entire situation of the church presupposed in the Pastoral Epistles seems to differ from what we know about the church in Paul's own day.

We have a good idea of what Paul's churches were like from such letters as 1 and 2 Corinthians, where he discusses the inner workings of his congregations, how they were organized and structured, and how they operated. By the time we get to the Pastoral Epistles, things have changed drastically.

Paul's churches were not hierarchically structured. There was no one leader or group of leaders in charge. They were communities of believers that were run according to the Spirit of God working through each member.

It is important to bear in mind that Paul was thoroughly apocalyptic in his views. He believed that Jesus' resurrection indicated that the end of the age was near. It would arrive any day, with the reappearance of Jesus from heaven; the dead would be raised and the living believers would be transformed into immortal bodies, and so live forever in the future kingdom.

What was to happen in the meantime, while believers awaited the coming of the Lord? They were to meet together in communities for worship, edification, education, and mutual support. How were these communities to be organized? Paul thought they were organized by God himself, through the Holy Spirit; this is spelled out in 1 Corinthians 12–14. When people were baptized into the Christian church, they not only "died with Christ" but also were given an endowment of the Holy Spirit, God's presence here on earth before the end came. Everyone at that point received some kind of "spiritual gift" that they could use to help out others in the community. Some people were given the gift of knowledge, others of teaching, others of giving, others of speaking prophecies from

God, others of giving revelations in foreign or angelic languages that were not generally understood ("speaking in tongues"), others of interpreting these revelations (the "interpretation of tongues"). These gifts were meant for the common good, so that the community of believers could function peacefully and harmoniously in these last days before the end.

Quite often, though, things did not go as planned, for example, in the church of Corinth. It was, truth be told, a real mess. Different spiritual "leaders" claimed to be more spiritually endowed than others and had their own sets of followers, leading to divisions in the church. These divisions had gotten completely out of hand: some members of the church were taking others to court and suing them. There was rampant immorality: some of the men in the church were visiting prostitutes and bragging about it in church; one man was cohabiting with his stepmother. The church services were pure chaos, as the "more spiritual" among the Corinthians had decided that the true sign of spirituality was the ability to speak in tongues and so were competing with one another during worship to see who could do so more loudly and more often than others. At the weekly communion meal—a real meal, not a matter of eating a wafer and taking a sip of wine—some members of the church were coming early and gorging themselves and getting drunk, and others had to come late (possibly the lower classes and slaves, who presumably had to work longer hours) and had nothing to eat or drink. Some members of the congregation were so convinced of their spiritual superiority that they claimed they had already been raised up with Christ and were ruling with him in the heavenly places (similar to the claim made much later by the author of Ephesians).

Paul deals with the problems in the church by addressing the church at large and pleading with all the members to change their ways. Why doesn't he address the bishop of the church, or the head pastor? Why doesn't he write a letter to the leader of the church to tell him to get his troops in line? Because there was no ultimate leader of the church. There were no bishops or head pastors. In Paul's churches, in this brief time between the resurrection of Jesus and the resurrection of all believers, the community was run by the Spirit of God working through each member.[25]

What happens when there is no official hierarchy, no appointed leaders, no one to take charge? What typically happens is what happened in Corinth. A good deal of chaos. How can such chaos be brought under control? Someone needs to take charge. Over time, that's eventually what happened in Paul's churches. After he himself had passed off the scene, his churches assumed the kind of shape that you would assume, where there was someone at the top, someone who gave the orders, someone who had leaders under him who were appointed to keep everyone pulling together, to make sure that only the correct teachings were being given, to discipline those who were not behaving properly.

You don't find this kind of church structure in Paul's day. You do find it in the Pastoral Epistles. These are letters written to the head pastors of the churches in two of Paul's communities. These epistles give instructions for bringing false teachers into line; directions for appointing bishops who were evidently in charge of the spiritual oversight of the church, and deacons who were in charge of almsgiving and taking care of the physical needs of the community; and admonitions about how people in different social circumstances (husbands and wives, parents and children, masters and slaves) were to conduct themselves, so that the church could survive for the long haul.

For Paul, on the other hand, there was not going to be a long haul. He thought the end was coming very soon. But the end didn't come, and his churches had to get organized to survive. They did get organized, and the Pastoral Epistles were written in the context of this new situation, probably two or more decades after Paul had passed off the scene. In the new situation, an author wrote the three letters, claiming to be Paul so as to have Paul's authority behind his message. But his message was not Paul's. Paul lived in a different day and age.

WHO WROTE THE OTHER BOOKS
OF THE NEW TESTAMENT?

Much of what has already been said can also be said of the remaining books of the New Testament. Some of them are anonymous, specifically the letter to the Hebrews and the books called 1, 2, and 3 John. As many authors already in the early church realized, there is no reason to think that Paul wrote Hebrews, but it was eventually included in the canon by church fathers who argued that it was Paul's. In fact, the writing style is completely different from Paul's; the leading themes of the letter are absent from Paul's other letters, and the mode of argumentation is not at all like his. And why should one think Paul wrote it? Unlike his own writings, this book is anonymous.

The so-called epistles of John also don't claim to have been written by John; epistles 2 and 3 are by someone who calls himself "the elder," and the author of 1 John doesn't say anything about himself. The author could be almost any leader of the church near the end of the first century.

Other books are homonymous. The author of James makes no claim to be any James in particular, let alone the James who is known from other traditions to have been Jesus' brother. The book of Jude claims to be written by a Jude who is the "brother of James," so this may be interpreted as a claim to be Jesus' brother, since according to Mark's Gospel two of his brothers were named James and Jude. But it is odd that if he wanted to be thought of as Jesus' own brother, he didn't come out and say so in order to invest his book with even more authority. Both Jude and James were common names in Jewish antiquity and in the Christian church. Later Christians who were establishing the canon claimed that these two were Jesus' relatives, but they themselves never say so.

It is also hard to believe that these letters could have been written by two lower-class Aramaic-speaking peasants from Galilee (whose more famous brother is not known to have been able to write, let alone compose a complicated treatise in Greek). The argument here is the same one set forth earlier for the Gospel of John: it is in theory possible that Jesus' brothers—raised in the backwoods of rural Galilee, working with their hands for a living, never having time or money for an education—decided later in life to acquire a Greek education and to take courses in literary composition, so that they could write these heavily rhetorical and relatively sophisticated books. But it seems somewhat unlikely.

The same thinking is applicable to the letters of 1 and 2 Peter. But these books, like the Deutero-Pauline epistles (2 Thessalonians, Colossians, and Ephesians) and the Pastoral Epistles, actually claim to be written by someone who did not write them. They are pseudonymous in the strong sense of the term: they appear to be forgeries.

What is certain is that whoever wrote 2 Peter did not also write 1 Peter: the writing styles are vastly different. Already in the early church there were Christian scholars who argued that Peter did not write 2 Peter. Today there is even less debate about the matter than there is about the Pastorals. The book called 2 Peter was written long after Peter's death, by someone who was disturbed that some people were denying that the end was coming soon (one can understand why there might be doubters as the years rolled by); this author wanted to disabuse these people of their false notions, and did so by claiming to be none other than Simon Peter, Jesus' right-hand man.

The book called 1 Peter is more hotly debated among scholars than 2 Peter. But again, how likely is it that a simple fisherman from rural Galilee suddenly developed skills in Greek literary composition? It is sometimes argued that Peter had someone else write the letter for him, for example, Silvanus, who is named in the letter (5:12). But the letter itself doesn't say that. And if someone else wrote the letter, wouldn't he, rather than Peter, be the real author? The sophisticated use of the Old Testament in this book suggests that whoever wrote it was highly educated and very well trained, unlike Simon Peter. And it is worth pointing out that we have an extraordinary number of books from early Christianity that claim to be written by Peter that were not written by him—for example, a Gospel of Peter, a letter of Peter to James, several "Acts" of Peter, and three different apocalypses of Peter. Forging books in Peter's name was a virtual cottage industry.

CONCLUSION: WHO WROTE THE BIBLE?

I return now to my original question: Who wrote the Bible? Of the twenty-seven books of the New Testament, only eight almost certainly were written by the authors to whom they are traditionally ascribed: the seven undisputed letters of Paul and the Revelation of John, which could be labeled homonymous, since it does not claim to be written by any particular John; this was recognized even by some writers of the early church.

My views about the authors of the New Testament are not radical within scholarship. To be sure, there are debates among scholars about this book or that. Some very fine scholars think that Paul wrote 2 Thessalonians, or that Jesus' brother James wrote James, or that Peter wrote 1 Peter. But the majority of critical scholars has long doubted these ascriptions, and there is scarcely any debate about some of the books of the New Testament, such as 1 Timothy and 2 Peter. These books were not written by their putative authors.

Doubts about the authorship of writings that became the canon were raised in the early church, but in the modern period, starting in the nineteenth century, scholars have pressed the arguments home with compelling reasoning. Even now many scholars are loath to call the forged documents of the New Testament forgeries—this is, after all, the Bible we're talking about. But the reality is that by any definition of the term, that's what they are. A large number of books in the early church were written by authors who falsely claimed to be apostles in order to deceive their readers into accepting their books and the views they represented

This view that the New Testament contains books written under false names is taught at virtually all the major institutions of higher learning except strongly evangelical schools throughout the Western world. It is the view taught in all the major textbooks on the New Testament used in these institutions. It is the view taught in seminaries and divinity schools. It is what pastors learn when they are preparing for ministry.

And why isn't this more widely known? Why is it that the person in the pew—not to mention the person in the street—knows nothing about this? Your guess is as good as mine.

Liar, Lunatic, or Lord?
Finding the Historical Jesus

A couple of years ago I started receiving some very peculiar e-mail messages from Sweden. I've never been to Sweden, and these were from people I had never met elsewhere. They all wanted to know if it was true that I thought Jesus never existed. I thought this was an odd question. Several years ago I had written a book about the historical Jesus, indicating what ancient sources give us information about his life and outlining what I thought we could say about the things he said and did. Not only did I think there was a historical Jesus, I also thought we could make historically credible statements about him. Why, then, was I being asked if it was true that I thought he never existed?

These e-mails were not aggressive attempts to convince me that he had existed. Just the opposite: these people did not believe he had existed and had heard that I, as a New Testament scholar, lent my support to their view. This view may seem strange to an American audience, where the majority of people think not only that Jesus existed but that he was, and is, the Son of God. But in parts of Scandinavia the majority of people thinks that Jesus is a completely fabricated figure, that he never actually existed but was invented by a group of people intent on starting a new religion.

After puzzling for some weeks over why anyone would put me in this camp, I came to realize what the source of the confusion was: a misinterpretation of an article that had been written about me in the *Washington Post* in March 2006.

The *Post* had decided to do a profile on me, my work, and my turn to agnosticism in light of my recently published book, *Misquoting Jesus*. The newspaper had sent a sharp and clear-minded reporter, Neely Tucker, down to Chapel Hill to tail me for a few days. We hung out in my office and talked, he came to see my study at home, we had some meals together, and he came to one of my undergraduate classes. On the basis of our acquaintance he wrote and published the profile, entitling it "The Book of Bart." I read the piece when it came out, found it mildly amusing, and then more or less forgot about it.

But there was a paragraph in Neely's article that could easily be misunderstood, and that's what had led to problems in Sweden. Neely had come to hear me lecture to my large undergraduate class on the New Testament on the day that I happened to be talking about the Gospel of John. I pointed out that day in class—as I have several times in earlier chapters—that John's is the only Gospel in which Jesus is explicitly identified as divine. To be sure, he is called the Son of God in all the Gospels. But to ancient Jews, being the "son of God" did not make a person God; it made the person a human being in a close relationship with God, one through whom God does his will on earth. The Gospel of John goes beyond this. In John, Jesus is the preexistent Word of God through whom the universe was created, who has become human (1:1–14); he is equal with God (10:30); he can claim God's own name for himself (8:58); he is himself God (1:1; 20:28). John's Gospel is the only one with this exalted a view of Christ.

While I was explaining this to my class, with Neely sitting in the back row of the auditorium, something came to my mind from the days when I was an evangelical Christian. At Moody Bible Institute I had taken a course on Christian apologetics, the intellectual defense (Greek *apologia*) of the faith. In that course we had studied the famous English apologist and scholar C. S. Lewis, in particular his arguments that Jesus must have been divine. In Lewis's formulation, since Jesus had called himself God, there were only three logical possibilities: he was either a liar, a lunatic, or the Lord. Lewis's thinking was that if Jesus was wrong in his claim—if he was not God—either he knew it or he did not know it. If he knew that he was not God but claimed he was, then he was a liar. If he was not God but genuinely thought he was, then he was crazy, a lunatic. The only other choice would be that he was right in what he claimed, in which case he really was the Lord.

Lewis goes on to argue that there are all sorts of reasons for thinking that Jesus was neither a liar nor a lunatic. The inevitable conclusion was that he must have been who he claimed to be. Jesus was the Lord God.

Back at Moody I had found this line of argumentation completely convincing, and for years I had used it myself in order to convince others of Jesus' divinity. But that was many years ago, and my thinking had changed drastically. (All of this—Moody Bible Institute, Christian apologetics, C. S. Lewis, Jesus' identity, my change of thought—all of it flashed through my mind in a split second while I was giving my lecture on John at Chapel Hill.) I had come to see that the very premise of Lewis's argument was flawed. The argument based on Jesus as liar, lunatic, or Lord was predicated on the assumption that Jesus had called himself God. I had long ago come to believe that he had not. Only in the latest of our Gospels, John, a Gospel that shows considerably more theological sophistication than the others, does Jesus indicate that he is divine. I had come to realize that none of our earliest traditions indicates that Jesus said any such thing about himself. And surely if Jesus had really spent his days in Galilee and then Jerusalem calling himself God, *all* of our sources would be eager to report it. To put it differently, if Jesus claimed he was divine, it seemed very strange indeed that Matthew, Mark, and Luke all failed to say anything about it. Did they just forget to mention that part?

I had come to realize that Jesus' divinity was part of John's theology, not a part of Jesus' own teaching.

As this flashed through my head in my lecture, I decided on the spot to lay it all out for my students (it's not part of my normal lecture on John), especially since I knew that a large number of people in the class were involved with Christian groups on campus and had heard this argument about Jesus necessarily being either a liar, a lunatic, or the Lord. I thought it might be useful for them to hear what historical scholars, as opposed to Christian apologists, might say about the matter. And so I explained, with Neely listening, the standard apologetic line from C. S. Lewis and then pointed out the historical problem: Jesus probably never called himself God. And to make my point, I suggested that in fact there were not three options but four: liar, lunatic, Lord, or legend. Of course I chose the fourth word to maintain the alliteration. What I meant was not that Jesus himself was a legend. Of course not! I certainly believe that he existed and that we can say some things about him. What I meant was that the idea that he called himself God was a legend, which I believe it is. This means that he doesn't have to be either a liar, a lunatic, or the Lord. He could be a first-century Palestinian Jew who had a message to proclaim other than his own divinity.

Neely reported this part of my lecture on the very first page of his article in the *Washington Post,* and the report can easily be misinterpreted; one *could* read it as saying that I think Jesus himself was a legend. Nothing could be further from the truth.

But how can I or any other New Testament scholar or historian know what Jesus actually said about himself or about anything else? This is obviously part of a much bigger question of who Jesus really was, what he really taught, what he really did, and what he really experienced. This is the subject of many, many books, some of them extremely erudite—and very long. I cannot cover the entire waterfront in this chapter, but I can deal with the most important issues as they are discussed by historians of early Christianity, and I can give you a taste of what I think we can know about the man Jesus, not just how he is portrayed in this Gospel or that, but what he himself actually was, in history—the historical Jesus.

OUR EARLY SOURCES OF INFORMATION ABOUT JESUS

Most people who are not conversant with biblical scholarship probably think that knowing about the historical Jesus is a relatively simple matter. We have four Gospels in the New Testament. To know what Jesus said and did, we should read the Gospels. They tell us what he said and did. So what's the problem?

The problem is in part that the Gospels are full of discrepancies and were written decades after Jesus' ministry and death by authors who had not themselves witnessed any of the events of Jesus' life.

To put the problem in perspective, it might be useful to think about the kinds of sources scholars love to have at their disposal if they are writing a historical account of a figure from the past, such as Julius Caesar, William the Conqueror, or Shakespeare. The only way to know about any of these figures is if we have some sources of information. We can't simply intuit what Julius Caesar or Jesus was like. So what kind of sources do scholars need in order to reconstruct the life of an important historical figure?

If scholars had their wish, they would have lots of sources; the more the better, since some or all of them might give skewed accounts. These sources should be contemporary with the events they describe, not based on later hearsay. They should include reports by disinterested people, not simply biased accounts. The sources are best if they are independent from one another, so that you know their authors haven't collaborated in coming up with a story. And yet they should be consistent and confirm what the others say, providing corroboration without collaboration.

What sources do we have for Jesus? Well, we have multiple sources in the Gospels of the New Testament. That part is good. But they are not written by eyewitnesses who were contemporary with the events they narrate. They were written thirty-five to sixty-five years after Jesus' death by people who did not know him, did not see anything he did or hear anything that he taught, people who spoke a different language from his and lived in a different country from him. The accounts they produced are not disinterested; they are narratives produced by Christians who actually believed in Jesus, and therefore were not immune from slanting the stories in light of their biases. They are not completely free of collaboration, since Mark was used as a source for Matthew and Luke. And rather than being fully consistent with one another, they are widely inconsistent, with discrepancies filling their pages, both contradictions in details and divergent large-scale understandings of who Jesus was.

How can sources like this be used to reconstruct the life of the historical Jesus? It's not easy, but there are ways.

The first step is to get a better handle on how the Gospel writers got their stories. If they were living three to six decades after the events they narrate, what were their sources of information? The short answer is that the Gospel writers received most of their information from the oral tradition, stories that had been in circulation about Jesus by word of mouth from the time he died until the time the Gospel writers wrote them down. To figure out how sources of this kind—contradictory accounts written decades later based on oral testimony—can be used by historians to establish what really happened with some degree of probability, we have to learn more about the oral traditions about Jesus.

The Oral Traditions

Even though it is very hard to date the Gospels with precision, most scholars agree on the basic range of dates, for a variety of reasons. Without going into all the details, I can say that we know with relative certainty—from his own letters and from Acts—that Paul was writing during the fifties of the common era. He was well-traveled in Christian circles, and he gives in his own writings absolutely no evidence of knowing about or ever having heard of the existence of any Gospels. From this it can be inferred that the Gospels probably were written after Paul's day. It also appears that the Gospel writers know about certain later historical events, such as the destruction of Jerusalem in the year 70 CE (possibly Mark, in 13:1; almost certainly Luke, in 21:20–22). That implies that these Gospels were probably written after the year 70.

There are reasons for thinking Mark was written first, so maybe he wrote around the time of the war with Rome, 70 CE. If Matthew and Luke both used Mark as a source, they must have been composed after Mark's Gospel circulated for a time outside its own originating community—say, ten or fifteen years later, in 80 to 85 CE. John seems to be the most theologically developed Gospel, and so it was probably written later still, nearer the end of the first century, around 90 to 95 CE. These are rough guesses, but most scholars agree on them.

This means that our earliest surviving written accounts of Jesus' life come from thirty-five to sixty-five years after his death.

What was happening during all the intervening years? It is quite clear what was happening to Christianity: it was spreading throughout major urban areas of the Mediterranean region. If the Gospels and Acts are right, immediately after the resurrection of Jesus his followers included maybe fifteen or twenty men and women who had been with him previously, in Galilee, and who came to believe that he had been raised from the dead. By the end of the first century—thanks to the missionary efforts of the apostles and of converts like Paul—the religion could be found in the villages, towns, and cities of Judea, Samaria, Galilee, and Syria; it had moved north and west into Cilicia and throughout Asia Minor (modern Turkey) and Macedonia and Achaia (modern Greece); it had made its way as far as Rome, the capital of the empire, and possibly as far west as Spain. It had also traveled south, possibly to North Africa and probably to parts of Egypt.

It is not that thousands and thousands of people were converting overnight. But over the years, dozens and dozens of people—probably hundreds—were converting in major urban areas. How did Christians convert people away from their (mainly) pagan religions to believe in only one God, the God of the Jews, and in Jesus, his son, who died to take away the sins of the world? The only way to convert people was to tell them stories about Jesus: what he said and did, and how he died and was raised from the dead.

Once someone converted to the religion and became a member of a Christian church, they, too, would tell the stories. And the people they converted would then tell the stories, as would those whom those people converted. And so it went, a religion spread entirely by word of mouth, in a world of no mass media.

But who was telling the stories about Jesus? In almost every instance, it was someone who had not known Jesus or known anyone else who had known Jesus. Let me illustrate with a hypothetical example. I'm a coppersmith who lives in Ephesus, in Asia Minor. A stranger comes to town and begins to preach about the miraculous life and death of Jesus. I hear all the stories he has to tell, and decide to give up my devotion to the local pagan divinity, Athena, and become a follower of the Jewish God and Jesus his son. I then convert my wife, based on the stories that I repeat. She tells the next-door neighbor, and she converts. This neighbor tells the stories to her husband, a merchant, and he converts. He goes on a business trip to the city of Smyrna and tells his business associate the stories. He converts, and then tells his wife, who also converts.

This woman who has now converted has heard all sorts of stories about Jesus. And from whom? One of the apostles? No, from her husband. Well, whom did he hear them from? His next-door neighbor, the merchant of Ephesus. Where did he hear them? His wife. And she? My wife. And she? From me. And where did I hear them from? An eyewitness? No, I heard them from the stranger who came to town.

This is how Christianity spread, year after year, decade after decade, until eventually someone wrote down the stories. What do you suppose happened to the stories over the years, as they were told and retold, not as disinterested news stories reported by eyewitnesses but as propaganda meant to convert people to faith, told by people who had themselves heard them fifth- or sixth- or nineteenth-hand? Did you or your kids ever play the telephone game at a birthday party? The kids sit in a circle, and one child tells a story to the girl sitting next to her, who tells it to the next girl, who tells it to the next, and so on, until it comes back to the one who first told the story. And it's now a different story. (If it weren't a different story the game would be a bit pointless.) Imagine playing telephone not among a group of kids of the same socioeconomic class from the same neighborhood and same school and of the same age speaking the same language, but imagine playing it for forty or more years, in different countries, in different contexts, in different languages. What happens to the stories? They change.

Is it any wonder that the Gospels are so full of discrepancies? John heard different stories than did Mark, and when he heard the same stories he heard them differently. The Gospel writers themselves evidently changed the stories of their sources (remember how Luke changed Mark's account of Jesus going to his death). If things could change that much just from one writer to the next, imagine how much they could change in the oral tradition.

One might be tempted to despair at establishing anything historical about Jesus, given the chaotic state of affairs. With sources like these, how can we know anything at all about the historical Jesus?

Despair may be a bit premature at this stage. There may be ways to apply rigorous methods of analysis to the sources to get around all the problems they present. One approach is to see whether there are any other sources of information about Jesus outside the Gospels that can be thrown into the mix. As it turns out, there are some sources—but they are not of much use.

Other Sources for Reconstructing the Life of Jesus

If you've watched enough Hollywood movies about Jesus, you may think that Jesus was one of the most talked about figures in the Roman Empire. After all, the Son of God who heals the sick, casts out demons, and raises the dead does not come along every day. And evidently the Roman authorities were fearful enough of his power to want to do away with him, fearful of this God-man in their midst. Possibly the orders actually came down from on high, from Rome itself.

Unfortunately, all that is pure fantasy. What I am about to say seems quite odd to most of us, since, after all, Jesus is by all accounts the most significant person in the history of Western Civilization. But he was not the most significant person in his own day. Quite the contrary, he appears to have been almost a complete unknown.

What do Greek and Roman sources have to say about Jesus? Or to make the question more pointed: if Jesus lived and died in the first century (death around 30 CE), what do the Greek and Roman sources from his own day through the end of the century (say, the year 100) have to say about him? The answer is breathtaking. They have absolutely nothing to say about him. He is never discussed, challenged, attacked, maligned, or talked about in any way in any surviving pagan source of the period. There are no birth records, accounts of his trial and death, reflections on his significance, or disputes about his teachings. In fact, his name is never mentioned once in any pagan source. And we have a lot of Greek and Roman sources from the period: religious scholars, historians, philosophers, poets, natural scientists; we have thousands of private letters; we have inscriptions placed on buildings in public places. In no first-century Greek or Roman (pagan) source is Jesus mentioned.

Scholars have never been sure what to make of that. Most simply suppose that Jesus wasn't all that important in his day. But whether or not that is right, the reality is that if we want to know what Jesus said and did, we cannot rely on what his enemies in the empire were saying. As far as we know, they weren't saying anything.

The first time Jesus is mentioned in a pagan source is in the year 112 CE. The author, Pliny the Younger, was a governor of a Roman province. In a letter that he wrote to his emperor, Trajan, he indicates that there was a group of people called Christians who were meeting illegally; he wants to know how to handle the situation. These people, he tells the emperor, "worship Christ as a God." That's all he says about Jesus. It's not much to go on if you want to know anything about the historical Jesus.

A bit more information is provided by a friend of Pliny's, the Roman historian Tacitus. In writing his history of Rome in the year 115, Tacitus mentions the fire, set by Nero, that took place in Rome in 64, for which the emperor blamed "the Christians." Tacitus explains that the Christians get their name from "Christus . . . who was executed at the hands of the procurator Pontius Pilate in the reign of Tiberius" (*Annals* 15.44). He goes on to say that the "superstition" of Christianity first appeared in Judea before spreading to Rome. Here at least is some confirmation of what we already knew from the Gospels of Jesus' death at the hands of Pilate. But Tacitus, like Pliny, gives us nothing to go on if we want to know what Jesus really said and did.

If we cast our net over all surviving Greek and Roman (pagan) sources for the first hundred years after Jesus' death (30–130 CE), these two brief references are all we find.[1]

In addition to pagan sources of the first century, we have non-Christian Jewish sources, though not nearly as many. But there is one, and only one, that does mention Jesus. This is the famous Jewish historian, Flavius Josephus, who around 90 CE wrote a twenty-volume history of the Jewish people from the time of Adam and Eve down to his own day. In this lengthy book he does not talk about Jesus at great length, but he does refer to him twice. In one reference he simply identifies a man named James as "the brother of Jesus, who is called the messiah" (*Antiquities of the Jews*, 20.9.1).

The other reference is more extensive, but it is also problematic. In it Josephus seems to confess that he himself is a Christian, but we know from his other works that he was not (he wrote an autobiography, among other things). Scholars have long known that Josephus's writings were not copied by Jews throughout the Middle Ages, since he was (probably rightly) considered a traitor to the Jewish cause in the disastrous war with Rome in which Jerusalem was destroyed in 70 CE. His writings were copied instead by Christians. And at the point where Josephus discusses Jesus, it appears that a Christian scribe made a few choice insertions, in order to clarify who Jesus really was. I have placed the sections possibly inserted by the scribe in brackets:

> At this time there appeared Jesus, a wise man [if indeed one should call him a man, for] he was a doer of startling deeds, a teacher of people who receive the truth with pleasure. And he gained a following both among many Jews and among many of Greek origin. [He was the Messiah.] And when Pilate, because of an accusation made by the leading men among us, condemned him to the cross, those who had loved him previously did not cease to do so. [For he appeared to them on the third day, living again, just as the divine prophets had spoken of these and countless other wondrous things about him.] And up until this very day the tribe of Christians, named after him, has not died out. (*Antiquities* 18.3.3)[2]

It is certainly worth knowing that the most prominent Jewish historian of the first century knew at least something about Jesus— specifically that he was a teacher who allegedly did wonderful deeds, had a large following, and was condemned to be crucified by Pontius Pilate. This account confirms some of the most important aspects of Jesus' life and death as recounted in the Gospels. But it doesn't indicate exactly what he did or said, or what circumstances led to his accusation and death, even if you include the bracketed comments.

There are no other non-Christian sources—Jewish or pagan—from the first hundred years after his death that mention Jesus.

There are, of course, later Christian sources—lots of other Gospels, for example—from the second and third centuries and later. We will be looking at these sources in the next chapter. There we will see that these other accounts are interesting in the extreme and well worth reading. But they do not, as a rule, provide us with reliable historical information. They are all later than the Gospels of the New Testament and are filled with legendary, though intriguing, stories of the Son of God.

One might think that the other books of the New Testament could provide us with additional information about Jesus, but here again there simply is not much to go on. The apostle Paul, for example, talks a lot about Jesus' death and resurrection, but says very little about Jesus' life—what he said and did before he died. In a few places he provides confirmation of what the Gospels report: that Jesus was a Jew who ministered to Jews; that he had brothers, one of whom was named James, and twelve disciples. He mentions Jesus' words at the Last Supper and two other sayings of Jesus: that his followers should not get divorced and that they should pay their preachers.[3] Apart from this Paul doesn't tell us much. The other writers of the New Testament tell us even less.

The results of this quick survey should be clear: if we want to know about the life of the historical Jesus, we are more or less restricted to using the four Gospels of Matthew, Mark, Luke, and John. These are not disinterested accounts by eyewitnesses, however. They are books written decades after the fact by authors who had heard stories about Jesus from the oral tradition, stories that had been altered and even made up over time. There were lots of discrepancies in these stories, and the Gospel writers themselves changed them as they saw fit. How is it possible to use such sources to find out what really happened historically? In fact, there are ways. Scholars have devised some methodological principles that, if followed closely and rigorously, can give us some indications of who Jesus really was.

Criteria for Establishing the Veracity of Historical Material

There is nothing overly complicated about these principles—they make sense, given everything that we have seen about the Gospel traditions so far. The first should seem a bit obvious:

1. *The earlier the better.* Since the traditions about Jesus changed over time as stories about him were told and retold, and as the written sources were altered, amplified, and edited, it makes sense that the earlier sources should be more trustworthy than the later ones. Gospels from the eighth century will not, as a rule, be as historically reliable as Gospels from the first century (although they may be terrifically fun to read).

John is the latest of the four New Testament Gospels and tends to be less historically reliable than the others. It presents views of Jesus that represent later developments within the tradition—for example, that he was the Passover lamb who died on the day the Passover lambs were slaughtered, or that he claimed to be equal with God. This doesn't mean that we can completely discount everything found in John; on the contrary, we need to apply the other criteria to its accounts as well. But generally speaking, earlier is better.

Our earliest surviving Gospel is Mark, and it may contain more reliable information than John. But Mark was not the only source for later Gospels. There was probably another Gospel source that may have been produced as early as Mark and that no longer survives. In an earlier chapter I pointed out that Matthew and Luke got many of their stories from Mark, which they used as a source. There are numerous other traditions about Jesus in both Matthew and Luke that cannot be found in Mark. Most, but not all, of these traditions are sayings of Jesus, for example, the Lord's prayer and the Beatitudes (found in Matthew and Luke, but not in Mark). Since the later Gospels could not have gotten these traditions from Mark, where did they get them? There are good reasons for thinking that Matthew did not get them from Luke, nor Luke from Matthew. And so, since the nineteenth century, scholars have maintained that they both got them from some other source. The German scholars who came up with this view called this other source *Quelle*, the German word for "source." This unknown additional "source" is called simply Q.[4]

Q then is the source of material found in Matthew and Luke but not found in Mark. This material appears to have come from a lost Gospel accessible to the two later Gospel writers. We do not know everything that was in Q (or that was *not* in Q), but whenever Matthew and Luke agree word for word on a story not found in Mark, it is thought to came from Q. So Mark and Q are our two earliest sources. Matthew used one or more other written or oral sources for his Gospel, and these we call Matthean sources, or M. The sources for material special to Luke we call L. So prior to the Gospels of Matthew and Luke there were four available sources: Mark, Q, M, and L (both M and L are possibly multiple sources). These are our earliest materials for reconstructing the life of Jesus.[5]

2. *The more the better.* Suppose there is a story of Jesus found in only one source; it is possible that the author of that source invented the tradition himself. But what if a story is found independently in more than one source? That story cannot have been made up by either source, since they are independent; it must predate them both. Stories found in multiple, independent sources therefore have a better likelihood of being older, and possibly authentic. (Note: if the same story is found in Matthew, Mark, and Luke, that is not *three* sources for the story, but one source: Matthew and Luke both got it from Mark.)

For example, both Matthew and Luke independently indicate that Jesus was raised in Nazareth, but their stories about how he got there differ, so one came from M and the other from L. Mark indicates the same thing. So does John, which did not use any of the Synoptics or their sources. Conclusion? It is independently attested: Jesus probably came from Nazareth. Another example: Jesus is associated with John the Baptist at the beginning of Mark, at the beginning of Q (Matthew and Luke both preserve portions of John's proclamation that don't appear in Mark), and at the beginning of John. Conclusion? Jesus probably associated with John the Baptist at the beginning of his ministry.

3. *It is better to cut against the grain.* One thing we have repeatedly seen is that discrepancies have been created in our stories about Jesus because different storytellers and authors changed the traditions in order to make them conform more closely with their own views. How might we account for traditions of Jesus that clearly do *not* fit with a "Christian" agenda, that is, that do not promote the views and perspectives of the people telling the stories? Traditions like that would not have been made up by the Christian storytellers, and so they are quite likely to be historically accurate. This is sometimes, confusingly, called the "criterion of dissimilarity." Any tradition of Jesus that is dissimilar to what the early Christians would have likely wanted to say about him is more likely authentic. Take the two previous examples. You can see why Christians might want to say that Jesus came from Bethlehem: that was where the son of David was to come from (Micah 5:2). But who would make up a story that the Savior came from Nazareth, a little one-horse town that no one had ever heard of? This tradition does not advance any Christian agenda. Somewhat ironically, then, it is probably historically accurate. Or take John the Baptist. In Mark, our earliest account, John baptizes Jesus. Would Christians have made this up? Remember, in the early Christian tradition it was believed that the person who was spiritually superior baptized the one who was spiritually inferior. Would a Christian make up the idea that Jesus was baptized by, and therefore inferior to, someone else? Moreover, John was baptizing "for the forgiveness of sins" (Mark 1:4). Would someone want to claim that Jesus needed to be forgiven for his sins? It seems highly unlikely. Conclusion? Jesus probably really did associate with John the Baptist at the beginning of his ministry, and probably was baptized by him.

4. *It has to fit the context.* Since Jesus was a Jew who lived in first-century Palestine, any tradition about him has to fit in his own his-

torical context to be plausible. Lots of our later Gospels—written in the third or fourth century, in other parts of the world—say things about Jesus that do not make sense in his own context. These things can be eliminated as historically implausible. But there are implausibilities even in our four canonical Gospels. In the Gospel of John, chapter 3, Jesus has a famous conversation with Nicodemus in which he says, "You must be born again." The Greek word translated "again" actually has two meanings: it can mean not only "a second time" but also "from above." Whenever it is used elsewhere in John, it means "from above" (John 19:11, 23). That is what Jesus appears to mean in John 3 when he speaks with Nicodemus: a person must be born from above in order to have eternal life in heaven above. Nicodemus misunderstands, though, and thinks Jesus intends the other meaning of the word, that he has to be born a second time. "How can I crawl back into my mother's womb?" he asks, out of some frustration. Jesus corrects him: he is not talking about a second physical birth, but a heavenly birth, from above.

This conversation with Nicodemus is predicated on the circumstance that a certain Greek word has two meanings (a double entendre). Absent the double entendre, the conversation makes little sense. The problem is this: Jesus and this Jewish leader in Jerusalem would not have been speaking Greek, but Aramaic. But the Aramaic word for "from above" does not also mean "second time." This is a double entendre that works only in Greek. So it looks as though this conversation could not have happened—at least not as it is described in the Gospel of John.

These then are some of the criteria that scholars use to examine the various traditions of Jesus, especially as they are found in the New Testament Gospels. The careful and rigorous application of these criteria can lead to some positive results. We probably *can* know some things about the historical Jesus. What, then, can we know?

JESUS THE APOCALYPTIC PROPHET

For over a century now, since the landmark publication of Albert Schweitzer's masterpiece, *The Quest of the Historical Jesus,*[6] the majority of scholars in Europe and North America have understood Jesus as a Jewish apocalyptic prophet.[7] A good deal of work on the subject has been done since Schweitzer, of course, who did not rigorously apply the various criteria that I have laid out (they were developed after his day). But his instincts appear to have been right.

The Teachings of Jesus

Like other apocalypticists of his day, Jesus saw the world in dualistic terms, filled with the forces of good and evil. The current age was controlled by the forces of evil—the Devil, demons, disease, disasters, and death; but God was soon to intervene in this wicked age to overthrow the forces of evil and bring in his good kingdom, the Kingdom of God, in which there would be no more pain, misery, or suffering. Jesus' followers could expect this kingdom to arrive soon—in fact, in their lifetimes. It would be brought by a cosmic judge of the earth, whom Jesus called the Son of Man (alluding to a passage in the Jewish Scriptures, Daniel 7:13–14). When the Son of Man arrived there would be a judgment of the earth, in which the wicked would be destroyed but the righteous rewarded. Those who were suffering pain and oppression now would be exalted then; those who had sided with evil and as a result were prospering now would be abased then. People needed to repent of their evil ways and prepare for the coming of the Son of Man and the Kingdom of God that would appear in his wake, for it was to happen very soon.

You don't hear this view of Jesus very often in Sunday School or from the pulpit. But it is the view that has been taught for many years in leading seminaries and divinity schools throughout the country. There are strong and compelling arguments for thinking of Jesus in these apocalyptic terms. Most important, the traditions that present Jesus this way, all of them from the New Testament Gospels, are the ones that pass our various criteria of authenticity.

We have already seen some of the evidence that this is the earliest view found in the Gospels. As I pointed out in a previous chapter, it is in the Synoptic Gospels that Jesus preaches the coming Kingdom of God. This Kingdom of God is not "heaven"—the place you go to when you die (as in later Christian tradition; I'll discuss this further in chapter 7). It is a real kingdom, here on earth, which will be ruled by God through his Messiah, a utopian kingdom where the first will be last and the last first. Only in the last Gospel, John, does Jesus no longer preach that this kingdom is arriving soon. And why is this teaching not in the last of our Gospels? No doubt because the kingdom never did arrive, and the later Gospel writer was forced to reinterpret Jesus' message for his own day. The earliest Gospel traditions, though, portray Jesus' message as about the coming kingdom.

In fact, not only is this message generally found in our earlier sources, it is a leading message of our very earliest sources, Mark and Q. In Mark, Jesus says:

> Whoever is ashamed of me and of my words in this adulterous and sinful generation, of that one will the Son of Man be ashamed when he comes in the glory of his Father with the holy angels. . . . Truly I tell you, there are some standing here who will not taste death until they see that the Kingdom of God has come in power. (Mark 8:38–9:1)

> And in those days, after that affliction, the sun will grow dark and the moon will not give its light, and the stars will be falling from heaven, and the powers in the sky will be shaken; and then they will see the Son of Man coming on the clouds with great power and glory. And then he will send forth his angels and he will gather his elect from the four winds, from the end of earth to the end of heaven. . . . Truly I tell you, this generation will not pass away before all these things take place. (Mark 13:24–27, 30)

The Son of Man is coming, he will judge the world, those who side with Jesus will be rewarded, others will be punished, and it will happen within Jesus' own generation. This apocalyptic message is found throughout our earliest accounts of Jesus' proclamation.

Consider what he says in Luke and Matthew—not in Mark, thus from Q:

> For just as the flashing lightning lights up the earth from one part of the sky to the other, so will the Son of Man be in his day. . . . And just as it was in the days of Noah, so will it be in the days of the Son of Man. They were eating, drinking, marrying, and giving away in marriage, until the day that Noah went into the ark and the flood came and destroyed them all. So too will it be on the day when the Son of Man is revealed. (Luke 17:24; 26–27, 30; cf. Matthew 24:27, 37–39)

> And you, be prepared, because you do not know the hour when the Son of Man is coming. (Luke 12:39; Matthew 24:44)

Jesus preaches a similar message in the material that Matthew drew from his M source(s):

> Just as the weeds are gathered and burned with fire, so will it be at the culmination of the age. The Son of Man will send forth his angels, and they will gather from his kingdom every cause of sin and all who do evil, and they will cast them into the furnace of fire. In that place there will be weeping and gnashing of teeth. Then the righteous will shine forth as the sun, in the kingdom of their father. (Matthew 13:40–43)

If one of our criteria is that we look for independent attestation of traditions of Jesus from multiple sources, the idea that Jesus preached the imminent arrival of the Son of Man in judgment on the earth passes with flying colors.

Just as important, some of these independently attested sayings appear to pass the criterion of dissimilarity. Consider, for example, the saying quoted in Mark 8:38: "Whoever is ashamed of me and of my words in this adulterous and sinful generation, of that one will the Son of Man be ashamed when he comes in the glory of his Father with the holy angels." It is no secret that the earliest Christians thought that Jesus himself was the future cosmic judge of the earth, as we saw in Paul. And so naturally when Christians read this verse from Mark, they think Jesus is talking about himself. But look at it closely. Jesus doesn't identify himself as the Son of Man. If you didn't know any better (and for this kind of argument, you have to bracket your preconceptions), you would think that he was actually differentiating between himself and the Son of Man. Whoever doesn't listen to Jesus will be judged when the Son of Man comes from heaven.

Would later Christians who were inventing sayings of Jesus make up one in which Jesus seemed to differentiate himself from the Son of Man? It seems unlikely. If Christians had made up this saying, they would not have phrased it this way; instead, they would have said something like, "Whoever is ashamed of me, the Son of Man, of that one will I, the Son of Man . . ." This means that the saying probably does actually go back to Jesus.

Or take another instance. In a saying drawn from Q, Jesus tells his disciples: "Truly I tell you, at the renewal of all things, when the Son of Man is seated on the throne of his glory, you who have followed me will also sit on twelve thrones, judging the twelve tribes of Israel" (Matthew 19:28; see also Luke 22:28–30). This saying about future judgment, and the future rulership of the Kingdom of God, is almost certainly authentic, something Jesus actually said. Why? Note whom he is addressing. The twelve disciples. That includes Judas Iscariot. Soon after the events of Jesus' death, there were *no* Christians who would be willing to say that Judas Iscariot would be one of the twelve rulers in the Kingdom of God. In other words, no Christian would have made up this saying later. That means it must go back to Jesus. Jesus believed his own disciples would be the rulers of the future, earthly, Kingdom of God.

A final instance of dissimilarity concerns the final judgment, when the Son of Man is sitting on his great throne and separates the sheep from the goats (this is M material, from Matthew 25). The "sheep" are allowed to enter their heavenly and eternal reward because of all the good deeds they did: feeding the hungry, clothing the naked, tending the sick; the "goats" are sent to eternal punishment because they failed to do good deeds. Would a later Christian make up this particular tradition? After Jesus died, his followers claimed that a person was made right with God and would receive an eternal reward by believing in Jesus' death and resurrection, not by doing good deeds. Thus, this story cuts against the grain of that teaching by indicating that one will be rewarded by doing good things. Ergo: this must go back to Jesus.

Jesus, in short, taught that the Son of Man was soon to arrive from heaven in judgment, and people needed to be ready for it by mending their ways and living as God wanted them to. This involved self-giving love for the sake of others. Thus Jesus is said to have quoted from the Scriptures: "Love your neighbor as yourself" (Matthew 22:39; quoting Leviticus 19:18). His formulation of this view is the Golden Rule, "Do to others as you would have them do to you" (Matthew 7:12). It is hard to state more concisely the ethical requirements of the law of God. Those who followed the dictates of Scripture would be rewarded in the coming judgment; those who did not would be punished. And when would this judgment come? In the disciples' own lifetime: "Some of you standing here will not taste death before they see that the Kingdom of God has come in power" (Mark 9:1); "this generation will not pass away before all these things take place" (Mark 13:30).

That this view fits in a first-century Palestinian context is clear to every historian of the period. Jesus was not alone in proclaiming the end of this age and the imminent appearance of the Son of Man. Other Jewish prophets had similar apocalyptic messages—even if the details varied from one prophet to another—including the Jews from roughly Jesus' day who left us the Dead Sea Scrolls, which are chock full of Jewish apocalyptic thinking.

Of even greater importance is the fact that this was the message of John the Baptist, before Jesus. John is recorded as saying in Luke 3:9 (from the Q source): "Even now the axe is lying at the root of the trees; every tree therefore that does not bear good fruit is cut down and thrown into the fire." This is an apocalyptic image of judgment. Humans are likened to trees that are cut down and burned if they do not do what they were designed to do: bear good fruit. And when will this destruction begin? It is imminent: the ax is ready to begin its work; it is "lying at the root of the trees." People need to begin to "bear good fruit"—that is, do what God commands them to do—or they, too, will be destroyed.

That is why it is important to know—based on multiple attestation and dissimilarity—that Jesus began his ministry by associating with John. Jesus was an apocalypticist from the beginning of his ministry. That he remained an apocalypticist is quite clear from our sources. Our earliest traditions are filled with apocalyptic sayings and warnings. More significant still, after Jesus' death his followers remained apocalyptically oriented. That is why they thought the end was coming in their day, that Jesus himself was soon coming back from heaven to sit in judgment on the earth. This is contained in Paul's writings, the earliest Christian documents we have. The early Christians, like Jesus before them, and John the Baptist before him, were apocalyptically minded Jews, expecting the imminent end of the age.

Jesus' ethical teachings need to be placed in that apocalyptic context. Many people understand Jesus as a great moral teacher, and of course he was that. But it is important to recognize *why* he thought people should behave properly. In our day, ethicists typically argue that people should behave in ethical ways so that we can all get along for the long haul, in happy and prosperous societies. For Jesus, there wasn't going to *be* a long haul. The end was coming soon, the Son of Man was to appear from heaven, imminently, in judgment on the earth, the Kingdom of God was right around the corner. The reason to change your behavior was to gain entrance to the kingdom when it came. It was not in order to make society a happy place for the foreseeable future. The future was bleak—unless you sided with Jesus and did what he urged, in which case you could expect a reward when God intervened in history to overthrow the forces of evil and set up his good kingdom on earth, which would happen very soon.

The Deeds and Activities of Jesus

Understanding Jesus as an apocalyptic prophet who anticipated the judgment of this world and the imminent appearance of the Kingdom of God helps us make sense of the deeds and activities of Jesus that can be established as historically probable, on the basis of our various criteria.

The Baptism

It is almost certain that Jesus began his public ministry by being baptized by John the Baptist. This is attested to in multiple independent sources, both early and later, and is not the kind of tradition that a later Christian would make up. I think the significance of the baptism makes sense only within an apocalyptic context. Jesus had lots of religious options available to him, as did other Jews of his day. Some Jews joined the Pharisees, who were intent on keeping the law of God as carefully and conscientiously as possible (that was why God had given the law—so it could be kept); others joined monastic communities like those of the Essenes, who produced the Dead Sea Scrolls, and were intent on preserving their own purity apart from the corrupting influences of the world around them; others sided with the Sadducees, aristocratic power players in Palestine who controlled the Temple and its sacrificial practices and who served as the liaison with the ruling Roman authorities; others were particularly zealous for the Holy Land and urged a religious and military rebellion against Rome, in order to establish Israel as a sovereign state within the land that God had originally given them.

Jesus did not join any of these groups. Instead he sided with John the Baptist, an apocalyptic prophet who was urging people to prepare for the day of judgment, which was to appear in the very near future. Why did Jesus side with John? Because he agreed with his message, not with the messages of all the others. Like John before him and his followers afterward, Jesus was an apocalypticist.

The Twelve Disciples

There can be little doubt that Jesus chose twelve followers to be a kind of inner circle around him. The twelve are attested to in various Gospel sources as well as by Paul and Acts. In addition, one saying, about the twelve ruling the twelve tribes of Israel in the kingdom, passes the criterion of dissimilarity. But why did Jesus choose twelve disciples? Why not nine? Or fourteen?

It was not so they could have a disciple-of-the-month club. It appears to have been a symbolic gesture on Jesus' part. Originally, in the Hebrew Bible, the people of God—the people of Israel—had consisted of twelve tribes. According to Jesus, these twelve tribes would be reconstituted in the coming Kingdom of God, when the true people of God were ruled by the twelve apostles. By choosing twelve close disciples, Jesus was indicating that those who follow him and his teachings would be the ones who enter into that future Kingdom of God. Not all Jews would be allowed into that kingdom. Only those who mended their ways and adhered to Jesus' teachings would survive the coming judgment. Choosing twelve, in other words, was a kind of cryptic apocalyptic message.

Jesus as a Healer and Exorcist

Later in this chapter I will discuss the problem of whether historians can say anything definite about whether Jesus actually performed miracles. For now it is enough to point out that he was widely *be-lieved* to have done miracles—healing the sick, casting out demons, and raising the dead. Traditions of Jesus' miracles occur in multiple independent sources. These traditions cannot pass the criterion of dissimilarity of course: storytellers in the early church naturally wanted the people they were trying to convert to understand that Jesus was not a mere mortal, but was especially empowered by God in his public ministry. No doubt stories of his great miracles were made up all the time, as is evidenced in later Gospels outside the New Testament, where the miracles that both he and his followers do are even more stupendous. But even early on, the stories were widespread, and what matters for my purposes at this point is that in the earliest stages of the tradition these miracle stories were interpreted in apocalyptic terms.

In the future kingdom there will be no forces of evil. Jesus overcomes evil now. There will be no demons; Jesus casts out demons now. There will be no disease; Jesus heals the sick now. There will be no natural disasters; Jesus calms the storms now. There will be no hunger; Jesus feeds the hungry now. There will be no death; Jesus raises the dead now.

When John the Baptist sent messengers from the prison where he was being held to ask Jesus if he is the prophet to come at the end of the age, or if another is to be expected, Jesus (according to Q) gives the response: "Go and tell John what you have seen and heard: the blind receive their sight, the lame walk, the lepers are cleansed, the deaf hear, the dead are raised, the poor have good news brought to them. And blessed is anyone who takes no offense at me" (Luke 7:22–23). The Kingdom of God is soon to appear, and is already beginning to be manifest in a small way in the deeds of Jesus. Jesus' activities are understood apocalyptically.

The Trip to Jerusalem

If a Christian theologian were asked why Jesus traveled to Jerusalem the last week of his life, she might say that it was so he could be crucified for the sins of the world. But, from a historical perspective, what was his motivation for going? If one understands Jesus as an apocalypticist, it makes perfect sense. According to our earliest sources, the Synoptic Gospels, Jesus had spent the bulk of his ministry preaching to Jews in the rural hinterlands of Galilee. He evidently did not spend much time, if any at all, in large cities, but went to small towns, villages, and hamlets throughout the north.

But he had an urgent message: the kingdom was soon to arrive with the coming of the Son of Man, and people needed to prepare.

Why, then, did he go to Jerusalem? Evidently in order to take his message to the heart of Judaism, the capital city, the home of the Temple, and to all the important social and political figures there, as well as to the masses. And why did he go during Passover? Because that is when the largest crowds would be there. As we saw in an earlier chapter, Passover in Jerusalem was a big event. It was the largest pilgrim festival in the Jewish year, when the number of people would swell the city beyond its normal capacity.

It was also the time when Jews would reflect back on the great events of the Exodus under Moses, recalling how God had intervened on their behalf. No doubt many Jews did this in anticipation that God would intervene yet again, and overthrow the overlords of the present (the Romans) much as he had overthrown the overlords in the past (the Egyptians). Some Jews thought this would happen through a political and military uprising. Others thought it would be a supernatural cosmic event, when God himself would destroy those opposed to him. Jesus was of the latter train of thought. He came to Jerusalem in order to proclaim this message. The Kingdom of God was almost here: people needed to repent and believe the good news.

It is no surprise that in our earliest sources—Matthew, Mark, and Luke—Jesus spends his last week in Jerusalem preaching a heavily apocalyptic message (see, for example, Mark 13 and Matthew 24–25). This is historically accurate. It is how Jesus spent his last week. But before doing so, he did something significant upon arriving in town, a symbolic act that conveyed his apocalyptic message.

The Cleansing of the Temple

Independently of one another, Mark and John tell the story of Jesus entering into the Temple and causing a ruckus. Mark's account is earlier, of course, and in Mark this event is more plausibly situated toward the end of Jesus' life rather than at the beginning. For Mark, in fact, the Temple event is what eventually led to Jesus' crucifixion.

The Temple was the focal point of all Jewish worship, as established in the Jewish Scripture. In Jesus' day, Jews from around the world would come to Jerusalem to perform the animal sacrifices prescribed by the law, which had to be done in the Temple, nowhere else. Of course, people coming from long distances would not be able to bring sacrificial animals with them; these had to be purchased on site. But they could not be purchased with normal Roman currency: Roman coins were stamped with an image of the emperor, who in parts of the empire was thought to be a divine being. For Jews there was only one God, and so they were not inclined to bring the image of Caesar into the holy Temple. In addition, the law proscribed the use of any "graven images," another reason that Roman coins could not be used. Some other kind of money had to be made available, and so there had to be a kind of currency exchange, where Roman coinage could be traded for Temple currency, which did not bear the image of Caesar. The Temple currency could then be used to purchase the necessary animals.

There were money changers who made these currency exchanges. When Jesus arrived in Jerusalem he saw all the exchange of money and the selling of animals, and evidently he found it scandalous: he overturned some money changers' tables and drove the animal sellers out of the Temple. It is hard to know just how thorough he was in this "cleansing of the Temple." It is difficult to believe that Jesus shut down the entire operation: the Temple precincts were approximately the size of twenty-five football fields, not a small contained space, and the Gospels do not portray this act as a miracle. Moreover, if he had created such an enormous scene, it is almost impossible to explain why he wasn't arrested on the spot, but only a week later. It looks as if our early sources have exaggerated some of the details.

It is also hard to know what, exactly, Jesus was objecting to. God's law required sacrifice; Jews had to have sacrificial animals; and they certainly couldn't use Roman currency for the exchange. Was Jesus simply put off by the idea that some people were profiting from the worship of God? It is at least possible, and that's how the Gospel writers themselves interpret the event.

But modern interpreters have suggested that something else was going on as well. One of the best attested sayings of Jesus found in a number of our independent sources is a prediction that at the coming onslaught, at the end of the age, the Temple itself would be destroyed (Mark 13:2; 14:58; 15:29). The Temple? The center of the worship of the God of Israel? Isn't that a blasphemous thought?

Some Jews evidently thought so. This is what ended up getting Jesus into trouble. But Jesus himself appealed to a prophet of the Hebrew Scriptures, Jeremiah, who also thought the Temple and the activities within it had grown corrupt. Like Jesus, Jeremiah inveighed against the Temple. Like him, he also paid a heavy price (see Jeremiah 7:1–15; 20:1–6).

Jesus thought that at the judgment that was soon to arrive, the Temple would be destroyed. Why, then, did he overturn the tables and cause a ruckus? It is now a standard opinion among critical scholars that Jesus was performing a symbolic act—a kind of enacted parable, if you will.[8] By overthrowing tables Jesus was symbolizing in a small way what was going to happen soon in a big way when the Son of Man arrived in judgment. God's enemies would be destroyed. And like many of the prophets of the Hebrew Bible, Jesus thought that among God's enemies were the Jewish leaders themselves, in charge of the

Temple, who had become corrupt and powerful. But a day of reckoning was at hand.

The Arrest of Jesus

So it comes as no surprise that these very authorities saw Jesus as a threat who needed to be gotten out of the way. Why wasn't Jesus arrested on the spot, but only a week later? My hunch is that the episode in the Temple was small and insignificant at the time, but that word eventually got around about what Jesus had done, and the leaders decided to keep an eye on him. What they saw and heard did not much improve their opinion of him. Jesus started gathering larger and larger crowds of people interested in his apocalyptic message of the coming judgment. Eventually the leaders became afraid that this could get out of hand. It was the Passover, after all, when the crowds were flocking into Jerusalem, many of them zealous for the traditions of Israel and eager for something to happen to change the dire straights they found themselves in under Roman rule. The Jewish leaders made arrangements to have Jesus arrested.

The tradition that Jesus was betrayed by one of the twelve, Judas Iscariot, is firmly rooted in our early sources and does not seem to be the sort of thing a later Christian would make up (Jesus had no more authority over those closest to him than *that*?). There has been a lot of speculation about why Judas did what he did: Was he eager for a political rebellion and disappointed that Jesus was uninterested in starting one? Did he think he could force Jesus' hand to call out to the crowds to come to his assistance and start the revolt? Did Judas need some cash on the spot? Was he simply a bad apple from the beginning?

Even more interesting, though, is the question of what it is that Judas betrayed. This gets us to the heart of the matter: is it possible that Judas did more than tell the authorities where they could find Jesus alone, apart from the crowd? Surely this is something they could discover for themselves by having him followed, without shelling out thirty pieces of silver. Did Judas reveal something more, something that the leaders could use in prosecuting Jesus and having him permanently taken out of the way? The answer to this question hinges on one of the key issues of this chapter, the one that I began it with: What did Jesus teach about himself?

What Jesus Taught About Himself

Throughout this chapter I have been insisting that Jesus did not teach that he was divine. He taught about God, not, for the most part, about himself. Specifically, he taught about the Kingdom of God that was soon to appear with the coming of the Son of Man in judgment on the earth, an event that Jesus declared would happen within his own generation. He taught the crowds that entering this coming kingdom meant accepting his teaching, which involved turning to God with all one's heart and loving one's neighbor as oneself.

But what did Jesus teach about himself? One reason this question has been so puzzling to so many scholars for so long is that when Jesus is eventually turned over to the Roman authorities and made to stand trial, the charge leveled against him is that he called himself the king of the Jews (Mark 15:2). This is odd because in our earliest sources Jesus never says any such thing about himself in any of his public proclamations. Why did the Roman authorities think this is what he was saying about himself, if in fact it was not what he was saying about himself? And why, when put on trial, didn't he simply deny the charge and get off the hook?

One can see why the authorities would take such a claim seriously: claiming to be king when only the Roman Caesar or someone the Romans appointed could be king was an act of political insurgency. This is why Jesus was killed, for fomenting a rebellion against Rome. But it appears from our early sources that he had nothing to do with a political rebellion. So how does one explain these data?

The answer lies in Jesus' apocalyptic teaching. He told his disciples that they, the twelve (including Judas), would be the rulers over the "twelve tribes of Israel" in this kingdom that was soon to appear. But who would be ruling over *them*? Every kingdom has a king. Who would be the king of the coming kingdom, once the Son of Man destroyed the forces aligned against God and established his reign on earth? Of course God would in some sense be the ultimate king, but through whom would he rule? Now it was Jesus who called the disciples and was their master. Would he be their master then?

I do not think that Jesus publicly declared himself a king during his ministry. Doing so would be an extremely dangerous and criminal act. And he did not think of himself as a king in the present age. But it is well attested that he taught the twelve disciples at greater length in private. And one of the things he taught them was that they would be rulers in the future kingdom.

All the pieces fall into place if Jesus taught his disciples in private that he would be their master not only now but in the age to come. When the kingdom arrived, he would be the king. In ancient Israel one of the designations of the future king was the term "Messiah," meaning anointed one of God. Jesus did not call himself the Messiah in public, although others may have thought of him in this way. But when Jesus spoke of himself as the Messiah in private with his disciples, he did not mean that he would drive out the Romans and set up Israel as a sovereign state in the land. He meant that God was going to overthrow the forces of evil and appoint him king.

That is why after his death his disciples continued to call him the Messiah. Jews at the time did not believe that the Messiah was supposed to die and then be raised from the dead. So even if Jesus' followers came to believe in the resurrection, this would not be a reason for them to call Jesus the Messiah. They therefore must have thought of him as the Messiah before he died. Why? Because that's what he had taught them.

Why did the Romans execute Jesus for calling himself king of the Jews if he never called himself that in public? Because they learned that he actually did think of himself this way. He meant it in a futuristic, apocalyptic sense, but they interpreted it in a present, political sense, and so ordered his execution. And how could they have learned this about Jesus, if it wasn't public knowledge? Someone must have told them, someone who was privy to his private instructions. It was one of the twelve.

Judas did not simply tell the authorities where to find Jesus. He told them that Jesus had been calling himself the (future) king of the Jews.

That is all the authorities needed to hear. From there on it was a done deal. The Jewish leaders, whom Jesus had aggravated by his apocalyptic preaching against them and their authority, questioned Jesus and turned him over to Pilate for trial. He asked Jesus if he was the king of the Jews, and Jesus could not very well deny it. Pilate ordered him crucified, and the sentence was carried out immediately.

EXCURSUS: THE RESURRECTION AND OTHER MIRACLES IN THE LIFE OF JESUS

I have said nothing particularly new or unusual in this chapter, except my claims about what Judas actually betrayed to the authorities, which is a more unusual interpretation. Otherwise, the views I've laid out are fairly standard fare. Different scholars will disagree on this point or that, of course. That's why there is always more and more scholarship. But my views of Jesus as an apocalyptic prophet are the ones I learned in seminary. They are the views of the majority of scholars in North America and Europe and have been for something like a century.[9] They are the views taught in leading institutions of higher learning in the country, including seminaries and divinity schools. They are the views that most mainline Christian pastors are taught, even if they tend not to be the views these pastors teach their own parishioners.

I want to close this chapter on a final issue of real importance to both the casual Bible reader and the scholar of early Christianity.

According to the Gospels, Jesus' story does not end with the crucifixion but with the accounts of his resurrection from the dead.

There was nothing miraculous about the crucifixion per se. Lots of people were being crucified, probably every day, throughout the Roman Empire. The only miraculous aspect of Jesus' death involves its theological interpretation, that Jesus died "for the sins of the world." A historian qua historian cannot pass judgment on this interpretation. We have no historical record that can prove why, from God's point of view, Jesus died. Historians have no access to God, only to what goes on here on earth, for which we have historical records. And there is nothing historically problematic about Jesus getting crucified.

There is something historically problematic with his being raised from the dead, however. This is a miracle, and by the very nature of their craft, historians are unable to discuss miracles. That is my thesis in this final section. This thesis seems counterintuitive to some people: if something actually happened, even a miracle, isn't it subject to historical investigation? Isn't the refusal to consider the possibility of a miracle an antisupernatural bias? Do you think atheists are the only ones who can do history?

The answer to all these questions is no. What I want to show is that because of the very nature of the historical disciplines, historians cannot show whether or not miracles ever happened. Anyone who disagrees with me—who thinks historians can demonstrate that miracles happen—needs to be even-handed about it, across the board. In Jesus' day there were lots of people who allegedly performed miracles. There were Jewish holy men such as Hanina ben Dosa and Honi the circle drawer. There were pagan holy men such as Apollonius of Tyana, a philosopher who could allegedly heal the sick, cast out demons, and raise the dead. He was allegedly supernaturally born and at the end of his life he allegedly ascended to heaven. Sound familiar? There were pagan demigods, such as Hercules, who could also bring back the dead. Anyone who is willing to believe in the miracles of Jesus needs to concede the possibility of other people performing miracles, in Jesus' day and in all eras down to the present day and in other religions such as Islam and indigenous religions of Africa and Asia.

But for now I want to focus on the miracles of Jesus. His resurrection wasn't the only miracle. According to the Gospels, Jesus' entire life was filled with miracles. He was born of a woman who had never had sex. As an adult he performed one miracle after the other—healing the blind, the lame, the deaf, the paralyzed; casting out demons; restoring to life those who had previously died. And at the end of his life came the biggest miracle of all: he was raised from the dead, never to die again.

Despite the prominence of miracles in the Gospel traditions, I don't think historians can show that any of them, including the resurrection, ever happened. This is not because of an antisupernatural bias. I'm not saying that miracles by definition cannot happen. That is what a lot of people do say, but it is not what I'm saying here. For the purpose of the argument, I'm willing to concede that maybe what we think of as miracles do happen.

And I am not saying that we cannot demonstrate that miracles happened merely because our sources of information are not completely trustworthy. To be sure, that, too, is true. Our first records of any of Jesus' public miracles were written thirty-five to sixty-five years after the fact, by people who had not seen any of these things happen, who were basing their stories on oral traditions that had been passed down for decades among people trying to convince others to believe in Jesus. And these records are absolutely filled with discrepancies, especially the resurrection narratives themselves. None of the accounts of Jesus' miracles can pass the criterion of dissimilarity.

But that is not why historians cannot show that miracles, including the resurrection, happened. The reason instead has to do with the limits of historical knowledge. There cannot be historical evidence for a miracle.

To understand why, we need to consider how historians engage in their craft. Historians work differently from the way natural scientists work. Scientists do repeated experimentation to demonstrate how things happen, changing one variable at a time. If the same experiment produces the same result time after time, you can establish a level of predictive probability: the same result will occur the next time you do the experiment. If I want to prove scientifically that bars of Ivory soap float in lukewarm water and that bars of iron sink, I simply need a hundred tubs of lukewarm water and a hundred bars of both soap and iron. When I toss the bars in, the soap will always float; the iron will always sink. That gives us a good sense of probability that I will get the same result when I do it the 101st time.

Historians have to work differently. Historians are not trying to show what does or will happen, but what *has* happened. And with history, the experiment can never be repeated. Once something happens it is over and done with.

Historians work with all kinds of evidence in order to show what probably happened in the past. You can never know for sure, although in some instances the evidence is so powerful that there is no doubt. There is no doubt in my mind that my basketball team, the Carolina Tar Heels, lost in the Final Four to the Kansas Jayhawks last month. I hate to admit it and I wish I were wrong, but the evidence (videotapes, newspaper reporting, eyewitness testimony) is simply too strong. Some people in Kansas might think that the results were miraculous, and some in Carolina might think that they were the result of evil cosmic powers, but the results themselves seem clear.

What about a game played a century ago? Well, there may be good evidence, but it won't be as good as the evidence regarding the outcome for the Tar Heels. What about a game played in the Roman Empire two thousand years ago? The outcome of that game would be harder to establish. Not as much evidence.

Given the nature of things, there is better evidence for some historical events than others, and the only thing historians can do is establish levels of probability. Some things we might as well call certain (UNC's loss in the Final Four). Others seem to most of us to be just as certain: the Holocaust, for example. Why do some people claim the Holocaust never happened? They argue that the evidence was all doctored. That's absolutely crazy, I agree. But the fact that otherwise apparently intelligent people can make the claim, and even convince a few others, shows that it is not completely impossible.

With many other historical events there is much less certainty. Did Lincoln write the Gettysburg address on an envelope? Did Jefferson have a long-term love affair with one of his slaves? Did Alexander the Great drink himself to death after becoming upset when his male lover died? Was Jesus born when Quirinius was the governor of Syria? Make up your own questions: there are billions.

There is nothing inherently implausible about any of these events; the question is whether they probably happened or not. Some are more probable than others. Historians more or less rank past events on the basis of the relative probability that they occurred. All that historians can do is show what *probably* happened in the past.

That is the problem inherent in miracles. Miracles, by our very definition of the term, are virtually impossible events. Some people would say they are literally impossible, as violations of natural law: a person can't walk on water any more than an iron bar can float on it. Other people would be a bit more accurate and say that there aren't actually any laws in nature, written down somewhere, that can never be broken; but nature does work in highly predictable ways. That is what makes science possible. We would call a miracle an event that violates the way nature always, or almost always, works so as to make the event virtually, if not actually, impossible. The chances of a miracle occurring are infinitesimal. If that were not the case it would not be a miracle, just something weird that happened. And weird things happen all the time.

By now I hope you can see the unavoidable problem historians have with miracles. Historians can establish only what probably happened in the past, but miracles, by their very nature, are always the least probable explanation for what happened. This is true whether you are a believer or not. Of the six billion people in the world, not one of them can walk on top of lukewarm water filling a swimming pool. What would be the chances of any *one* person being able to do that? Less than one in six billion. Much less.

If historians can only establish what probably happened, and miracles by their definition are the least probable occurrences, then more or less by definition, historians cannot establish that miracles have ever probably happened.

This is true of the miracles of Mohammed, Hanina ben Dosa, Apollonius of Tyana—and Jesus.

But what about the resurrection? I'm not saying it didn't happen. Some people believe it did, some believe it didn't. But if you do believe it, it is not as a historian, even if you happen to be a professional historian, but as a believer.

There can be no historical evidence for the resurrection because of the nature of historical evidence.

Some evangelical Christian scholars argue just the opposite, that given the empty tomb and the eyewitness testimony of those who claimed to see Jesus alive after he was dead, there is good evidence that he was really raised. But to make this claim is fundamentally to misunderstand what historians can and cannot do. Historians can only establish what probably happened in the past. They cannot show that a miracle, the least likely occurrence, is the most likely occurrence. The resurrection is not least likely because of any anti-Christian bias. It is the least likely because people do not come back to life, never to die again, after they are well and truly dead. But what if Jesus did? If he did, it's a miracle, and it's beyond historical demonstration.

Many Christians don't want to hear this, but the reality is that there are lots of other explanations for what happened to Jesus that are more probable than the explanation that he was raised from the dead. None of these explanations is very probable, but they are *more* probable, just looking at the matter historically, than the explanation of the resurrection.

You could come up with dozens of implausible (but not impossible) explanations yourself. Let me give just two.

Why was the tomb supposedly empty? I say supposedly because, frankly, I don't know that it was. Our very first reference to Jesus' tomb being empty is in the Gospel of Mark, written forty years later by someone living in a different country who had heard that it was empty. How would he know? Anyhow, suppose that it was empty. How did it get that way? Suppose—here is my wild hypothesis— that Jesus was buried by Joseph of Arimathea in Joseph's own family tomb, and then a couple of Jesus' followers, not among the twelve, decided that night to move the body somewhere more appropriate. Only Matthew indicates there was a guard at the tomb; what if there wasn't? But a couple of Roman legionnaires are passing by, and catch these followers carrying the shrouded corpse through the streets. They suspect foul play and confront the followers, who pull their swords as the disciples did in Gethsemane. The soldiers, expert in swordplay, kill them on the spot. They now have three bodies, and no idea where the first one came from. Not knowing what to do with them, they commandeer a cart, take the corpses out to Gehenna, outside town, and dump them. Within three or four days the bodies have deteriorated beyond recognition. Jesus' original tomb is empty, and no one seems to know why.

Is this scenario likely? Not at all. Am I proposing this is what really happened? Absolutely not. Is it more probable that something like this happened than that a miracle happened and Jesus left the tomb to ascend to heaven? Absolutely! From a purely historical point of view, a highly unlikely event is far more probable than a virtually impossible one.

Why, then, did some of the disciples claim to see Jesus alive after his crucifixion? I don't doubt at all that some disciples claimed this. We don't have any of their written testimony, but Paul, writing about twenty-five years later, indicates that this is what they claimed, and I don't think he is making it up. And he knew at least a couple of them, whom he met just three years after the event (Galatians

1:18–19). But does the fact that some people claimed to have seen Jesus alive mean that he really did come back from the dead? Is that the most probable occurrence? It can't be—by definition it is the least probable. What would be more probable? Nearly any explanation you can think of.

Let me suggest one. It is an extremely well-documented phenomenon that people sometimes have visions of their loved ones after they died. A man sees his wife in his bedroom a month after she was buried; a woman sees her dead daughter; a girl sees her dead grandmother. Happens all the time. It is extremely well documented.[10] In many instances the person having this experience can talk to the dead person, can give them a hug and feel them. There are documented instances of multiple people having some such visionary experience together, and not just visions of relatives. The blessed Virgin Mary appears to groups of people all the time—there are thousands of eyewitnesses. Do I think that she really has appeared to them? No. Or that the grandmother really did come back from the dead to visit her granddaughter's bedroom? No. Maybe these things happened. But it is unlikely. In fact, from the historian's point of view, it is virtually impossible. But people claim they happen all the time.

Jesus' closest followers, and later Paul, claimed they saw him alive afterward. Does it mean he was really raised from the dead? No, it means that they, like so many thousands of other people, had a real-seeming, tangible experience of a person after he died. The disciples had not done any research into postmortem visionary experiences. They experienced what they experienced, and they interpreted it in terms that they knew: Jesus was alive. He must have been raised from the dead. Where is he now? He's not here—he must have ascended to heaven.

Is my explanation of why they claimed what they did very probable? No. But it's not impossible. From a strictly historical point of view, it is more probable than an actual resurrection.

I am decidedly *not* saying that Jesus was not raised from the dead. I'm not saying the tomb was not empty. I'm not saying that he did not appear to his disciples and ascend into heaven. Believers believe that all these things are true. But they do not believe them because of historical evidence. They take the Christian claims on faith, not on the basis of proof. There can be no proof. Historians can only establish what probably happened in the past, and by definition, miracles are the least probable of occurrences.

How We Got the Bible

Even though I was a conservative evangelical Christian when I arrived at Princeton Theological Seminary in the late 1970s, I was not a completely ignorant, head-in-the-sand fundamentalist. I did have a liberal arts education, a bachelor's degree in English literature, and some training in history, classics, and philosophy. I also knew something about the world and didn't think that everyone who disagreed with me on a point of doctrine was going to roast in hell. I've known more conservative Christians. But I was pretty conservative.

Among other things, I continued to be convinced that the Bible was not just a collection of authoritative books that could guide a Christian's views about what to believe and how to behave. I was convinced that the Bible was the very Word of God, inerrant in everything that it taught. This was the view that I had been taught at Moody Bible Institute, where I had majored in "Bible Theology"; even with my more progressive education in the liberal arts at Wheaton, I held on to this view. At least for a while.

Various aspects of my study of the New Testament began to eat away at this view. One of the issues that I had to confront was a very basic question that is somewhat damning in its simplicity, a question that everyone who believes that the Bible is the verbally inspired Word of God has to confront. Which Bible?

Is the inspired Bible the one that we actually use? The King James Version? Some people continue to insist so, even if it does seem to be a rather silly view: do you mean that for all those centuries before the King James translators got to work, Christians did not have access to God's inspired word? What was God thinking? Some other modern translation then? The Hebrew and Greek texts from which these English translations are made? If one chooses the last option, what does one do about the fact that we don't have the original Hebrew and Greek texts of any of the books of the Bible, but only later copies of these texts, all of which have mistakes?

At Moody I had been taught that the inspired words were the words of the originals, the so-called autographs. Sure, scribes had modified these words over the years, but before they were modified they were the perfectly inspired Word of God. As I explain in *Misquoting Jesus*, eventually this view came to seem problematic to me. Why would God have inspired the words of the Bible if he chose not to preserve these words for posterity? Put differently, what should make me think he had inspired the words in the first place if I knew for certain (as I did) that he had not preserved them? This became a major problem for me in trying to figure out which Bible I thought was inspired.

Another big problem is one that I don't deal with in *Misquoting Jesus*. If God inspired certain books in the decades after Jesus died, how do I know that the later church fathers chose the right books to be included in the Bible? I could accept it on faith—surely God would not allow noninspired books in the canon of Scripture. But as I engaged in more historical study of the early Christian movement, I began to realize that there were lots of Christians in lots of places who fully believed that other books were to be accepted as Scripture; conversely, some of the books that eventually made it into the canon were rejected by church leaders in different parts of the church, sometimes for centuries.

In some parts of the church, the Apocalypse of John (the book of Revelation) was flat out rejected as containing false teaching, whereas the Apocalypse of Peter, which eventually did not make it in, was accepted. There were some Christians who accepted the Gospel of Peter and some who rejected the Gospel of John. There were some Christians who accepted a truncated version of the Gospel of Luke (without its first two chapters), and others who accepted the now noncanonical Gospel of Thomas. Some Christians rejected the three Pastoral Epistles of 1 and 2 Timothy and Titus, which eventually made it in, and others accepted the Epistle of Barnabas, which did not.

If God was making sure that his church would have the inspired books of Scripture, and only those books, why were there such heated debates and disagreements that took place over three hundred years? Why didn't God just make sure that these debates lasted weeks, with assured results, rather than centuries?[1]

In this chapter I want to talk about the problems that arose for me in thinking of the Bible as the inspired Word of God. The first problem is that we don't have the originals of any of the writings of the New Testament (since I already have devoted an entire book to the subject, I can keep this part of the discussion short).[2] The second problem involves how the canon of twenty-seven books was eventually formed.

THE "ORIGINAL" TEXT OF THE NEW TESTAMENT

Even though *Misquoting Jesus* seemed to stir up a bit of a hornet's nest, at least among conservative evangelical Christians, its overarching theses were almost entirely noncontroversial. I would summarize them as follows:

- We don't have the originals of any of the books of the New Testament.

- The copies we have were made much later, in most instances many centuries later.

- We have thousands of these copies, in Greek—the language in which of all the New Testament books were originally written.

- All of these copies contain mistakes—accidental slips on the part of the scribes who made them or intentional alterations by scribes wanting to change the text to make it say what they wanted it to mean (or thought that it did mean).

- We don't know how many mistakes there are among our surviving copies, but they appear to number in the hundreds of thousands. It is safe to put the matter in comparative terms: there are more differences in our manuscripts than there are words in the New Testament.

- The vast majority of these mistakes are completely insignificant, showing us nothing more than that scribes in antiquity could spell no better than most people can today.

- But some of the mistakes matter—a lot. Some of them affect the interpretation of a verse, a chapter, or an entire book. Others reveal the kinds of concerns that were affecting scribes, who sometimes altered the text in light of debates and controversies going on in their own surroundings.

- The task of the textual critic is both to figure out what the author of a text actually wrote and to understand why scribes modified the text (to help us understand the context within which scribes were working).

- Despite the fact that scholars have been working diligently at these tasks for three hundred years, there continue to be heated differences of opinion. There are some passages where serious and very smart scholars disagree about what the original text said, and there are some places where we will probably never know what the original text said.

The conservative evangelical response to my book surprised me a bit.[3] Some of these critics criticized *Misquoting Jesus* for "misleading" people—as if facts such as those I have just cited could lead someone down a slippery slope toward perdition. A number of critics indicated that they didn't much appreciate my tone. And a whole lot of them wanted to insist that the facts I laid out do not require anyone to lose their faith in the Bible as the inspired word of God.

That last point is one with which I might take issue: there are certain views of the inspiration of Scripture, such as the one I had pounded into me as a late teenager, that do not stand up well to the facts of textual criticism. For most Christians, who don't have a conservative evangelical view like the one I had, these textual facts can be interesting, but there is nothing in them to challenge their faith, which is built on something other than having the very words that God inspired in the Bible. And I certainly never intended to lead anyone away from the Christian faith; critics who have suggested that I myself stopped being a Christian once I realized there were differences among our manuscripts are simply wrong and being ridiculous.[4]

In any event, as I indicated, these theses themselves were almost entirely noncontroversial. Who can deny that we have thousands of manuscripts? Or hundreds of thousands of variants? Or that lots of the variants involve spelling? Or that scholars continue to debate what the original text was in lots of places? All of these statements are factually true.

The one statement that has stirred up controversy is my claim that some of these variations are significant. This view has been objected to by some conservative evangelicals and no one else that I know of. That gives me pause—why is this criticism coming only from people with a particular set of theological views? The typical response has been two-pronged: critics have charged that (1) the vast majority of textual alterations don't matter at all, and I've misled people into thinking that they do; and (2) *none* of the variants is terrifically significant; they have all been known for a long time and none of them counts for much of anything.

I'm not completely sure how to respond to the first criticism, since I have always insisted that most textual variants are insignificant (for example, right away on page 10 of *Misquoting Jesus*). I think maybe the objection is that I don't say this enough, and that by focusing on the variants that do matter, I mislead people into thinking that the situation is worse than it is. I get the sense from these critics that they would have preferred me to write mainly about the insignificant textual changes that don't matter for anything. Now wouldn't *that* be an interesting book?

It is the second criticism that I want to respond to at length. It simply is not true, in my opinion, that none of the textual variants actually matters for very much. Some of them matter, a lot.

In response to the assertion, made by conservative evangelicals, that not a single important Christian doctrine is affected by any textual variant, I point out:

a. It simply isn't true that important doctrines are not involved. As a key example: the only place in the entire New Testament where the doctrine of the Trinity is explicitly taught is in a passage that made it into the King James translation (1 John 5:7–8) but is not found in the vast majority of the Greek manuscripts of the New Testament. I would suggest that the Trinity is a rather important Christian doctrine. A typical response to this rebuttal is that the doctrine of the Trinity can be found in Scripture without appealing to 1 John 5:7–8. My reply is that this is true of every single Christian doctrine. In my experience, theologians do not hold to a doctrine because it is found in just one verse; you can take away just about any verse and still find just about any Christian doctrine somewhere else if you look hard enough.[5]

b. It seems to me to be a very strange criterion of significance to say that textual variants ultimately don't matter because they don't affect any cardinal Christian doctrine. Why is Christian doctrine the ultimate criterion of significance?

Suppose, for example, that we discovered a manuscript of the Gospel of Matthew that for some reason was lacking chapters 4–13. Would that be significant? I should think so. But would it affect anyone's doctrine? Not at all. Or take an even more extreme example. Suppose we all woke up tomorrow morning and found that every trace of the books of Mark, Philippians, James, and 1 Peter had been removed from every New Testament on the planet. Would that be significant? It would be huge! Would it affect any Christian doctrine? Not in the least.

c. Most important, some of the textual variants do matter deeply, for things other than "cardinal Christian doctrines."

1. Some matter for how to interpret entire books of the New Testament. Take a couple of variants in the Gospel of Luke. First, did Luke think that Jesus was in agony when going to his death, or that he was calm and controlled? It depends entirely on what you make of the textual variant in Luke 22:43–44, where Jesus allegedly sweated great drops as if of blood before his arrest. Leave the verses in, as some manuscripts do, and Jesus is obviously in deep agony. Take them out and there is no agony, either in this passage or anywhere else in Luke's Passion narrative, as we saw earlier when we noticed that Luke had eliminated all of Mark's references to Jesus' being in pain, uncertain up to the end. Second, did Luke understand that Jesus' death was an atonement for sin? It depends on what you do with Luke 22:19–20. Everywhere else in Luke, as we saw in chapter 3, Luke has eliminated Mark's references to Jesus' death as an atonement. The only remnant of that teaching is in some manuscripts of the Lord's Supper, where Jesus says that the bread is his body to be broken "for you" and the cup is his blood poured out "for you."

But in our earliest and best manuscripts, these words are missing (much of v. 19 and all of v. 20). It appears scribes have added them to make Luke's view of Jesus' death conform to Mark's and Matthew's. I'd say that's rather important—unless you think that Luke's views on the subject don't really matter.

2. Some variants, including those just mentioned, are terrifically important for knowing what traditions about Jesus were in circulation among the early Christians. Did Jesus have an encounter with an adulterous woman and her accusers in which he told them, "Let the one without sin among you be the first to cast a stone at her," and in which he told her, after all her accusers had left, "Neither do I condemn you. Go and sin no more"? It depends on which manuscripts of John you read. After his resurrection, did Jesus tell his disciples that those who came to believe in him would be able to handle snakes and drink deadly poison without being harmed? It depends on which manuscripts of Mark you read.

3. Some variants are crucial for understanding what was going on in the communities of the scribes who were copying the texts. Some scribes, for example, omitted the prayer of Jesus spoken while being crucified, "Father forgive them, for they don't know what they were doing" (Luke 23:34). Early Christians interpreted this as a prayer of forgiveness for the Jews, ignorant of what they had done. No wonder some scribes omitted the verse in the context of Christian anti-Judaism in the second and third centuries, when many Christians believed that Jews knew exactly what they were doing and that God had in no way forgiven them. Or as an example from Paul: it appears that

Paul's injunction to women to be "silent" in the churches and "subordinate" to their husbands was not originally part of 1 Corinthians 14 (vv. 34–35) but was added by later scribes intent on keeping women in their place. Is that significant or not?

d. Finally, I have to say that I actually don't believe it when conservative evangelicals say that the textual variations in the New Testament don't matter very much. If they don't matter, why do such conservative evangelical seminaries as Dallas Theological Seminary (headed by one of my outspoken critics on the matter) and New Orleans Baptist Theological Seminary sponsor multi-million-dollar projects to examine the Greek manuscripts of the New Testament? If the differences in the manuscripts don't matter, why bother to study them? If they are completely insignificant, why devote one's career to examining them? If they are altogether immaterial, why devote millions of dollars to investigating them? I wonder what such people say when they're out raising money for their projects: "We'd like you to invest five hundred thousand dollars to help us study the manuscripts of the New Testament, because we don't think they have any significance"?

I think it is quite obvious that the manuscripts do matter. They matter for how we interpret the New Testament; they matter for knowing about the historical Jesus; they matter for understanding the history of the Christian church after Jesus' death. Those who argue that they don't matter either are trying to provide comfort to those who might be disturbed by learning the historical facts, or are fooling themselves.

THE FORMATION OF THE CANON OF SCRIPTURE

The problem of thinking that in the Bible we have the very words inspired by God is bigger, however, than the fact that we don't always know what those words were. There is also the problem of knowing whether the books in our Bibles are the ones that God wanted to be Scripture in the first place. How do we know that only the right books got in? How do we know that some inspired books were not left out?[6]

Some of my students tend to think that the Bible just kind of descended from heaven one day in July, a short time after Jesus died. The New Testament is the New Testament. Always has been and always will be. You can go into any store in any part of the country, or any part of the Western world, and buy a New Testament, and it is always the same collection of twenty-seven books, the four Gospels followed by Acts followed by the epistles and ending with the Apocalypse. Surely it has always been that way.

But it has not always been that way. Quite the contrary, the debate over which books to include in the Bible was long and hard fought. As difficult as this is to believe, there never was a final decision accepted by every church in the world; historically there have always been some churches in some countries (Syria, Armenia, Ethiopia) that have slightly different canons of Scripture from the one we have. Even the twenty-seven-book canon with which all of us are familiar did not ever get ratified by a church council of any kind—until the anti-Reformation Catholic Council of Trent in the sixteenth century, which also ratified the Old Testament Apocrypha, in response to the widespread Protestant rejection of these books as noncanonical.[7] In a strange way, the canon, far from being definitively decided upon at some point of time, emerged without anyone taking a vote.

Not that it happened by accident. The canon was formed through a process of a long series of debates and conflicts over which books ought to be included. These debates were fueled not only by a general sense that it would be a good thing to know which books are authoritative, but even more by a very real and threatening situation that early Christians confronted. In the first few centuries of the church, lots of different Christian groups espoused a wide range of theological and ecclesiastical views. These different groups were completely at odds with each other over some of the most fundamental issues: How many Gods are there? Was Jesus human? Was he divine? Is the material world inherently good or evil? Does salvation come to the human body, or does it come by escaping the body? Does Jesus' death have anything to do with salvation?

The problem in the development of the canon of Scripture was that each and every one of the competitive groups of Christians—each of them insisting they were right, each trying to win converts—had sacred books that authorized their points of view. And most of these books claimed to be written by apostles. Who was right? The canon that emerged from these debates represented the books favored by the group that ended up winning. It did not happen overnight. In fact, it took centuries.

The Wild Diversity of the Early Christian Church

To put the process of canonization into its proper context, we need to know something about the wild diversity of the early Christian movement during its early centuries. You might think that from the beginning, Christianity was always basically one thing: a religion descended from Jesus, as interpreted by Paul, leading to the church of the Middle Ages on down to the present. But things were not at all that simple. About a hundred fifty years after Jesus' death we find a wide range of different Christian groups claiming to represent the views of Jesus and his disciples but having completely divergent perspectives, far more divergent than anything even that made it into the New Testament.

Who were some of these groups?

The Ebionites

The Ebionites were a group of Christians who were converted Jews who insisted on maintaining their Jewishness and on following the laws God had given Moses, as found in the Hebrew Bible, all while believing that Jesus was the Messiah sent from God for the salvation of the world. We do not know where their name comes from. Most scholars think that it derives from the Hebrew word *ebyon*, which means "the poor." Possibly these Christians followed Jesus' command to give up everything for the sake of the Gospel and had taken on voluntary poverty as part of their religious devotion, much like the first followers of Jesus as described in the book of Acts (Acts 2:44–45; 4:32). The Ebionites almost certainly claimed to be the spiritual descendants of these first followers and like them understood that faith in Jesus did not entail a break with Judaism but the proper interpretation of it, the religion revealed to Moses by God on Mount Sinai.

Some scholars have thought that the Ebionites may have held views very much like those of the first followers of Jesus, such as his brother James or his disciple Peter, both leaders of the church in Jerusalem in the years after Jesus' death. James in particular appears to have held to the ongoing validity of the Jewish law for all followers of Jesus. His view, and evidently that of the Ebionites later, was that Jesus was the Jewish Messiah sent from the Jewish God to the Jewish people in fulfillment of the Jewish law. Therefore, anyone who wanted to follow Jesus had to be Jewish. If a gentile man converted to the faith, he had to be circumcised, since circumcision always had been the requirement of a male to become a follower of the God of Israel, as God himself demanded in the law (Genesis 17:10–14).

Eventually the apostle Paul came along and insisted the opposite, that the God of Jesus was the God of all people and that gentiles did not have to become Jewish to follow Jesus. For Paul, doing what the law required could not put a person into a right standing with God, and trying to keep the law was pointless when it came to salvation. Paul ended up winning this argument, but for centuries there were Christians who disagreed with him, including the Ebionites. They did not view Paul as the great apostle of the faith; he was the one who had gotten the fundamentals of the faith precisely wrong.

The Ebionites were strict Jewish monotheists. As such, they did not think that Jesus was himself divine. There could be only one God. Instead, Jesus was the human appointed by God to be the Messiah. He was not born of a virgin: his parents were Joseph and Mary, and he was a very righteous man whom God had adopted to be his son and to whom he had given a mission of dying on the Cross to atone for the sins of others.

You might wonder why the Ebionites didn't just read their New Testaments to see that Jesus was born of a virgin, was himself divine, had abrogated the Jewish law, and was correctly proclaimed by Paul. They couldn't read the New Testament because there was as yet no New Testament. The Ebionites had their own sacred books, along with the Hebrew Bible, that proclaimed their points of view, including a Gospel that looked very much like our Gospel of Matthew (the most "Jewish" of our Gospels), but without its first two chapters, which narrate the virgin birth.

The Marcionites

At the opposite end of the theological spectrum were the Marcionites, followers of Marcion, a famous preacher-theologian of the second century from Asia Minor, who spent a few years in Rome before being expelled from the church and moving back to Asia Minor, where he established numerous churches in lots of cities.

Unlike the Ebionites, Marcion understood Paul as the great hero of the faith, the one apostle who actually understood Jesus and his relation to the Jewish law. As we have seen, Paul drew a distinction between the law given by Moses, which could not bring salvation, and the gospel of Jesus, which could. Marcion thought that this distinction was absolute: the Jewish law and the gospel of Jesus had nothing in common. The law was one thing (for Jews), the gospel was another (for Christians).

Marcion wrote a book called the *Antitheses* (literally, "Contrary Statements") that showed the absolute dichotomy between the God of the Old Testament and the God of Jesus. The God of the Old Testament was a wrathful, vengeful God of judgment; the God of Jesus was a loving and merciful God of salvation. How different were these two Gods? Marcion drew a logical conclusion: these were two different Gods.

The God of the Old Testament had created this world, chosen Israel to be his people, given them his law, and then condemned them, and everyone else, to eternal punishment when they disobeyed. The God of Jesus had nothing to do with this creation, Israel, or the law, and came into this world to save people from the wrath of the Old Testament God. He did this by having Jesus die on the cross, to take the wrath of God upon himself. Those who have faith in Jesus can therefore escape the clutches of the vengeful God of the Jews.

In this interpretation, Jesus was not and could not be a human being. That would make him physical, part of the physical creation, a creature of the creator God. According to Marcion, Jesus only seemed to be a human but was actually a divine being, pure and simple. Marcion's opponents called this view of Christ "docetism," from the Greek word *dokeo* ("to seem, to appear"). Jesus appeared in the likeness of human flesh, as Paul says (Romans 8:3); he did not really become flesh.

Consequently, per Marcion, the followers of Jesus were not to be associated with Jews or Judaism in any form. They were to be followers of Jesus and of Paul, the one apostle who understood Jesus.

Marcion had his own list of sacred books, but obviously not those of the Ebionites. His canon consisted of the ten letters of Paul that he knew (all of our thirteen, apart from the Pastoral Epistles) and a form of the Gospel of Luke. All of these books, though, are problematic in terms of the support they offer for Marcion's views, since they quote the Old Testament (the book of the "other" God) and seem to assume that the Creation was made by the true God. Marcion believed that all of these books had been altered by the scribes who copied them, who did not understand the truth of the Gospel. And so Marcion produced his own version of his eleven books of Scripture (he did not, of course, include the Old Testament in his canon), a truncated version that eliminated the scribal changes that tied Jesus to the creator God.

The Various Groups of Gnostics

Scholars debate whether or not the Christians called Gnostics constitute one group or a bunch of roughly similar groups, or a number of groups without much in common. I won't go into all of the scholarly debates here, but simply indicate that I think there were multiple groups of Gnostics that had some basic theological views in common and that it is heuristically useful to think about these groups together, as "Gnostic." (Of course there were differences, too, otherwise they would not be separate groups.)[8]

They are called Gnostic, from the Greek *gnosis*, "knowledge," because they maintained that knowledge, not faith, was necessary for salvation. But knowledge of what? Knowledge of how this world came into existence and, yet more important, of who you really are. Specifically, you need to know who you are, where you came from, how you got here, and how you can return.

The assumption of the various Gnostic groups was that some of us do not come from here, on this earth, and do not belong here. We come from another realm, a heavenly place, and we have become entrapped in the evil confines of our bodies. We need to learn how to escape, and for that we need secret knowledge (*gnosis*).

The Gnostics believed that this world is not the creation of the one and only true God. Instead, there are many divine beings in the heavenly realm, even if all of them were generated from the ultimate divinity, and this world was an afterthought, the creation of lower, inferior, and ignorant divinities. Its creation was a kind of cosmic disaster, the result of a catastrophe that took place in the divine realm. In part the world was created in order to provide a place of imprisonment for elements of the divine. Some of us have these sparks of the divine within us. We need to learn the truth about this world and the world above, and about our true identity, in order to escape and return to our heavenly home.

What does this have to do with being a follower of Jesus? In the Christian Gnostic systems (there were also non-Christian varieties), Jesus is a divine being who has come down from the divine realm in order to communicate the secret knowledge of salvation to the spirits who have been entrapped here. This knowledge includes an account of how the divine realm itself came into being, how the catastrophic material creation came to exist, and how elements of the divine managed to become entrapped here. Without Jesus we could not have this knowledge. He really is the savior of our souls.

Of course Jesus himself could not be an entrapped spirit. Some Gnostics agreed with Marcion that Jesus was a divine being who only appeared to be human. He came to earth in order to convey his secret teachings. Most Gnostics thought differently, however; according to them, Jesus himself was a human being who was temporarily inhabited by a divine being, the Christ, for his public ministry between the time of his baptism—when the Christ entered into him in the form of a dove—and the time before his death. That's why on the cross Jesus cried out, "My God, my God, why have you forsaken me?" It was then that the divine Christ left Jesus to die alone. But he raised Jesus from the dead, after which he continued to deliver his secret teachings to his close disciples before ascending back to the heavenly realm.

This may not sound like the kind of Christianity you learned about in Sunday School, but it was very popular in many regions of the early church. Salvation came not by having faith in Jesus' death and resurrection but by understanding the secret teaching that he revealed. Since the teaching was secret, the public instruction that Jesus gave was not his real message, or at least it was carefully coded so that only the insiders, those with the divine spark within, could fully understand it. His real message came in private revelations that he gave to his closest followers. Many of the Gnostic books reveal this divine knowledge.

We are fortunate that a number of these books have turned up in modern times, especially when a cache of Gnostic writings, commonly called the Gnostic Gospels, was discovered in the wilderness of Egypt near the town of Nag Hammadi in 1945. They convey a picture of Christianity quite unlike anything most of us were reared on or ever even heard before. And the reason for this is obvious: the Gnostics were losers in the struggle over who would decide the "right," the official, form of Christianity for all posterity.

The Proto-Orthodox Christians

Ultimately, only one group of Christians won in the struggle to gain converts. Their victory was probably sealed sometime in the third century. When the Roman emperor Constantine converted to Christianity in the early fourth century, he converted to this victorious form of the faith. When Christianity later became the official religion of the empire, about fifty years after Constantine, it was this form that was accepted by nearly everyone—with lots of variation of course. Alternative views have always been around.

Once it won the battles, this form of Christianity declared not only that it was right, but that it had been right all along. The technical term for "correct belief" is "orthodoxy" (in Greek, *orthos* means "right"; *doxa* means "opinion"). The "orthodox" Christians, that is, the ones who won the struggle, labeled all the competing perspectives heresies, from the Greek word for "choice." Heretics are people who choose to believe the wrong belief, a nonorthodox belief.

What should we call the group of Christians who held to the views that eventually won out, before the victory was sealed? I usually call them the "proto-orthodox," the spiritual ancestors of those whose views later became orthodox.

The proto-orthodox are the second- and third-century Christians we are best informed about, since it was their writings, not the writings of their opponents, that were preserved for posterity. This would include such writers as Justin Martyr, Irenaeus, Tertullian,

Hippolytus, Clement of Alexandria, and Origen—figures well known to students of early Christianity. These authors were responsible for shaping the views that eventually became orthodox. They did so in no small part by arguing against all contrary sides at once, leading to certain kinds of paradoxical affirmations. For example, they agreed with the Ebionites that Jesus was fully human, but disagreed when they denied he was God. They agreed with the Marcionites that Jesus was fully divine, but disagreed when they denied he was human. How could the proto-orthodox have it both ways? By saying that Jesus was both things at once, God and man. This became the orthodox view.

The major orthodox doctrines are the ones that eventually made it into the Christian creeds: there is one God, he is the creator of all there is; therefore, the Creation is inherently good, even if flawed by sin. Jesus his son is both human and divine, and he is not two beings (as the Gnostics held), but one; he brought salvation not through secret knowledge but by shedding his real blood.

Like all of their opponents, the proto-orthodox had a range of books that they considered sacred authorities and that they saw as authorizing their particular perspectives. Some of these books eventually made it into the canon. The major debates within proto-orthodox circles concerned which of the proto-orthodox books to accept, but all proto-orthodox agreed that none of the heretical books could possibly have been written by any of the apostles and so were not to be included in the canon of Scripture.

SOME NONCANONICAL SCRIPTURES

All of the Christian groups had books that were considered sacred Scripture. Most of the books revered at one time or another by one group or another have not survived, but dozens did survive or were rediscovered in modern times. Here is a choice sampling of the literature that was revered in the early centuries of the church but that didn't get into the canon.

The Gospel of the Ebionites

There may have been more than one Christian group called Ebionite. Three Gospels have come down to us that appear to have been used by various Ebionite groups. One is the truncated version of the Gospel of Matthew mentioned earlier. Another is known simply as the Gospel of the Ebionites. It no longer survives intact, but we know about it through the quotations of a fourth-century heresy hunter, Ephiphanius. What he tells us is quite intriguing. Apparently this group of Ebionites believed that Jesus was the perfect sacrifice for sins, which meant that the Jewish sacrifices in the Temple were no longer required. And so they were Jews who no longer believed in Jewish sacrifice; they did, however, keep the other aspects of the law.

In the ancient world, about the only time a person would eat meat was when an animal had been ritually slaughtered by a priest, as a sacrifice to the gods or to God. Since this particular group of Ebionites no longer believed in sacrifice, they became, on principle, vegetarians. This choice of food is reflected in the way they told their Gospel traditions. For example, when the disciples ask Jesus where they are to prepare the Passover meal for him, in this Gospel he replies, "I have no desire to eat the meat of this Passover lamb with you." Even more interesting is that in this Gospel, John the Baptist's diet apparently changed. In the canonical Gospels he is said to have subsisted on locusts and wild honey. By changing one letter in the Greek word "locust" (which is, after all, a meat), the Ebionite Gospel stated that John was eating pancakes and wild honey—a much better choice, some of us might think.

The Coptic Gospel of Thomas

Among all the archaeological discoveries of noncanonical texts in modern times, none is more significant than the Gospel of Thomas, found among the Gnostic Gospels at Nag Hammadi. Like the other books found at the same time, it is written in Coptic, an ancient

Egyptian language.⁹ It is significant both because of its unusual character and because of its relative antiquity: it is one of the earliest noncanonical Gospels yet discovered and most likely dates from just a few decades after the Gospel of John.

Unlike the Gospels of the New Testament, which narrate the words and deeds of Jesus up to his death and resurrection, the Gospel of Thomas contains only a group of sayings of Jesus. Altogether the Gospel presents 114 discrete sayings. Most are introduced with the words "And Jesus said . . ." Many of these sayings are similar to teachings of Jesus in the Gospels of the New Testament. For example, one finds here the parable of the mustard seed and the saying of the blind leading the blind, in slightly different forms. But around half of the sayings, depending on how you count, are unlike the canonical accounts. Most of these unique sayings sound bizarre to people raised on biblical accounts of Jesus' teaching. For example, here it is recounted that he said, "The dead are not alive, and the living will not die. In the days when you consumed what is dead, you made it what is alive. When you come to dwell in the light, what will you do? On the day when you were one you became two. But when you become two, what will you do?" (saying 11).

What is one to make of the unusual sayings of the Gospel of Thomas? For the past ten or fifteen years there have been heated scholarly discussions on just this point, with some scholars thinking that these sayings make the most sense if placed within the thought-world of some form of early Christian Gnosticism, and others arguing that they are not Gnostic at all. I myself take the former view. These sayings do not promote the Gnostic myth, but that does not mean they are not best understood gnostically, just as a lot of Marxist writings do not lay out the tenets of Marxism. A gnostic framework explains a lot of this Gospel.¹⁰

In it Jesus indicates that his hearers have a spark of the divine that had a heavenly origin. This world we live in is a cesspool of suffering that he calls a corpse. A person's inner being (the light within) has tragically fallen into this material world and become entrapped

here (sunk into "poverty"), and in that condition has become forget-
ful of its origin (become "drunk"). It needs to be reawakened by
learning the truth of both this world and its own heavenly origins.
Jesus is the one who conveys this truth. Once the spirit within learns
the truth, it will strip off this material body (symbolized as clothes
to be removed) and escape this world, returning to the divine realm,
whence it came.[11]

The most striking feature of the Coptic Gospel of Thomas is that
it does not narrate Jesus' death and resurrection. Salvation does not
come by believing in Jesus' death but by understanding his secret
teachings: "Whoever finds the interpretation of these sayings will
not taste death" (saying 1).

The Acts of Thecla

According to the proto-orthodox theologian and apologist Tertullian, the church leader who forged the Acts of Thecla was caught in
the act and severely disciplined by being removed from his position
of authority. This unhappy result does not appear to have had much
effect on the success of his endeavor. Stories about Thecla continued
to circulate long after the book had first been put into publication,
some time in the second half of the second century. For centuries
after that, Thecla was a household name throughout parts of Christendom, and in some places she vied with the Blessed Virgin Mary
herself as the most revered saint.

But the forger did not make up his stories out of whole cloth. He
evidently drew on oral traditions then in circulation concerning the
apostle Paul and his most famous female convert. The Acts of Thecla
tell the history of their association.

Thecla is said to have been a wealthy young upper-class woman
engaged to be married to one of the leading men of the city. Thecla
lives next door to the house where the Christians meet, and when
Paul comes to town he preaches there, a sermon that Thecla can hear
from her upstairs window. She sits enraptured for days on end. On

this occasion Paul preaches the gospel of sexual renunciation: people should remain celibate and will thereby inherit the kingdom of God.

Thecla is persuaded by this message to convert, much to the consternation of her fiancé, who was anticipating a long and happy married life together. She breaks off the engagement and becomes a follower of Paul, which leads to a number of very strange and intriguing episodes in which Thecla is threatened with martyrdom, only to escape by the supernatural intervention of God. Possibly the most memorable incident occurs when she is thrown to the wild beasts for embracing the Christian faith; desperate to be baptized before her ultimate demise (Paul had put off baptizing her), she leaps into a vat of "man-eating seals" and baptizes herself in the name of Jesus. God sends down a thunderbolt to kill the seals, she escapes, and more adventures ensue.

The Acts of Thecla is now found in a collection of traditions about Paul's missionary escapades known broadly as the Acts of Paul.

Third Corinthians

Also in the Acts of Paul are two noncanonical letters, one written to the apostle by his converts in Corinth and the other the reply written by him. This exchange is called 3 Corinthians, to differentiate it from 1 and 2 Corinthians in the New Testament.

The occasion for the correspondence is spelled out in the Corinthians' letter, where they say that two Christian teachers, Simon and Cleobius, have arrived in town and have been teaching that God is not the creator of the world, that the Jewish prophets are not from God, that Jesus did not come in the flesh, and that the flesh of believers will not be raised at the resurrection. (These teachings seem to reflect some kind of Gnostic point of view.) What are the Corinthians to make of such teachings?

Paul responds by addressing himself to the heretical views one by one, showing that they do not accord with the truth of the Gospel.

He emphasizes that the material world is indeed the Creation of the one God, who spoke through the prophets and has now sent Jesus into the world in the flesh "so that he might set free all flesh through his flesh, and might raise us from the dead as fleshly beings."

This is a proto-orthodox, antignostic production. Not well known to most Christians in the West, it had a remarkable reception in other parts of the world. In Armenia and parts of Syria it was accepted as canonical Scripture, even though, as well known to scholars, it was written at least a century after Paul's death.

The Letter of Barnabas

According to both Paul and the book of Acts, one of his close apostolic companions was a man named Barnabas, about whom we are otherwise poorly informed. About seventy years after both Paul and Barnabas died, some anonymous author wrote a "letter"—actually more of a theological treatise—that eventually came to be attributed to Barnabas, no doubt in order to promote its reputation among Christian readers. Some proto-orthodox Christians were quite insistent that the book belonged in the canon of Scripture, and it is found among the New Testament writings in our earliest complete manuscript of the New Testament, known as the Codex Sinaiticus, dating from the middle of the fourth century.

Christians of modern times might express some relief that Barnabas was not eventually included among the books of sacred writ. Even more than the books that did get into the New Testament, this letter is virulently and unashamedly anti-Jewish in its views. In fact, it is largely a discussion of the Jewish religion and the Jewish Scripture.

Its overarching theme is that Jews are not the people of God because they rejected the covenant that God made with Moses on Mount Sinai, for down below they were making and worshipping the golden calf. As a result, God rejected them. The laws he gave Moses were misinterpreted by the Jewish people, who were not the covenantal people at all. And they are still misinterpreted by them since they think the laws given to Moses were meant to be taken literally. They were actually symbolic laws meant to direct people about how to live. For example, the prohibition on eating pork did not mean that one could not eat any pork; it really meant not to live like pigs. Moreover, according to Barnabas these laws look forward to Jesus, whose followers are the true people of God.

In short, says Barnabas, the Old Testament is not a Jewish book. It is a Christian book. And the covenant God made with the Jewish ancestors is not a covenant for the Jews. It is a covenant for the followers of Jesus.

The Apocalypse of Peter

Another book considered canonical in some proto-orthodox circles was the Apocalypse (or Revelation) of Peter. This book cannot be found in any of the surviving manuscripts of the New Testament, but is mentioned as belonging, or potentially belonging, to the canon in several early church writings. Whatever its canonical status, it is an intriguing narrative, the first surviving account from early Christianity of someone being given a guided tour of heaven and hell.

Most of us are familiar with this motif from Dante's *Divine Comedy*. Dante did not make up the idea, however; he had lots of predecessors, and so far as we can tell from the written record, the Apocalypse of Peter was the first.

The account begins with Jesus talking to his disciples on the Mount of Olives, discussing with them what would happen at the end of all things (Mark 13; Matthew 24–25). Peter asks Jesus about the afterlife, and Jesus begins to explain it all to him. At this point it is not completely clear whether Jesus' explanation is so graphic that Peter can visualize what he is describing or whether Jesus takes him on an actual tour. But the reader is treated to a vivid description of both the realm of the blessed, in heaven, and the realm of the damned, in hell.

By far the most interesting part of the tour is the description of hell. It is a bit difficult to describe at any length the ecstasies of the blessed: they are, after all, extremely happy, and there's only so much one can say about it. It is quite easy, on the other hand, to let one's imagination roam when portraying the various torments of the damned. And this book is nothing if not imaginative.

Those being eternally tormented are punished appropriately for the sin they most often committed while living. Habitual liars are hanged by their tongues over eternal flames; women who braided their hair to make themselves attractive to men in order to seduce them are hanged by their hair over the fires; the men who gave in to their seductions are hanged by . . . a different body part. As one might expect, the men cry out, "We did not know that we should come to eternal punishment!"

And so it goes. The point of the narrative is quite clear: anyone who wants to enjoy the blessings of heaven and escape the torments of hell needs to live a proper, moral, and upright life. Otherwise the flames of hell are waiting.

The Coptic Apocalypse of Peter

There is another Apocalypse of Peter that is decidedly not proto-orthodox. Rather, it is a Gnostic text, discovered along with the Gospel of Thomas at Nag Hammadi, that provides a firsthand account of the crucifixion of Jesus. To those familiar with the accounts of the New Testament, this narrative will seem very bizarre indeed.

After Peter receives a secret revelation from Jesus, he has a vision that he cannot understand. He is standing on a hill talking with Jesus when he sees Jesus down below being arrested and then crucified. More peculiar still, he also sees a figure above the cross who is happy and laughing. He asks Jesus, standing next to him, what it is he is seeing, and Jesus explains. The one the soldiers are crucifying is merely his outer shell; the one above the cross is his true self, the spiritual being who cannot suffer.

This odd image is closely tied to the Gnostic understanding of Christ spelled out earlier, in which the man Jesus was temporarily inhabited by the divine Christ. Here the Christ is laughing precisely because the people crucifying him don't understand what they are doing. They are simply killing the body, the clay vessel, that the divine being had inhabited, but they can't hurt him, the real Christ. He is incorporeal and above all pain and suffering. And he finds the ignorance of his enemies hilarious.

It is no surprise that a text like this had no chance of making it into the proto-orthodox canon, since it celebrates a view of Christ that the proto-orthodox vigorously denounced as heretical.

THE DEBATES LEADING TO THE ESTABLISHMENT OF THE CANON

There were lots of other books considered sacred by one or another group that I have not been able to discuss here. Some were proto-orthodox, others were not: Gospels allegedly by or embodying the perspective of Jesus' brother James, his disciple Philip, Mary Magdalene, Judas Iscariot, and many more. There were books of Acts that describe the missionary endeavors of John, Andrew, Peter, Thomas, and others. There were letters allegedly from Paul to the Christians of Laodicea and correspondence with the Roman philosopher Seneca; letters allegedly from Peter and James; letters from one of the first bishops of Rome, Clement; Apocalypses and Secret Revelations of Paul, John, James, and a Roman Christian named Hermas. But the ones I've discussed can at least give you an idea of what was being written, and read.

The Case of the Gospel of Peter

With all these books floating around, many of them representing a very wide range of theological points of view, how did the proto-orthodox go about deciding which ones to include in their canon of Scripture? An instructive anecdote is told by the fourth-century historian Eusebius, the so-called father of church history. Eusebius tells a story about a second-century bishop named Serapion and his encounter with a Gospel allegedly written by none other than Jesus' right-hand man, Simon Peter.

Serapion was the bishop of the large church of Antioch, in Syria. As part of his official duties he occasionally made the rounds among the towns and villages under his jurisdiction. According to Eusebius, on one occasion Serapion visited the Christian church in the village of Rhossus and while there learned that there were some disputes among the Christians involving a Gospel by Peter. Without reading the book himself, Serapion reasoned that if Peter had written a Gospel, it must be acceptable, and so he told the church members to go ahead and read it.

When he returned home to Antioch, however, some informers came forward to tell him that this was a heretical book, used by docetic Christians—Christians who, like Marcion and some Gnostics, denied that Jesus was fully human but only appeared to be. Serapion obtained a copy of the book to evaluate its teaching. In his opinion most of the book was orthodox in its views, but there were some passages that were questionable, open to a docetic interpretation.

He fired a letter off to the church in which he detailed the problems with the book and concluded that in light of its dubious passages it could not actually have been written by Peter. He forbade the church to continue using it.

Eusebius tells this story and actually quotes portions of Serapion's letter. Unfortunately, he does not quote the passages that Serapion cited from the Gospel that made it appear potentially heretical. This is a real shame, since a fragmentary copy of a Gospel allegedly written by Peter turned up in modern times, and it looks very much like the Gospel that Serapion discussed. But since Eusebius preserves none of his quotations of the book, we can't know for sure whether it is the same book or not.

The modern discovery occurred during the winter of 1868–69, when a French archaeological team was digging in an ancient cemetery in Akhmim, Egypt. They uncovered the tomb of a person they took to be a monk who was buried with a book. The book contained sixty-six pages on which were transcribed portions of four texts— it was a small anthology. One of the texts was a Greek copy of the proto-orthodox Apocalypse of Peter, but the most sensational text was a Gospel, written in the first person, allegedly by Simon Peter.

Regrettably the text is fragmentary. It begins in the middle of a sentence, in an account of Jesus' trial before Pontius Pilate, and it ends in the middle of a sentence, in a story that appears to be an account of Jesus appearing to his disciples after his resurrection. Between these two partial sentences is a narrative of Jesus' trial, condemnation, death, and resurrection.

The account is like the Gospels of the New Testament in many ways. But just as they all differ from one another, so, too, this account differs from each of them. For one thing, the Jewish leaders and Jewish people are portrayed far more negatively here than even in the canonical accounts. It is the Jewish king, Herod, not the Roman governor, Pilate, who condemns Jesus to death. The Jewish leaders are fully culpable in his execution. The Jewish people realize that they are now under the judgment of God, that in fact their city of Jerusalem might now be destroyed in judgment (later Christians interpreted the destruction of Jerusalem in 70 CE as God's punishment for the death of the Messiah).

Probably the most striking feature of the account is that it gives a narrative of the resurrection. The four Gospels of the New Testament indicate that Jesus was buried and on the third day the women find the tomb empty, but there is no account of Jesus coming out of the tomb. This Gospel does narrate the event, however—and quite an amazing account it is. In the middle of the night two angels descend from heaven and the stone is seen to roll away from the tomb of its own accord. The angels enter and then come out with their heads reaching up to the sky, supporting a third figure. It is obviously Jesus, whose head reaches above the sky. Behind them the cross emerges from the tomb. A voice comes from heaven asking if the Gospel has been preached to those "who are asleep" (the dead). And the cross replies, "Yes!"

A giant Jesus and a walking, talking cross. It's hard to believe that this Gospel was ever lost. Is it the one known to Serapion? Most scholars have concluded that it is. It is a Gospel allegedly by Peter. It is for the most part theologically acceptable, in proto-orthodox terms, but there are some passages that could be interpreted in a docetic way. The body of Jesus does not seem like a real human body at the resurrection, for example, and we are told that earlier, while Jesus was being crucified, "he was silent as if he felt no pain." Maybe he really didn't feel pain. Maybe this is docetic. Even if it is *not* docetic, it is at least possible to see how someone might interpret it as docetic, which is what Serapion seems to imply. My hunch is that this is a fragmentary copy of the text available to Serapion at the end of the second century.

What is most important for our purposes here is how Serapion decided whether or not the book was acceptable for use in the church— whether it should be considered an authoritative book of Scripture. Since, for Serapion, the book was susceptible to a docetic interpretation, it was potentially heretical. And because it was potentially heretical, it could not have been written by Peter, who naturally would not advance any theological view that ran counter to the proto-orthodox position. Since it was not by Peter, it could not be considered Scripture. For Serapion, a book could be Scripture only if it taught orthodox doctrine and was written by an apostle.

These two criteria were the most important among the proto-orthodox leaders who decided which books should make up the canon of the New Testament.

An Early Attempt at the Canon: The Muratorian Canon

The decision about which books should make up the canon was not made overnight. Not until the end of the fourth century—some three hundred years after most of the books of the New Testament had been written—did anyone of record indicate that he thought the New Testament consisted of the twenty-seven books we have today, and only those books.

By then debates had been going on for a very long time. The very first attempt that we know of to set down a list of books that the author, who was anonymous, believed formed the Christian Scriptures comes from about the time of Serapion. This fragmentary list is called the Muratorian Canon, named after L. A. Muratori, the eighteenth-century Italian scholar who discovered it in the city of Milan.

The fragment is a simple list of books with occasional comments by the author about the books he lists. It is written in truly awful Latin, which most scholars have taken to be a wretched attempt to translate the text from Greek. The fragment itself dates from the eighth century, but it is usually thought that the list originated at the end of the second century, probably near Rome.[12] The first part of the list is missing. After a few words from the end of a sentence describing one of the Gospels, the author continues by speaking of Luke as "the third book of the Gospel." He continues by naming John as the "fourth," and goes from there. It is almost certain, since Luke and John are the third and fourth Gospels, that the list began with Matthew and Mark.

The unknown author includes twenty-two of our twenty-seven books as canonical—all except Hebrews, James, 1 and 2 Peter, and 3 John. But he also includes the Wisdom of Solomon and the proto-orthodox Apocalypse of Peter. He indicates that the apocalypse known as The Shepherd of Hermas is acceptable for reading but not as part of the church's sacred Scriptures. He goes on to reject two letters allegedly from Paul, those to the Alexandrians and the Laodiceans, which he indicates are forgeries made by the followers of Marcion. He then mentions other forgeries written by other heretics, including some Gnostics.

The Muratorian Canon is especially valuable if it really does come from the second century,[13] because this would indicate that at least one proto-orthodox author was interested in knowing which books could be accepted as canonical Scripture; it shows that there was a concern to eliminate from Scripture any forgeries or heretical documents; and it shows that there was already the acceptance in some circles of books that eventually were to become canonical, although a couple of other books were included as well.

But the matter continued to be debated for centuries. We know this in part from manuscripts we have of the New Testament. Once we get into the sixth and seventh centuries, manuscripts containing books that were considered parts of the New Testament usually do not include anything besides canonical books, but this is not true of earlier periods. The Codex Alexandrinus, a famous manuscript of the fifth century, includes as part of the New Testament the books of 1 and 2 Clement, allegedly written by the man Peter had appointed to be the bishop of Rome. And the Codex Sinaiticus, from the fourth century, includes both the letter of Barnabas and The Shepherd of Hermas. Earlier still is our first copy of the books of 1 and 2 Peter and Jude, found in a manuscript called P^{72}, since it was the seventy-second papyrus manuscript of the New Testament to be catalogued. In addition to these three books, the manuscript contains numerous others, including a Gospel allegedly written by Jesus' brother James, "The Nativity of Mary," more frequently known as the Proto-Gospel of James; 3 Corinthians; and a homily by the church father Melito on the Passover.

What were the power dynamics involved with deciding which books should be in and which out? To make fuller sense of the development of the canon, we need to know more about how the proto-orthodox Christians emerged victorious in their struggles for dominance over other groups within the early church. This takes us straight into the relationship between orthodoxy and heresy.

ORTHODOXY AND HERESY IN THE EARLY CHURCH

From the very beginning, when the competition for converts began, there were different Christian groups claiming to represent "the truth" as told by Jesus and his apostles. Our very earliest Christian author, Paul, talks at length about Christian missionaries who preached "another gospel," which of course for him was a false Gospel (Galatians 1:6–9). Naturally, his opponents thought that they were right and that he was the one who had gotten it wrong. They believed their views were those of Jesus and his original disciples. And they no doubt had writings to prove it. But these writings have all been lost to posterity. Only Paul's letters opposing their views survive.

What was the relationship among the various groups of Christians from Paul's day down through the second and third Christian centuries? For most of Christian history, the relationship was understood through the lens of the fourth-century orthodox church father Eusebius, whose ten-volume work, *The Church History*, contains a good deal of information about the progress of Christianity from its inception to the time of Constantine.

Eusebius's View of Orthodoxy and Heresy

Since Eusebius's *Church History* is our only source of information about much of what happened in the second and third Christian centuries, it is no surprise that Eusebius's perspective shaped how Christian scholars through the ages understood the relationship of orthodoxy and heresy in the period. As a member of the Christian group that won out over the others, Eusebius maintained that the views he and like-minded Christian leaders of the fourth century held were not only right (orthodox) but also that they were the same views Jesus and his apostles had promoted from day one.

To be sure, there were occasional dissenters, as willful heretics tried to pervert the original message of Jesus. To Eusebius, anyone

promoting one of these alternative perspectives (including the Ebionites, Marcion, the various Gnostics) was inspired by wicked demons
and represented only a fringe movement in the great forward progress of orthodoxy. For Eusebius, certain beliefs were and always had
been orthodox: the belief that there was only one God, the creator of
all; that the material world was created good; that Jesus, God's son,
was both human and divine. These were the original beliefs of the
church and had always been the majority view.

Heresies, then, were seen to be offshoots of orthodoxy that came
along as the demons tried to work their nefarious purposes in the
church and pervert the truth. Heresy was always secondary (coming
after orthodoxy), derivative (altering the views of orthodoxy), and
perverted. But God was ultimately triumphant, and the truth suppressed these heretical movements, until the orthodox Christian
religion became a powerful force near the time of the emperor
Constantine.

Walter Bauer's Bombshell

This was the view that virtually every scholar of the church accepted until the early twentieth century. All that changed with
the publication of one of the most important books to be written
about early Christianity in modern times, Walter Bauer's *Orthodoxy
and Heresy in Earliest Christianity* (1934; originally published in
German). Bauer took issue with Eusebius on a number of key points
and reconceptualized what had happened in the struggle for theological dominance in the early church.

Bauer looked at our earliest evidence for Christianity in a range
of geographical regions throughout early Christendom—for example, in Egypt, Syria, Asia Minor, and Rome.[14] He found that if the
sources are studied in minute detail, they tell a very different story
from the one told by Eusebius. In many places of early Christianity,
forms of Christian belief that were later labeled heretical were the
original form of Christianity, and in some parts of the church so-called

heretics outnumbered those who agreed with the orthodox form of the faith. In some places Marcionite Christianity was dominant; in other places, one or another of the Gnostic systems prevailed.

Moreover, a number of Christian groups saw no sharp divisions between what would later be called heresy and what would be called orthodoxy. The clear theological distinctions of Eusebius's day were not original to the faith, but were created later when the battle lines were drawn up. Some people who were later considered heretics would have been seen, and were seen, as completely orthodox in their own day.

The way Bauer saw it, the church of the second and third centuries was not made up of one massive and dominant movement known as orthodoxy, with heretical groups at the fringes. Early on there were all sorts of groups with all sorts of views in lots of different places. Of course, all of these groups believed that their views were right, that their beliefs were orthodox.

But in the struggle to win converts, only one group eventually won out; this was the group that was particularly well represented in the city of Rome. The Roman Christians asserted their influence on other churches; as the church in Rome, the center of the empire, this community was larger, wealthier, and better organized than other Christian groups.

This Roman group acquired more converts than any of the others, eventually stamped out all of its competition, declared itself orthodox, argued that its views really were those of Jesus and the apostles, claimed that it had always been the majority view, and then—as a final coup de grâce—rewrote the history of the conflict. What emerged was a Christianity characteristic of the Roman church. It was Roman Christianity—Roman *catholic* (meaning universal) Christianity.

Eusebius stands at the end of this process. It was his rewriting of history that made all later historians think that his group had always been the majority opinion. But it did not really happen that way.

In the Aftermath of Bauer

Needless to say, Bauer's book created quite a storm, and the winds of controversy have not died down yet. Many scholars, especially those who considered themselves heirs of the Christian orthodoxy embraced by Eusebius, rejected Bauer wholesale. But other scholars were convinced, and continue to be convinced.[15]

Among critical scholars today the majority opinion seems to be that in many, many details of his analysis Bauer is wrong, or at least that he has overplayed his hand. He sometimes makes dubious arguments and in places attacks the surviving sources with inappropriate inquisitorial zeal. And Rome may not have been as central to the process as he would have it.

But Bauer's basic portrayal of Christianity's early centuries appears to be correct. There were lots of early Christian groups. They all claimed to be right. They all had books to back up their claims, books allegedly written by the apostles and therefore representing the views of Jesus and his first disciples. The group that won out did not represent the teachings of Jesus or of his apostles. For example, none of the apostles claimed that Jesus was "fully God and fully man," or that he was "begotten not made, of one substance with the Father," as the fourth-century Nicene Creed maintained. The victorious group called itself orthodox. But it was not the original form of Christianity, and it won its victory only after many hard-fought battles.

This view of things has been confirmed by almost every archaeological discovery made since Bauer's time. To be sure, most of these finds come from Egypt, but that is just an accident of climate: Egypt's dry sands allow documents to survive almost permanently. The finds come from different parts of Egypt, and there is no guarantee that a document found in Egypt originated there, given what we know about the extensive travel and interchange of books that occurred throughout the empire.

Amazingly, virtually every time a new document is found, it is "heretical" rather than "proto-orthodox."[16] These include such nonorthodox works as the Nag Hammadi treatises discovered in 1945; a book called the Gospel of the Savior (found in Egypt), uncovered in a museum in Berlin in the 1990s; and the most recent discovery, the Gnostic Gospel of Judas, found in the late 1970s and first published in 2006.[17] Why don't proto-orthodox (noncanonical) texts ever appear? Were the heretics the only ones doing any writing? Or was heresy much more widely spread and significant than Eusebius knows or lets on?

It appears that alternative views of Christianity were dominant during certain time periods and in some locations, most demonstrably in Egypt, but probably in lots of other places as well. Eventually these views were stamped out. How did it happen? What were the weapons that the proto-orthodox used in their quest to gain converts and displace their opponents, leading to the emergence of their doctrines as orthodoxy?

THE WEAPONS OF THE CONFLICT

When one reads through the ancient discussions of orthodoxy and heresy, it becomes clear that the proto-orthodox had three major weapons that it used to combat Christian views that it considered aberrant: the clergy, the creed, and the canon.

The Clergy

Unlike some other Christian groups, the proto-orthodox Christians insisted that there should be a rigid hierarchy in the churches, in which one leader, the bishop, was given authority over the congregation. The bishop had groups of leaders under him: elders (called presbyters), who evidently were most directly involved with the spiritual needs of a congregation, and deacons (literally, "ministers"), who may have been more involved with the congregation's physical needs, such as alms giving and the like. Already by the early second century, a proto-orthodox author such as Ignatius of Antioch could argue quite vociferously that church members were to "regard the bishop as the Lord himself" (Ignatius, *To the Ephesians*, 6.1).

Anyone with that much power could obviously shape things in his church the way he wanted. Other Christian groups, such as many of the Gnostics, were not as interested in centralized power. Gnostics believed that everyone in the true church had a spark of the divine within and could receive the secret knowledge that brings salvation. As a result, many Gnostics were egalitarian. But not the proto-orthodox. Taking their lead from what was already a movement in this direction in the Pastoral Epistles, they insisted on having clearly designated leaders who could make decisions. Having the right person in power made a difference. The proto-orthodox used their influence wherever possible to make sure that the bishop toed the line theologically, and insisted that the bishop exercise his control over the thinking of the church. An example of this is Serapion's exercise of power over the church at Rhossus described earlier.

The Creed

Proto-orthodox Christians began to insist that there was only one true faith, the one they subscribed to. Some of their views began to take on a paradoxical cast, as they insisted, for example, that Jesus was fully divine (against the Ebionites) and fully human (against the Marcionites) but only one person, not two (against the Gnostics). They insisted that there was only one God. But Jesus himself was also God. They insisted that the true God had created this world, even though sin had corrupted the world.

I will be dealing more with the development of several important theological views in the next chapter. For now I want to emphasize that over time the proto-orthodox developed a set of beliefs that it insisted were standard and had to be accepted by everyone in the church. We find early traces of this development in the writings of late-second- and early-third-century church fathers, such as Irenaeus and Tertullian, who argued that a "rule of faith" came down from the apostles, which was to be accepted by all Christians. This rule included important ideas that became the backbone of orthodoxy and negated other views: there is only one God; he is the creator; Christ is human but also divine.

These views eventually came to be crystallized in the creeds— statements of faith—that were written by orthodox Christians of the fourth century, including those that came to be known as the Apostles' Creed and the Nicene Creed, which are still recited in churches today.

By having a set of beliefs that everyone was required to accept and that the bishop enforced, the proto-orthodox intended to weed out those who subscribed to what they considered false beliefs. But on what basis did they make their theological decisions? They claimed, at least, to base their views on divinely inspired texts, the books of the canon.

The Canon

In a sense, the Christian church, in all its varieties, started out with a body of Scripture. Jesus was a Jewish teacher who taught his Jewish disciples a particular understanding of the Jewish Scriptures. The Jewish Bible was the original Christian canon. It is not completely clear which books that later came to be the Old Testament were accepted as Scripture in Jesus' day; almost certainly they included the law of Moses (the first five books), the prophets, and a number of the other books, such as the Psalms. Jews were in the process of formulating their canon at the same time as the Christians.

It was not long after Jesus' death, however, that Christians started appealing to other authorities as standing on a par with Scripture. Jesus' words themselves functioned as a kind of scriptural authority for his followers. And writers like Paul, even though he didn't think of himself as writing the Bible, considered their own writings to have authority over their congregations. Eventually two kinds of Christian authorities emerged: Gospels—containing Jesus' words, but also much more—and the writings of apostles.

The problem the proto-orthodox had to face from early on was that so many books claimed to be written by apostles. How were they to decide which ones really were apostolic, and therefore authoritative? No one from the early church actually lays out a set of criteria to be followed, but by reading such ancient accounts as Eusebius's story of Serapion and the account in the Muratorian Canon, it becomes evident that four criteria were particularly important:

- *Antiquity.* By the second and third centuries it was clear to many of the proto-orthodox that even if a recently penned writing was important, useful, and trustworthy, it could not be seen as sacred Scripture. Scriptural books had to be ancient, going back to the original decades of the Christian church.

- *Catholicity.* Only those books that were widely used throughout the proto-orthodox church could be accepted as Scripture. Books that had only local appeal might be valuable, but they could not be considered part of the canon.

- *Apostolicity.* This is one of the most important of the criteria. For a book to be considered Scripture it had to have been written by an apostle or a companion of an apostle. That's why the Gospels were attributed to particular people: Scripture was not acceptable if it was anonymous or if it had been written by any ole person. The books needed to have an apostolic origin. In many cases it was difficult to make this judgment. Serapion decided that the Gospel of Peter was not really written by Peter, even though it claimed to be. He did not reach this conclusion by the kind of historical analysis that a modern critic might use. The basis of his decision was quite simple— his preexisting ideas: the book was not sufficiently orthodox, and so could not have been written by Peter.

- *Orthodoxy.* Serapion's use of a theological criterion is indicative of how such judgments were typically made. The most important gauge for whether a book could be considered sacred

Scripture was whether it promoted a view that the proto-orthodox considered to be acceptable theologically. Books that were not orthodox were nonapostolic; and if they were nonapostolic they could not be scriptural.

In the long and protracted debates over canon, it was not hard for the proto-orthodox to weed out books that were clearly unorthodox, including all of the Gnostic Gospels, for example. Even though it was claimed that Gospels had been written by Thomas, Philip, Mary Magdalene, and others, these claims could not be sustained. The evidence was a priori: the books were heretical, and apostles would never write heresy.

There were numerous other books, too, that stood on the fringes, books that looked perfectly orthodox and that made apostolic claims, but that were not obvious candidates for inclusion. Some of these were the Apocalypse of Peter, the letter of Barnabas, and 1 Clement.

The first time any author from Christian antiquity lists our twenty-seven books and indicates that they are the only twenty-seven books of the canon comes in the year 367 CE. The author is Athanasius, the famous bishop of Alexandria, Egypt. Years earlier Athanasius had played a role in the Council of Nicaea, the first church council to be called by a Roman emperor, Constantine, to resolve important theological issues in the church. After Athanasius became bishop of the important church in Alexandria, he wrote a letter every year to the congregations under his jurisdiction, in order to inform them when the feast of Easter was to be celebrated that year (they didn't have years mapped out in advance, like today). In his thirty-ninth "Festal Letter," Athanasius, as was his wont, gave his readers a good deal of additional pastoral advice, including a list of books that could be read in church. He listed all the books of our New Testament.

Two points are worth making. This list of Athanasius's did not end all discussion of the matter. For centuries various churches continued to accept slightly different lists. The Armenian church continued to accept 3 Corinthians as canonical. Even in Athanasius's own church of Alexandria there were Christian leaders who had somewhat different views.[18] But for the most part, moving into the fifth century and later, Athanasius's canon became the canon of the orthodox church at large. These books and only these books were copied by scribes who reproduced the Scriptures throughout the Middle Ages. And even though no worldwide church council ever ratified Athanasius's list for over a millennium, popular usage provided a kind of de facto ratification, down to the time of the invention of printing. Once Bibles could be easily printed, after the invention of movable type in the fifteenth century, the canon was a done deal. From here on out there were no doubts concerning which books were to be included, and in which order. Today, wherever you buy a New Testament in the English-speaking world, it will be the same group of books, in the same sequence.

The second point to make is rather obvious. It took at least three hundred years of debate before the question of the canon even began to reach closure. The decisions that were eventually made were not handed down from on high, and they did not come right away. The canon was the result of a slow and often painful process, in which lots of disagreements were aired and different points of view came to be expressed, debated, accepted, and suppressed. Whatever Christian theologians and other believers might maintain about the divine impetus and guidance behind the canonization of Scripture, it is also clear that it was a very human process, driven by a large number of historical and cultural factors.

CONCLUSION

Sometimes when I give lectures on the formation of the Christian canon, I am asked whether there are any books that I would like to see removed from the canon, and any that I would like to see added. It's a delightful question to think about, but my first response is always to say that no matter what scholars say, the canon is never going to change. The New Testament has twenty-seven books now and it will always have twenty-seven books, world without end.

When pressed I do admit that there are a few books that I would not mind seeing omitted. At the top on my list would probably be 1 Timothy, forged in Paul's name by someone living later, who was so vehemently opposed to women actively involved in the churches that he ordered them to be silent and to "exercise no authority over a man." If they want to be saved, he indicates, it will be through "bearing children." That's great—women have to be silent, submissive, and pregnant. Not exactly a liberated view, and one that has done a world of damage over the years. I wouldn't be sorry to see it taken out.

What would I put in? It'd be nice to have a giant Jesus and a walking-talking cross, but the Gospel of Peter carries too much other baggage, including a scary dose of anti-Judaism. Maybe I would include one of the infancy Gospels, where Jesus works his miraculous powers, often with more than a touch of mischievousness, starting as a five-year-old. But that, too, would probably start getting people upset. At the end of the day, the canon is the canon, and there's little point in thinking how we might want to change it. Better to figure out how to encourage interpretations of it that don't lead to sexism, racism, bigotry, and all kinds of oppression.

When I started studying the Bible as a teenager, with more passion than knowledge (lots of passion; no knowledge), I naturally assumed that this book was given by God. My early teachers in the Bible encouraged that belief and drove it home for me, with increasingly sophisticated views about how God had inspired Scripture, making it a kind of blueprint for my life, telling me what to believe, how to behave, and what to expect would happen when this world came to a crashing halt, soon, with the appearance of Jesus on the clouds of heaven.

Obviously I no longer look at the Bible that way. Instead I see it as a very human book, not a divinely inspired one. To be sure, a good many parts of it are inspiring, but I no longer see God's hand behind it all. We don't have the originals that any of these authors wrote, only copies that have been changed by human hands all over the map. And the books that we consider Scripture came to be formed into a canon centuries after they were written. This was not, in my opinion, the result of divine activity; it was the result of very human church leaders (all of them men) doing their best to decide what was right.

Most believing Christians and Christian theologians see the process differently, insisting that God's hand was constantly at work behind the long, drawn-out process. As a historian I have no real way, ultimately, to evaluate that claim. What I can say is that however divine the process was (or was not), it was certainly a very human one, with the decisions being made by humans who based their decisions on a lot of factors. They wanted the churches to be unified in the face of opposition from the outside. They wanted everyone in the church to agree on important aspects of Christian doctrine. They didn't want troublemakers in their midst. They wanted to be assured that they had the one orthodox teaching that had been handed down by Jesus to his apostles and on to posterity. They wanted to know they were right.

Their desires for certainty butted up against some unfortunate historical realities. There were other people who also wanted to know that they were right, and these other people had beliefs that stood directly at odds with what they themselves believed. Who, really, was right? The formation of the canon is in some sense a movement to decide that issue. The final decisions were not a foregone conclusion. For centuries there continued to be Christians who insisted that this, that, or the other book had a rightful place in the canon. But eventually, by the beginning of the fourth century, the options were narrowed in proto-orthodox circles; somewhat later there were no options at all. Because of a series of historical, cultural, political, and social factors that informed and guided the debates, one canon of Scripture finally emerged, centuries after the process began. It is still the canon we have with us today, and it will be the canon of the church for as long as the church survives.

Who Invented Christianity?

In the American South, where I live, Christianity is very much about the Bible. Most Christians come from churches that preach the Bible, teach the Bible, adhere (they claim) to the Bible. It is almost "common sense" among many Christians in this part of the world that if you don't believe in the Bible you cannot be a Christian.

Most Christians in other parts of the world—in fact, the vast majority of Christians throughout the history of the church—would find that common sense to be nonsense. For most Christians, Christian faith is about believing in Christ and worshipping God through him. It is not about belief in the Bible. When I tell people that in churches here I'm often met with firm disbelief—how could so many Christians, they wonder, get it so wrong. But it's true. Just look at the Christian creeds that are still recited throughout the world today, the Apostles' Creed and the Nicene Creed. Not a word about the Bible. In traditional Christianity the Bible itself has never been an object of faith.

In the South, it is true, more people revere the Bible than read it. This became clear to me a few years ago when I started asking my undergraduate classes about their views of the Bible. I get the same response every year. The first day of class, with over three hundred students present, I ask: "How many of you would agree with the proposition that the Bible is the inspired Word of God?" *Whoosh!* Virtually everyone in the auditorium raises their hand. I then ask, "How many of you have read one or more of the Harry Potter books?" *Whoosh!* The whole auditorium. Then I ask, "And how many of you have read the entire Bible." Scattered hands, a few students here and there.

I always laugh and say, "Okay, look. I'm not saying that I think God wrote the Bible. You're telling me that you think God wrote the Bible. I can see why you might want to read a book by J. K. Rowling. But if God wrote a book . . . wouldn't you want to see what he has to say?" For me it's just one of the mysteries of the universe: how so many people can revere the Bible and think that in it is God's inspired revelation to his people, and yet know so little about it.

Throughout this book I've been talking about historical-critical problems with the Bible: contradictions in details, discrepancies on major points of view, authors claiming to be apostles when they weren't, historical problems in the reconstruction of the life of Jesus, and so on. These are not problems that I have made up or discovered on my own. They are problems that scholars have been talking about for two hundred years, that professors in universities and seminaries have known and taught for as long as any of us has been alive, that most pastors learn in seminary. These are problems that are well known to anyone who has engaged in serious research into the Bible but that the average person on the street or the average person in the pew has never heard of.

My overarching argument has been that the Bible, my field of study and expertise, is a very human book. For the past twenty years, though, much of my serious research has been devoted to a different but related field—the development of Christianity in the second and third Christian centuries, after the books of the New Testament were written.

And so in this final chapter I want to go further afield to look not just at the New Testament (although that will be part of this examination as well) but also at the formation of the Christian religion more generally. My thesis here is that not only is the Bible a very human book, but that Christianity as it has developed and come down to us today is a very human religion.

The Christian claim that their religion is also divinely inspired is a theological view that historians have no way of evaluating; historians don't have access to God, only to what happens here on earth in front of our eyes—or in front of someone else's eyes. I personally do not accept this view any longer (though I once did); but as you will see in the final chapter, the historical findings I am discussing here do not necessarily lead to my personal agnostic conclusions. But they should lead all people to see the human element in the development of the Christian religion.

We saw in the previous chapter that the canon of Scripture was a human creation, as Christians struggled over the question of which books to include in the New Testament, struggles that involved long, protracted, and often heated debates over what was the proper form of belief (orthodoxy) and what was improper (heresies). What else did Christians invent on the way to making Christianity into the religion it became? In this chapter I will consider some of the key aspects of the Christian religion and see how they emerged historically. All of these are extremely important identifying features of the emergent Christian religion.

A SUFFERING MESSIAH

The belief in a suffering Messiah is absolutely central to the Christian religion. The term "Messiah" is simply the Hebrew equivalent of the Greek term "Christ." I have to tell my students this because some of them think that Christ was Jesus' last name—Jesus Christ, born to Joseph and Mary Christ. Christ eventually *did* become such a common designation for Jesus that it started to function as his name, but originally "Jesus Christ" meant "Jesus is the Messiah."

Christians' Views of the Messiah

Calling Jesus the Messiah seems so natural and obvious to many Christians that they don't understand why Jews don't accept him as the Messiah. In the Christian tradition it is believed that the prophets of the Jewish Bible constantly and repeatedly make predictions about what the Messiah would do, be like, and experience, and Jesus fulfilled all of these prophecies. It was predicted that he would be born of a virgin (and for them, Jesus was), that he would be born in Bethlehem (Jesus was), that he would be a great healer (Jesus was), that he would ride into Jerusalem on a donkey (Jesus did), that he would be rejected by his own people (Jesus was), that he would suffer a horrible death by execution (Jesus did), and that he would rise from the dead (Jesus did).

For many Christians, since all of these predictions of the prophets of the Old Testament were fulfilled by Jesus, it is obvious that he must be the Messiah. Many Christians wonder why Jews refuse to believe it. How can Jews fail to accept the claims of Christ? Why don't they believe? Are they just being stubborn? Are they hardheaded? Can't they read? Are they stupid?

Jewish Expectations of the Messiah

Why is it that the vast majority of Jews has always rejected that Jesus is the one who was predicted—a savior sent from God in order to suffer for others, so as to bring salvation, and then be raised from the dead?

The answer is actually quite simple. In the Jewish tradition, before the appearance of Christianity, there was no expectation of a suffering Messiah.

But doesn't the Bible constantly talk about the Messiah who would suffer? As it turns out, the answer is no. Since the beginning, Christians have frequently cited certain passages in the Old Testament as clear prophecies of the future suffering Messiah, passages such as

Isaiah 53 and Psalm 22, in which someone suffers horribly, sometimes expressly for the sins of others. These passages, Christians have claimed, are clear statements about what the Messiah would be like. Jews who do not believe in Jesus, however, have always had a very effective response: the Messiah is never mentioned in these passages. You can check it out for yourself: read Isaiah 53 or Psalm 22 (I'll quote the relevant verses later in this chapter). The term "Messiah" never occurs in them. In Jewish tradition, these passages refer not to the Messiah but to someone else (or to lots of someone elses).

Before Christianity there were no Jews that we know of who anticipated a Messiah who would suffer and die for the sins of others and then be raised from the dead. What then would the Messiah be like? We know from Jewish documents written around the time of Jesus that there were various expectations of what the Messiah would be like. In none of these expectations was he anything like Jesus.

The term "Messiah" literally means "anointed one." It was used of various figures in the Old Testament—for example, priests and kings—who were ceremonially anointed with oil as a symbol of divine favor, indicating that God had set them apart to perform their tasks (1 Samuel 10:1; Leviticus 4:3, 5). The classical Jewish view of the Messiah derived from the ancient Israelite view of kingship.

According to traditions found in ancient Israel, God promised King David that there would always be a descendant of David sitting on the throne of Israel (1 Samuel 7:14–16). But the vicissitudes of history created a disconfirmation of this promise. The nation of Judah, over which the Davidic monarch had reigned for over four hundred years, was destroyed by the Babylonians in 586 BCE. There was no longer a Davidic king sitting on the throne. But God had promised that there always would be. How could the promise be reconciled with the historical reality?

Some Jews thought that God would make good on his promise by restoring an anointed king to rule Israel when he was finished punishing his people for their disobedience. This would be the Messiah, the newly anointed one, a great warrior-king like David who would overthrow the enemies of Israel and establish Israel once again as a sovereign state in the land. This hope ebbed and flowed over the years, as the Babylonians were succeeded by the Persians, then the Greeks, then the Egyptians, then the Syrians, then the Romans: all of them controlling the land of Israel, and no descendant of David on the throne, down to the time of Jesus.

In the days of Jesus, many Jews were probably not thinking much about a future Messiah, just as most Jews today aren't. Those Jews who were expecting a Messiah, however, believed that God would fulfill his promise, a promise found in such messianic passages as Psalm 2:1–9 in the Hebrew Bible:

> Why do the nations conspire and the peoples plot in vain? The kings of the earth set themselves and the rulers take counsel together, against the LORD and his anointed [literally "Messiah"], saying, "Let us burst their bonds asunder, and cast their cord from us." He who sits in the heavens laughs; the LORD has them in derision. Then he will speak to them in his wrath, and terrify them in his fury, saying, "I have set my king on Zion, my holy hill." I will tell of the decree of the LORD: He said to me, "You are my son; today I have begotten you. Ask of me and I will make the nations your heritage and the end of the earth your possession. You shall break them with a rod of iron, and dash them in pieces like a potter's vessel.

The obvious expectation is for a great and powerful king in the line of David who will be the Son of God just as David's successors were (see 2 Samuel 7:14). That this expectation of a future political Messiah was alive and well in the days of Jesus is evident from Jewish writings of the time. One particularly clear statement of the expectation of this Messiah comes from outside the Bible, in a book called the Psalms of Solomon, written some decades before Jesus' birth. Notice what kind of person the Messiah would be:

See, Lord, and raise up for them their king, the son of David, to rule over your servant Israel in the time known to you, O God. Undergird him with the strength to destroy the unrighteous rulers, to purge Jerusalem from gentiles, who trample her to destruction; in wisdom and in righteousness to drive out the sinners from the inheritance; to smash the arrogance of sinners like a potters' jar; to shatter all their substance with an iron rod; to destroy the unlawful nations with the word of his mouth. . . . He will gather a holy people whom he shall lead in righteousness. . . . And he will have gentile nations serving him under his yoke, and he will glorify the Lord in a [place] prominent [above] the whole earth. And he will purify Jerusalem and make it holy as it was even from the beginning. . . . And he will be a righteous king over them, taught by God. There will be no unrighteousness among them in his days, for all shall be holy, and their king shall be the Lord Messiah. (Psalms of Solomon 17:21–32)

That the Messiah would be a powerful warrior-king was the expectation of many Jews in Jesus' day.

But there were other Jews who had other expectations about what the future deliverer of Israel would be. Especially in the apocalyptic tradition, within which Jesus and his followers stood, it was sometimes thought that the future savior would not be merely an earthly king. He would be a cosmic judge of the earth, sent from God to overthrow the forces of evil with a show of strength. This divine figure was called a variety of things in different texts, including "the Son of Man" (based on a reading of Daniel 7:13–14). Consider the two following Jewish texts, dating roughly from the time of the beginning of Christianity:

And they [the people of God] had great joy, and they blessed and praised and exalted because the name of the Son of Man had been revealed to them. And he sat on the throne of his glory, and the whole judgment was given to the Son of Man, and he will cause the sinners to pass away and be destroyed from the face of the earth. And those who led astray the world will be found in chains, and will be shut up in the assembly-place of their destruction, and all their works will pass away from the face of the earth. And from then on there will be nothing corruptible, for that Son of Man has appeared and has sat on the throne of his glory, and everything evil will pass away and go from before him. (1 Enoch 69)

As I kept looking the wind made something like the figure of a man come up out of the heart of the sea. And I saw that this man flew with the clouds of heaven; and everywhere he turned his face to look, everything under his gaze trembled. . . . After this I looked and saw that an innumerable multitude of people were gathered together from the four winds of heaven to make war against the man who came up out of the sea. . . . When he saw the onrush of the approaching multitude, he neither lifted his hand nor held a spear, or any weapon of war; but I saw only how he sent forth from his mouth something like a stream of fire, and from his lips a flaming breath . . .[which] fell on the onrushing multitude that was prepared to fight, and burned up all of them, so that suddenly nothing was seen of the innu-merable multitude but only the dust of ashes and the smell of smoke. (4 Ezra 13:1–11)

A great and powerful warrior-king, or an even more powerful cosmic judge of the earth—this is what some Jews expected of the Messiah. Other Jews had yet different expectations of what a future savior might be like.[1] But the one thing that all the Jewish expecta-tions had in common was this: the future Messiah would be a figure of grandeur and real power, who would overthrow God's enemies in a show of strength and rule over God's people, and the other nations of earth, with a rod of iron.

And who was Jesus? A virtually unknown itinerant preacher from the hinterlands of Galilee who got on the wrong side of the law and was crucified as a political insurgent. Jesus did not overthrow the Romans. The Romans crushed him like a gnat. Calling Jesus the Messiah was for most Jews beyond laughable; it was virtually (or really) a blasphemy against God. *Jesus* is the Messiah? The preacher who got crucified? *That* is God's Messiah? Yeah, right.

When I try to explain to my students how absurd the claim sounded to most Jews, I often resort to an analogy. The gut reaction that many Jews had to the claim that Jesus was the Messiah is comparable to what your reaction would be if I insisted in all earnestness that the Branch Davidian leader David Koresh, who was killed by the FBI at Waco, is the Lord of the universe. David Koresh? Yes, he is the savior of the world and the Lord of all! Oh, sure—what are you, crazy? (I get in trouble for making this analogy every semester; at least one student will say on his or her course evaluation, "I can't believe that Ehrman thinks David Koresh is the Lord of the universe!")

The Basis for the Christians' Claims

If there was no expectation among Jews that the Messiah would suffer and die for sins, why is it that Christians believe in a suffering Messiah? Here's the way it worked historically. Prior to Jesus' death some of his followers evidently thought that he was the Messiah; this conviction shows up throughout the Gospels. But obviously if they said "Jesus is the Messiah," they meant it in a traditional Jewish sense, for example, that he would be the king who would establish the throne once more in Israel and rule over his people. (Remember, though, that Jesus himself appears to have understood the term in a different, apocalyptic, sense).

This hope that Jesus could be the Messiah was radically disconfirmed by the events of history: Jesus never did raise an army, never did drive the Romans out of the promised land, never did establish Israel as a sovereign state. Instead, he got crucified. This showed his followers that their faith in him had been unfounded.

But then they, or at least some of them, came to believe that God had raised Jesus from the dead. This reconfirmed their earlier notion: Jesus really is the one chosen by God! He is God's own son! He is the one upon whom God has shown his special favor, God's anointed one, our savior. He *is* the Messiah!

This reconfirmation forced the earliest Christians into a new understanding of what it meant to be the Messiah. Their logic was impeccable. Jesus is the Messiah. Jesus suffered and died. Therefore, the Messiah had to suffer and die.

But what was one to do with the fact that there were no Jewish prophecies that the Messiah would suffer and die? The earliest Christians began searching the Scriptures for hints of their new belief, and they found them, not in passages that referred to the Messiah but in other passages that describe the suffering of God's righteous one. Christians concluded, and argued, that these passages were actually referring to the Messiah, even though the Messiah is never mentioned in them and even though no one had ever thought, before this, that they referred to the Messiah. But for Christians, such passages as Isaiah 53:1–6 were clear messianic predictions:

> He was despised and rejected by others; a man of suffering and acquainted with infirmity; and as one from whom others hide their faces he was despised, and we held him of no account. Surely he has borne our infirmities and carried our diseases. Yet we accounted him stricken, struck down by God, and afflicted. But he was wounded for our transgressions, crushed for our iniquities; upon him was the punishment that made us whole, and by his bruises we are healed. All we like sheep have gone astray, we have all turned to our own way, and the LORD has laid on him the iniquity of us all.

Jesus' suffering and death were foretold by the prophets. In fact, the first Christians were convinced that there were passages that described the actual crucifixion of the Messiah, such as Psalm 22:1–18:

My God, my God, why have you forsaken me? . . . I am a worm, and not human; scorned by others, and despised by the people. All who see me mock at me; they make mouths at me, they shake their heads. . . . I am poured out like water and all my bones are out of joint; my heart is like wax; it is melted within my breast; my mouth is dried up like a potsherd, and my tongue sticks to my jaws; you lay me in the dust of death. For dogs are all around me; a company of evildoers encircles me. My hands and feet have shriveled; I can count all my bones. They stare and gloat over me. They divide my clothes among themselves, and for my clothing they cast lots.

Originally this passage had nothing to do with a future Messiah, and Jews did not interpret it as a reference to one. But once Jesus' followers came to believe that he was the Messiah, it was only natural that they saw in such passages references to what the Messiah would experience. The debates over Jesus' messiahship ensued. Jews insisted these passages were not referring to the Messiah (and they had a point, since the Messiah is never mentioned in them); Christians insisted that they were. And so the fireworks began.

But what about all the other prophecies that Jesus was said to fulfill: that his mother would be a virgin, that he would be born in Bethlehem, that he would ride into Jerusalem on a donkey, and so on? It is important to remember that our accounts of what Jesus did and experienced have come down to us in Gospels written many years after the fact, based on orally transmitted stories about him that had been in circulation for decades. The people telling the stories of Jesus were not ignorant of the Jewish Scriptures. Some of them knew the Scriptures well, and they told the stories of Jesus in light of what the Scriptures predict. And so, accounts of Jesus' birth, his ministry, his Triumphal Entry, his Passion, and his resurrection were often told with the predictions of Scripture in mind, by storytellers who believed that in Jesus all the promises had been fulfilled.

For example, both Matthew and Luke indicate that Jesus was born in Bethlehem, but they have him born by means of different, contradictory plot devices. Why do they both want him to be born in Bethlehem? Because the Old Testament indicates that a savior will come from Bethlehem (Micah 5:2). But didn't everyone know that he came from Nazareth? Yes, say both Matthew and Luke, Jesus actually grew up in Nazareth. But he was born in Bethlehem, and here is how it happened. The problem is their accounts contradict each other. What does this show? The Christians told stories about Jesus in light of what they believed about him, making sure that at every point, his life fulfilled Scripture, since he was, after all, the suffering Messiah.

In reality, the idea that Jesus was the suffering Messiah was an invention of the early Christians. It is no wonder that the apostle Paul, writing decades after Christians had come up with this idea, indicates that it is the greatest "stumbling block" for Jews (1 Corinthians 1:23). Even though this is the very foundation for all Christian belief, to many Jews it was a ridiculous claim.

Paul saw this claim as valid precisely because it was so foolish (1 Corinthians 1:1:18–25). God's ways are not humans' ways. God has saved the world through a crucified Messiah, as no one would have or could have expected. For Paul this was the central point and the key to the salvation that God had brought to the world (1 Corinthians 15:3–5; Romans 1–3). Through the death of the Messiah God had made salvation available to all people, Jews and gentiles. And Paul pushed this point a step further: it was *only* through the death of the Messiah that a person could be right with God—not, say, through the Jewish law.

But Paul did not make up the idea that the Messiah had to be crucified. The idea had been invented much earlier, as soon as Jesus' original followers came to believe that God had raised him from the dead. Paul inherited this idea when he converted to become a follower of Jesus. It was this idea that eventually led Christianity to break off from Judaism to become its own religion, a religion that stood in direct opposition to Judaism, the religion of Jesus himself.

CHRISTIANITY AS A DISTINCT, ANTI-JEWISH RELIGION

One of the most pressing and intriguing questions that historians of early Christianity have had to face is how the thoroughly Jewish religion of Jesus so quickly transformed itself into a religion of gentiles. How did Christianity move from being a sect within Judaism to becoming a virulently anti-Jewish religion in less than a century?

The Religion of Jesus and His Earliest Followers

We have already seen that there was nothing about Jesus' message or his mission that stood outside Judaism. He was a Jew, born to Jewish parents, raised in a Jewish culture; he became a teacher of the Jewish law, gathered around himself a group of Jewish followers, and instructed them in the essence of what he saw to be the true worship of the Jewish God.

Jesus was an apocalyptic Jewish prophet. He anticipated that the God of the Jews was soon to intervene in history, overthrow the forces of evil, and set up his good kingdom on earth. In order to enter this kingdom, Jesus told the Jewish crowds, they needed to do what God had commanded in the Jewish law. Specifically they needed to carry out the two greatest commandments of the law: love God with all their heart, soul, and strength (quoting Deuteronomy 6:4–6) and love their neighbors as themselves (quoting Leviticus 19:18). "On these two commandments," urged Jesus, "hang all the law and the prophets" (Matthew 22:40).

When one reconstructs the actual sayings and deeds of Jesus, they all stand firmly within this Jewish apocalyptic framework. It was only his later followers who saw him as starting a new religion. He appears to have had no intent to start a new religion. His was the religion of the Jews, correctly interpreted (in opposition, of course, to other interpretations, such as those of the Pharisees and Sadducees).

Some of his later followers retained the Jewish character of his proclamation. As the Christian religion developed in other directions, however, these followers came to be labeled heretics. This is one of the real ironies of the early Christian tradition, that the original form of the religion came to be cast out and denounced.

The followers of Jesus known as the Ebionites urged that Jesus never intended to abrogate the law; since he was the Jewish Messiah sent from the Jewish God to the Jewish people in fulfillment of the Jewish law, and since he himself wholeheartedly embraced the Jewish law, his followers needed to be Jewish—and needed to keep the law. If the law says that the males among the people of God are to be circumcised, then they must be circumcised. If it says the people of God are to keep kosher, they must keep kosher. If it tells them to keep the Sabbath, they must keep the Sabbath. The Ebionites claimed that this was the view promoted by Jesus' own brother, James, the leader of the Church in Jerusalem. Scholars have conceded that they may have been right.

A similar view seems to be preserved in the Gospel of Matthew. To be sure, this Gospel expresses the belief that the death and resurrection of Jesus are key to salvation, as the Ebionites themselves insisted. But it also indicates that Jesus taught his followers that they needed to keep the law if they wanted to enter the kingdom of heaven. In fact, they had to keep it even better than the leaders of the Jews themselves (Matthew 5:17–20). Jesus in this Gospel is portrayed as a teacher of the law who conveys its true meaning to his followers. He never urges them to break any of the laws. He urges them to follow him by observing the law.

The Anti-Jewish Teachings of Jesus' Later Followers

This view of what it meant to follow Jesus was destined to lose out in the struggles over core beliefs in the early church. The apostle Paul's views were different from those of the Ebionites (who saw Paul as the archenemy), of Matthew, and of Jesus himself. Paul was quite vociferous in claiming that the law can have no role in having a right standing before God. Any gentile who came into the church was decidedly not to start keeping the law of the Jews. Paul thought that if a gentile man was circumcised, he was not only doing something unnecessary but was denying the grace of God, which offered salvation as a gift through the death of Jesus, not through the law and the covenant of circumcision. Such a man was actually in danger of losing his salvation (Galatians 5:4).

Did Paul and Matthew see eye to eye on keeping the law? Evidently not. Did Paul and Jesus advocate the same religion? It is a key historical question, and the answer is hard to deny. Jesus taught his followers to keep the law as God had commanded in order to enter the kingdom. Paul taught that keeping the law had nothing to do with entering the kingdom. For Paul, only the death and resurrection of Jesus mattered. The historical Jesus taught the law. Paul taught Jesus. Or, as some scholars have put it, already with Paul the religion *of* Jesus has become the religion *about* Jesus. (Although, as I have pointed out, Paul did not invent this new take on Jesus but inherited it.)

Later Christians pushed Paul's distinction even further. And so we have seen that Marcion insisted that Paul's distinction between law and Gospel was an absolute one. The law has nothing to do with the Gospel. The law was given by the God of the Jews to the Jewish people, and it leads only to their (and everyone else's) damnation. The Gospel came from the God of Jesus; it was the way of salvation, through Jesus' death, and brought deliverance from the wrathful God of the Old Testament. For Marcion there were literally two Gods, and the God of the law has nothing to do with the God of Jesus. The Old Testament belongs to the wrathful God of the Jews. It is a Jewish book and nothing more. It is not part of the Christian canon and is to be completely rejected.

Other Christian thinkers from around the time of Marcion took just the opposite view, which ironically led to even more virulent forms of anti-Judaism. A key example is the letter of Barnabas (see chapter 6). For Barnabas, the Old Testament is a Christian, not a Jewish, book. The Jews misunderstand its teachings, and always have. They are a hardhearted, ignorant, willful, and disobedient people, and have been since the days of Moses. According to Barnabas, the Jewish people broke the special covenant that God made with them as soon as it was given. When Moses smashed the first set of the Ten Commandments, that was the end of the Jews' covenant with God. God never restored the covenant to them. It was with the followers of Jesus that he made the "new covenant."

Barnabas tells his Christian readers in Letter of Barnabas, 4:6–7:

Watch yourselves now and do not become like some people by piling up your sins, saying that the covenant is both theirs [the Jews] and ours [the Christians]. For it is ours. But they permanently lost it . . . when Moses had just received it.

As a result, says Barnabas, the Jews have always misinterpreted their law, thinking that it was to be taken literally, including rules about what foods could or could not be eaten. These laws were never meant literally but as spiritual descriptions of how people were to live. The Jewish religion is built on a false understanding of the Jews' own law.

Barnabas has a remarkable ability to find Christ and the Christian message throughout the pages of the Old Testament. Just one example: He argues that circumcision, the sign of the covenant given to the father of the Jews, Abraham, was always misinterpreted by Jews as indicating that they were to cut off the foreskin of their baby boys. That was never what it was about. Instead, circumcision means that a person has to believe in the cross of Jesus. How does Barnabas prove his point? He notes that in the Old Testament, Abraham leads his army of 318 servants into battle, but prepares them for victory by first circumcising them (Genesis 14:14; 17:23). What, asks Barnabas, is the significance of the fact that there were 318 circumcised servants? It is a symbolic number.

Recall that ancient languages used letters of the alphabet for numerals: the symbol for the first Greek letter, alpha, was *1*; beta was *2*; gamma, *3*. (Barnabas is basing his interpretation on the Septuagint—the Greek translation of the Hebrew Bible.) The number 318 is made up of the Greek letters tau, iota, and eta. Barnabas points out that the tau, which looks like our letter *t*, is in the shape of the cross, and iota and eta are the first two letters in the name of Jesus. Circumcision is not about foreskins. It is about the Cross of Jesus.

What happens when a Christian author states that the Jews have never understood their own religion, and that the Old Testament is a Christian, not a Jewish, book? It is an obvious attempt to rob Judaism of all its validity. And that was Barnabas's goal. His book is anti-Jewish to the core.

As time went on, Christian anti-Judaism got worse and worse, as Christian authors began to accuse Jews of all sorts of villainous acts, not just of misinterpreting their own Scriptures. Some Christian authors argued that destruction of the city of Jerusalem, the heart of Judaism, by the Romans in 70 CE was God's judgment on the Jews for killing their own Messiah. Eventually Christian authors appeared on the scene who took the logic a step further. As Christians began to see Jesus himself as divine, some maintained that by being responsible for Jesus' death, Jews were in effect guilty of killing God.

This charge of deicide first occurs in the writings of a late-second-century author named Melito, who was bishop of the city of Sardis. A sermon that Melito preached at some unspecified Easter celebration was discovered in the mid-twentieth century. In Melito's church, Easter was celebrated at the time of the Jewish Passover, and so this sermon is called his Passover homily. In it he reflects on the Jews' guilt in killing Jesus, their own God, in rhetorically powerful but frightful language:

This one was murdered. And where was he murdered? In the very center of Jerusalem! Why? Because he had healed their lame and had cleansed their lepers, and had guided their blind with light, and had raised up their dead. For this reason he suffered. (chapter 72)

Why, O Israel, did you do this strange injustice? You dishonored the one who had honored you. You held in contempt the one who held you in esteem. You denied the one who publicly acknowledged you. You renounced the one who proclaimed you his own. You killed the one who made you to live. Why did you do this O Israel? (chapter 73)

It was necessary for him to suffer, yes, but not by you; it was necessary for him to be dishonored, but not by you; it was necessary for him to be judged, but not by you; it was necessary for him to be crucified, but not by you, not by your right hand, O Israel! (chapters 75–76)

Therefore, hear and tremble because of him for whom the earth trembled. The one who hung the earth in space is himself hanged; the one who fixed the heavens in place is himself impaled; the one who firmly fixed all things, is himself firmly fixed to the tree. The Lord is insulted, God has been murdered, the king of Israel has been destroyed by the hand of Israel. (chapters 95–96)

Explaining the Rise of Christian Anti-Judaism

How did it get to this point? How did the passionately Jewish religion of Jesus become the virulently anti-Jewish religion of his followers?

You can probably trace the logical progression of Christian anti-Judaism from the information provided in this chapter. A rift naturally occurred as soon as Christians insisted that Jesus was the Messiah, that the Messiah had to suffer for sins, that the death of the Messiah was the means by which God made people right with Him, that the law could play no role in the act of salvation, and that Jews therefore had either to believe in Jesus as the Messiah or be rejected by God. Believers in Jesus were right with God; everyone else, including faithful Jews, stood under God's curse. We find this view in Paul, but he didn't invent it; it was already being propounded before he came on the scene. It is no wonder that Paul, when he was still a non-Christian Jew, found the followers of Jesus so offensive.

The logic of this position more or less drove some Christians to say that by rejecting God's Messiah, Jews had rejected God. The natural corollary was that God had rejected them.

Christian thinkers could argue that the Jewish Scriptures themselves indicate that the Jewish people had been rejected by God. The Old Testament prophets repeatedly warn the ancient Israelites that since they have violated God's will and law, he is turning on them in judgment. Such prophets as Amos, Hosea, and Isaiah say that God has rejected his people because of how they have chosen to live. The early followers of Jesus latched on to this view and made it into a kind of general principle. The culmination of Jewish hardheartedness and willfulness was the rejection of their own Messiah. For God this was the last straw. No longer were the Jews the chosen people of God. They had been replaced by the followers of Jesus.

This was not because God had gone back on his word or his promises. The Jews themselves were at fault. We find some of this anti-Jewish sentiment already in the pages of the New Testament. Paul deals at length with the rejection of the Jews, although he thinks that all of Israel will eventually come to see the error of its ways, come to believe in Jesus, and be saved (Romans 9–11, especially 11:1–26). Other authors were not so sure. The Gospel of John blames "the Jews" in quite graphic terms for rejecting and killing Jesus (chapters 19–20); and in one frightful passage he actually indicates that the Jews are not the children of God but the children of the Devil (John 8:42–44). It's hard to be saved if Satan is your father.

Starting in the middle of the second century the vitriol becomes even more extreme. Christian authors such as Justin Martyr and

Tertullian wrote treatises directly meant to oppose the Jews and their religion. They argue that the Jews misunderstand the meaning of their own religion and their own law, that they don't recognize the prophecies referring to Jesus, that they reject their own Messiah sent from God and thus reject God himself. According to Justin the sign of circumcision was never meant to set the Jews apart as the people of God; it was meant to show who was worthy of persecution.[2] Such anti-Jewish tractates continue on long after the second century, becoming a steady diet for Christian readers down through the centuries.

It comes as a surprise to some readers to learn that this kind of anti-Judaism did not exist in the Roman, Greek, or any other world before the coming of Christianity and is therefore a Christian invention. To be sure, some Roman and Greek authors maligned the Jews for what seemed bizarre customs—mutilating the penises of their boys, refusing to eat pork, being so lazy as not to work on one day of the week (the Sabbath). But Roman and Greek authors maligned *everyone* who was not Greek or Roman, and the Jews were not singled out.[3] Until Christianity appeared. Then Judaism came to be seen not just as a set of odd and risible practices but as a religion that was perverse and corrupt. Jews were no longer simply strange. They were willful and evil. As a people they had rejected God, and in response he had rejected them.

These views may have seemed harmless enough in the days of Paul, Barnabas, Justin Martyr, Tertullian, and even Serapion. After all, Christianity in these times was a tiny religion in the context of a very large empire. Jews outnumbered Christians many times over, and Christians had no social or political power. In those days the rhetorical attacks against Jews did not lead to physical attacks.

All that changed as Christianity grew and eventually came to be adopted by none other than the Roman emperor, Constantine. When Constantine converted to Christianity, at the beginning of the fourth century, Christians already outnumbered Jews and were about 10 percent of the population of the Roman Empire. But unlike the

Jews, who never were persecuted as a people in the empire, Christians were still a persecuted minority.[4] All of that changed when Constantine converted. It became popular and fashionable to be a Christian. Conversions started occurring en masse. By the end of the fourth century, fully half of the empire would claim to be Christian, and the Roman emperor, Theodosius, proclaimed Christianity to be the empire's official religion.

This turn of affairs played a pivotal role in Jewish-Christian relations.[5] Since the early days of the church, antipathy toward Jews had been expressed at the rhetorical level; soon it became a matter of action. Roman officials who were now Christian took the rhetoric of their predecessors seriously, and saw the Jewish people literally as enemies of the truth who were to be punished for their rejection of Jesus. The official policies of the empire in the fourth century did not require the persecution of Jews, but people in power, such as Christian governors of Roman provinces, often looked the other way or privately condoned it. Synagogues were burned, properties were confiscated, and Jews were publicly mocked and sometimes subjected to mob violence.

And so we have one of the great ironies of the early Christian tradition. The profoundly Jewish religion of Jesus and his followers became the viciously anti-Jewish religion of later times, leading to the horrific persecutions of the Middle Ages and the pogroms and attempted genocides that have plagued the world down to recent times.[6] Anti-Semitism as it has come down to us today is the history of specifically Christian reactions to non-Christian Jews. It is one of the least savory inventions of the early church.

THE DIVINITY OF JESUS

When I was in college I had already for many years believed that Jesus was God, that this was and always has been one of the most central and fundamental tenets of the Christian tradition. But when I began studying the Bible seriously, in graduate school, I began to

realize that this was not the original belief of Jesus' earliest followers, nor of Jesus himself.

When Did Jesus Become the Son of God?

We have seen that the Gospels of the New Testament, three of which
do not call Jesus God, were written many years after Jesus lived
and died. There are other portions of the New Testament that were
written earlier. It has long been thought by scholars that some of the
speeches of the apostles in the book of Acts may represent views that
were popular among Jesus' early followers, years before Luke wrote
them down; in other words, parts of these speeches had been circu-
lating as part of the oral tradition in the decades before Luke wrote
his Gospel and Acts. In none of these speeches in Acts is Jesus spoken
of as divine. And it is striking that some of the speeches embody a
very primitive belief that it was specifically at the resurrection that
God bestowed a special status on Jesus. To the Christian storytellers,
who came up with these speeches long before Luke recorded them,
Jesus was a flesh-and-blood human being who was exalted to a special position when God raised him from the dead.

For example, consider Peter's speech on the day of Pentecost in
Acts 2. He speaks of "Jesus of Nazareth, a man attested to you by God
with deeds of power, wonders, and signs that God did through him."
Here Jesus is a human miracle worker, empowered by God but not
God himself. According to Peter in this passage, the Jewish people in
Jerusalem rejected Jesus and crucified him, but God raised him from
the dead. And then comes a key line, the climax of the speech:

> Therefore let the entire house of Israel know with certainty that God
> has made him both Lord and Messiah, this Jesus whom you crucified.
> (Acts 2:36)

Only after his death, at his resurrection, did God make Jesus Lord
and Messiah. A speech that Paul delivers in Acts 13 speaks of Jesus as

one who was rejected by the Jewish people of Jerusalem who "asked Pilate to have him killed." But God then "raised him from dead." Paul goes on to proclaim, in Acts 13:32–33, "the good news,"

> that what God had promised to the our ancestors he has fulfilled for us, their children, by raising Jesus; as also it is written in the second Psalm, "You are my Son; today I have begotten you."

At what point does Jesus come to be "begotten" as the Son of God? At his resurrection: "*Today* I have begotten you."

This appears to be the oldest form of the Christian faith. Jesus was a man who was empowered by God to do mighty things; he was rejected by the Jewish leaders and killed; but God vindicated him by raising him from the dead and giving him an exalted status.

It was not long before some followers of Jesus reasoned that he must have been the Son of God, not just after the resurrection but during his entire public ministry. It was no longer the resurrection that made Jesus God's son, but the baptism. Thus, in our earliest Gospel, Mark, right off the bat Jesus is baptized by John; coming up out of the waters he sees the heavens split apart and the Spirit descending upon him as a dove; and he then hears the voice from heaven, "You are my beloved Son, in whom I am well pleased" (Mark 1:11; there is no birth narrative in Mark).

For ancient Jews, being the "Son of God" did not mean being divine (see chapter 3). In the Old Testament, "son of God" can refer to a number of different kinds of individuals. The very human king of Israel was called the son of God (2 Samuel 7:14), and the nation of Israel was thought of as the son of God (Hosea 11:1). Being the son of God normally meant being the human intermediary for God on earth. The son of God stood in a special relationship with God, as the one God had chosen to do his will. In Mark, Jesus is the son of God because he is the one God has appointed as the Messiah, who is to die on the cross to bring about atonement as a human sacrifice. But there is not one word in this Gospel about Jesus actually being God.

Whereas the earliest Christians appear to have thought that Jesus became God's son at his resurrection (and also the Messiah and the Lord), as put forth in the speeches in Acts, others eventually came to think that he was already God's son at his baptism.

The progression of this idea does not stop there, however. Some years after Mark was written, the Gospel of Luke appeared; now Jesus is not merely the Son of God at the resurrection or starting with his baptism; he is the son of God for his entire life. And so, in Luke, unlike in Mark, we have an account of Jesus being born of a virgin. As we saw in an earlier chapter, Luke understands that it is at the point of his conception that Jesus becomes the son of God—literally, God impregnates Mary through his Spirit. Mary learns this from the angel Gabriel at the Annunciation:

> The Holy Spirit will come upon you, and the power of the Most High will overshadow you; therefore the child to be born from you will be holy; he will be called the Son of God. (Luke 1:35)

The "therefore" is very important in this sentence (one should always ask, what is the "therefore" there for?). It is because Mary conceives through the Holy Spirit of God that Jesus can be called the Son of God. This is the moment in which Christ comes into existence for Luke. He is the Son of God because God is literally his Father. As a result, he is the Son of God not only after the resurrection or for his public ministry but for his entire life.

The last of our Gospels to be written, John, pushes the Son-of-God-ship of Jesus back even further, into eternity past. John is our only Gospel that actually speaks of Jesus as divine. For John, Christ is not the Son of God because God raised him from the dead, adopted him at the baptism, or impregnated his mother: he is the Son of God because he existed with God in the very beginning, before the creation of the world, as the Word of God, before coming into this world as a human being (becoming "incarnate").

And so we have the exalted words of the opening of John's Gospel (John 1:1–14):

In the beginning was the Word, and the Word was with God, and the Word was God. He was in the beginning with God. All things came into being through him, and without him not one thing came into being. . . . And the Word became flesh and dwelt among us, and we have seen his glory, glory as of the Father's only Son, full of grace and truth.

This is the view that became the standard Christian doctrine, that Christ was the preexistent Word of God who became flesh. He both was with God in the beginning and was God, and it was through him that the universe was created. But this was not the original view held by the followers of Jesus. The idea that Jesus was divine was a later Christian invention, one found, among our Gospels, only in John.

The Divinity of Christ in John's Community

What led Christians to develop this view? The Gospel of John does not represent the view of one person, the unknown author of the Gospel, but rather a view that the author inherited through his oral tradition, just as the other Gospel writers record the traditions that they had heard, traditions in circulation in Christian circles for decades before they were written down. John's tradition is obviously unique, however, since in none of the other Gospels do we have such an exalted view of Christ. Where did this tradition come from?

Scholars have long puzzled over this question, and a kind of consensus has emerged among interpreters of the Gospel of John over the past twenty-five or thirty years. This is a view that was developed by two giants of New Testament interpretation at the end of the twentieth century, one a Protestant and the other a Roman Catholic, both of them teaching at Union Theological Seminary in New York. J. Louis Martyn and Raymond Brown both argued that the exalted Christology in John's Gospel derives from changes in the understanding of Christ that occurred within John's Christian community, prior to his writing his Gospel. These changes were affected by the social experiences of the community.[7]

The theory behind this view is that every community—whether a family unit, a close-knit town, a fraternity or sorority, a civic organization, or a church—has traditions that it tells about itself in order to help constitute itself as a community. Communities have stories in common. And the way it tells its stories is related to the things that happen to it as a community.

Take a simple example. Suppose that in your family there was one real troublemaker, your younger brother. He was always getting into trouble and making mischief. Twenty years later, when you tell the stories of what he was like as a kid, the stories are always molded by what happened afterward. Suppose Tommy grew up to be a successful investment banker, the pride and joy of the family. When you tell the stories about him as a young brat, it is always with a smile on your face—"Ah, Tommy. He was always in trouble, that kid. You remember that time . . . ?" But suppose things turned out differently. What if Tommy grew up to be an ax murderer? Now you might tell the very same stories very differently, with tears in your eyes. "Tommy, Tommy. We never could control that kid; he was always trouble. You remember that time . . . ?"

The way you tell your community's traditions reflects the events that have happened in the meantime. Suppose you have a set of traditions from a certain community that are told a certain way, but you don't have any other access to what happened in that community historically? In theory you could take the way they tell their stories and work backward to figure out what has happened to lead them to tell the stories the way they do. That's what Louis Martin and Raymond Brown did with the traditions in the Gospel of John. They reconstructed the history of John's community as a way of explaining why they told the stories about Jesus as they did.

What is striking in John is that some of the stories about Jesus, such as the one in the very opening passage (1:1–18), have a highly exalted view of him as divine (called a "high Christology"), and other passages speak of Christ in very human terms, not at all as divine but rather as a human being chosen by God to fulfill his purposes on earth (a "low Christology"; see, for example, John 1:35–52). Why do you have both of these views in the Gospel of John? You might think it is because John understands Jesus as both human and divine. But what is striking is that some passages speak of Jesus one way, and others speak of him in the other way. Martyn and Brown argued that the passages that speak of Jesus in human terms (the low Christology) were the oldest traditions embodied in the Gospel, and the passages that speak of Jesus in exalted terms (the high Christology) were ones that developed later, as experiences in the community led the Johannine Christians to start thinking of Jesus as someone who was not of this world but of the world of God.

There isn't space to go into all the details here, but I can say that Martyn and Brown showed what these experiences were. John's community appears to have started out as a Jewish sect within the Jewish synagogue that accepted Jesus as the Jewish Messiah. Because of this belief they were eventually forced to leave the synagogue, and they started their own community as believers in Jesus. But they had to explain this to themselves: Why have we been rejected? Why do our families and friends not see the truth about Jesus? Why don't they understand him?

Drawing on their knowledge of how new communities are formed, Martyn and Brown argued that this new community came to believe that it alone had the truth and that the others could not see it. Why? Because this truth came from heaven, and those outside the community were thinking only in earthly terms. Jesus, who was the truth, himself came from heaven, and since those who stand in error are earthly they cannot recognize the one who comes from above. Only John's community has the truth. The others are in error. Only John's community stands in the light. The others live in darkness. Only John's community recognizes the one who comes from above. The others can see only what happens here below.

The community started thinking of Jesus in more exalted terms to explain their own rejection by the synagogue. They began to argue that to be right with God, one needed to accept this one who had come from God. One needed to have a new birth, a birth "from above." Those outside the community were dead and would never have life. They were not the children of God; they were the children of the Devil.

As the community developed its views, Jesus became more and more exalted. Eventually, when the Gospel was written, the author incorporated a range of traditions that had been in circulation among them, both those that were their original views, in which Jesus was fully human, and those that came later, in which he was himself divine. And thus there developed the view that Jesus was God.

Other Paths to the Same Destination

The path that John's community took to arrive at the view that Jesus was divine was not the same as other communities who arrived at the same place. Here I can give only a very brief sense of how it might have worked in one community or another.

As we have seen, early on there were traditions about Jesus that referred to him as the Son of God. This idea would mean different things to different groups. Some Jews who came to believe in him would have thought that like King David and some other great men of God, Jesus was intimately related to God; he was the man through whom God worked and who mediated his will on earth. But what would the same idea mean to pagans who converted to believe in Jesus? In pagan mythologies there were lots of people thought to be sons of God. These people were believed to be half human and half divine because they had one mortal parent and one immortal one. These groups would make comparisons between Jesus and their pagan traditions. Examples include the Greek demigod Heracles (the Roman Hercules; compare Luke's version of Jesus' birth). These semidivine figures were often thought capable of great miracles (compare the Gospel stories of Jesus' ministry), and at the end of their lives they went to live with the gods in heaven (compare the story of Jesus' ascension). Anyone who came into the Christian faith with this understanding of what it meant to be the son of God could easily have thought of Jesus as a semidivine being, not like the traditional "Jewish" son of God, who was completely human.

Another path to seeing Jesus' divinity starts not with the idea of Jesus as the Son of God but with Jesus as the Son of Man. Jesus himself spoke of the coming of the Son of Man, a cosmic judge of the earth who would bring judgment in his wake, based on his understanding of Daniel 7:13–14. Once his followers came to believe that Jesus was raised from the dead, however, they thought that he himself would be the one who would come from heaven to sit in judgment on the earth. This is Paul's view, expressed in 1 Thessalonians 4–5. Paul was writing to gentiles, not to Jews, and so he does not use the title Son of Man. But that is how he understood Jesus: as the future judge to come from heaven. If the Son of Man was a kind of divine figure, and Jesus was the Son of Man, that makes him a divine figure who lives with God.

Or consider a third way. During Jesus' life his followers thought of him as their master and called him lord, as slaves called their masters, or employees called their employers. After his followers came to believe in his resurrection, however, the term "lord" took on a different connotation. God had given Jesus an exalted status. He was the ruler—not an earthly ruler but a heavenly ruler. He had been made "the Lord." Soon Christians thought that he was the Lord of all, ruling from heaven. But who could rule from heaven but a divine figure? Moreover, early Christians realized that it is God himself who is called the Lord in the Old Testament. They came to think that Jesus had been exalted to a divine status. And soon they reasoned that if he was divine, he must have existed before he appeared on earth.

This view is already found in our earliest author, Paul, who speaks of Jesus as the one who was with God before he came into the world and who had a level of equality with God; but he chose instead to come into the world to suffer death for the sake of others, after which God exalted him again, brought him to heaven, and "gave him the name that is above every name, that at the name of Jesus every knee should bow." In the Old Testament it is only to God that every knee shall bow (Isaiah 45:23). Now it is to Jesus as well (Philippians 2:6–11).

The view of Jesus as divine did not develop in every early Christian community at the same time or in the same way. For centuries there continued to be some communities that did not hold to this view, such as the Ebionites. In some communities the view came into being remarkably early (evidently in Paul's). In others there is no evidence that it happened at all (Matthew or Mark's). In others it took several decades (John's). But by the second and third centuries it became quite a common doctrine as these various communities exchanged views. Jesus was not simply the Jewish son of God whom God had exalted at his resurrection. He was himself God. This was one of the most enduring theological creations of the early Christian church.

THE DOCTRINE OF THE TRINITY

The belief in the divinity of Jesus created an obvious problem for early Christian theologians who wanted to reject the pagan notion that there are many gods, and stay within the firm monotheistic tradition of Judaism. As the Jewish Scriptures indicate,

> Thus says the LORD, the King of Israel . . .
> I am the first and I am the last;
> besides me there is no God. (Isaiah 44:6)

But what were Christians holding to the divinity of Christ to think? If Christ is God and God is God, are there not two Gods?

How Many Gods? Some of the Responses

As is true of all the theological questions of the early Christians, there was a range of answers to this question. The Jewish-Christian Ebionites were adamant on this point: since there can be only one God, Christ is not God. For Christ to be God, there would be two Gods. To the Ebionites, Jesus is the Messiah (in Jewish circles the Messiah was *never* thought to be God), the man God had chosen to fulfill his will on earth by dying for sins. He was therefore special before God, adopted by God to be his son. But he was a man from first and last, not at all divine.

The Marcionites took the opposite view: Jesus was not human at all, precisely because he was God. God cannot be a human any more than a human can be a rock. Divinity and humanity are two different things, not to be confused. But the Marcionites evidently did not think that Jesus and God the Father were two different Gods. Instead, the two different Gods were the God of the Jews, the wrathful God of the Old Testament, and the God of Jesus, the God of love and mercy. It is hard to know how Jesus related to this latter God, since none of the church fathers who quote Marcion's writings ever spell the matter out. But in some places it appears that Jesus may have been thought of as God himself, come to earth.

The various groups of Gnostics had no difficulty in declaring that Christ was a divine being. For them there were lots of divine beings, and Christ was one of them. The God who declared that he alone was God and "there is no other" (Isaiah 45:18) was not the true God. He was the lower, inferior divinity who created the world. Far above this jealous and ignorant divinity was the higher divine realm in which all the divine beings dwelt.

All of these alternative approaches to the problem were eventually rejected as heretical. But how then was one to deal with the problem? If one wanted to remain monotheistic, as the proto-orthodox clearly wanted to do, and yet insist on the deity of Christ, as they also wanted to do, how was it possible without compromising one view or the other?

Two Hetero-Orthodox Solutions

In the history of scholarship on early Christianity, orthodoxy (the "right belief") is sometimes set against "heterodoxy" (meaning "a different belief"). Using this parlance, heterodoxy is the same as heresy. Of course, as noted, everyone considers themselves orthodox—everyone thinks they are right. People who think their beliefs are wrong change what they believe in order to believe the right beliefs. Or, as one wag has put it, orthodoxy is my doxy and heterodoxy is your doxy.

As early Christianity developed there were various attempts to explain how Jesus can be divine if there is only one God. Most of these attempts, while acceptable in some times and places, eventually came to be ruled out of court. For some proto-orthodox thinkers they were perfectly acceptable, for others they were heretical. So I've invented a term for them: "hetero-orthodox" solutions. The two best known are Patripassianism (as it was called by its opponents) and Arianism.

Patripassianism

From the writings of such church fathers of the second and third centuries as Hippolytus and Tertullian, we know that at one time the most popular view among Christian thinkers and church leaders was one that self-consciously and aggressively asserted the oneness of God. This view held that there was only one God and that Jesus is the incarnation of God here on earth. In other words, God the Father and God the Son are not two separate entities. God the Son is God the Father when the latter becomes incarnate.

This view goes under a number of names in the history of theology. Sometimes it is called modalism, since it teaches that the one God has different modes of existence. To illustrate: I am a son in relationship to my father, a father in relationship to my son, and a husband in relationship to my wife. I'm not three people but one person, defined differently in my different relationships. God was the creator of all things and he became a human; he was not two Gods but one God.

Sometimes this view is known as Sabellianism, named after Sabellius, a particularly notorious but historically rather unimportant person who eventually was excommunicated for holding this opinion. And sometimes it is given the derisive term invented by the heresy hunter Tertullian to encapsulate its view: Patripassianism—a term that literally means "the Father suffers." Tertullian mocked the view because it maintained that it was God the Father himself who died on the Cross, in the form of the son.

Tertullian tells us that in his own day, the end of the second century, this view was endorsed by two of the bishops of Rome (two of the early popes) along with most of the Roman church. It was in response to this view that Tertullian and others like him started developing the idea that God the Father is a different person from God the Son. They are both God, but nonetheless there is only one God. How can that be? Ultimately it is a mystery. But this was to become the orthodox teaching, with refinements and serious tweakings after Tertullian's day. Christ is God, and so is God the Father; but the two are one.

Moreover, since Jesus in the Gospel of John speaks of the Holy Spirit coming to earth as "another Advocate" (John 14:16) after he returns to heaven, the Spirit also is God. He, too, is not the same as God the Father or God the Son. And so there is a "triune" God. Three persons, one God.

This might sound all very confusing, but Tertullian is adamant on the point. In his attack on the Patripassianists, he especially wants to insist that God the Father and God the Son and God the Spirit are distinct. As he says:

The Father is one, and the Son is one, and the Spirit is one; . . . they are distinct from one another. . . . the Father is not the same as the Son, since they differ one from the other in the mode of their being. (Tertullian, *Against Praxeas*, 9)

He continues with what strikes many people today as impeccable reasoning:

A father must have a son, in order to be a father; so likewise a son, to be a son, must have a father. It is, however, one thing to have, and another thing to be. For instance, in order to be a husband, I must have a wife; I can never myself be my own wife. (*Against Praxeas*, 10)

He then throws down the gauntlet to the Patripassianists, with the kind of satirical wit that he became famous for:

If you want me to believe him to be both the Father and Son, show me some other passages where it is declared, 'The Lord said to himself, "I am my own Son, today have I begotten myself." (*Against Praxeas*, 11)

And yet Tertullian wants to insist that even though the three persons of the godhead are distinct, they are not different in substance. All are God. And so he speaks of "the unity of the trinity" and argues that they differ "on the ground of personality, not of substance—in the way of distinction, not of division. . . . I hold one only substance in their coherent and inseparable [persons]" (*Against Praxeas*, 12).

With the passing of time, these kinds of nuanced distinctions become increasingly technical. But already, in response to the modalists of his day, Tertullian had begun to speak of a trinity, one God manifest in three different persons.

Arianism

In some passages of Tertullian, however, it becomes clear that even though he thinks the Father is God and the Son is God, and that there is only one God, there is nonetheless a kind of hierarchy. The Father is greater than the Son, even though they are of the same substance. Otherwise he wouldn't be the Father.

For well over a century theologians continued to debate this question of the relationship of the Father to the Son. This was at the heart of the debate generated in the early fourth century by Arius, a famous Christian teacher in Alexandria, Egypt, a leading center of theological reflection. By the time of Arius, the proto-orthodox Christians had for the most part succeeded in wiping out, or at least completely marginalizing, such early Christian heresies as the Ebionites, the Marcionites, and the various groups of Gnostics. Just about everyone in the Christian church at large agreed that Jesus was himself divine, but that there was only one God. But how exactly did it work? How could they both be God?

Arius had a very simple solution for which he could claim considerable support from the New Testament and from earlier Christian thinkers: Christ was a divine being, but he was subordinate in power and essence to God the Father. Originally there was only one God, but in eternity past, God begat a second divine being, his son, Christ. Christ was the one through whom God created the universe, and it was Christ who became human at the incarnation.

In this view there was a time in eternity past before which Christ did not exist. He came into being at some point. And even though he was divine, he was not equal to God the Father; since he was the Son, he was subordinate to God the Father. They were not "of the same substance"; they were in some ways "similar" in substance.[8]

This view was exceedingly popular in its day, but a number of Christian theologians took exception to it. The best-known opponent was a young deacon in the church of Alexandria, Athanasius, whom we met in connection with the New Testament canon, in chapter 6. Athanasius and others like him argued that Christ was of the very same substance as God the Father, that they were complete equals, and that there never was a time when Christ did not exist.

This may seem like a bit of nitpicking to modern people, but at the time it was an enormous dispute between the Arians and those who were opposed to them. Much of the Christian Church was divided over the issue of whether Jesus was of the same substance as the

Father—the Greek term was *homoousias* ("same substance"). Or was he only of "similar substance," *homoiousias?* As later historians pointed out, this appears to be a debate over the letter *i*. But that letter packed a significant punch it its day. The church was split over it.

All of this mattered in part because the Roman emperor Constantine had converted to Christianity and wanted to use this new religion to help unify his fractured empire. A split religion could not bring unity. The religion had to be united first. And so the emperor called a meeting in Nicaea of the most important Christian bishops in the empire, in order to debate the issues and to make a judgment to be binding on all Christians. This was the famous Council of Nicaea of the year 325 CE.

In the end the council voted for Athanasius's position. Contrary to what is sometimes said, it was nearly a unanimous decision, not a close vote. Still, even after that day the debates continued, and for a while in the fourth century it looked as though the Arians were going to emerge victorious after all. But eventually the orthodox position was that of Athanasius. There are three persons in the Godhead. They are distinct from each other. But each one is equally God. All three are eternal beings. And they all are of the same substance. This, then, is the doctrine of the Trinity.

It is quite a development from anything found in the New Testament, where there is no explicit statement of anything of the sort. Not even in a document like the Gospel of John, where Jesus is thought of as divine, is there any discussion of three being one in substance. As you might expect, later scribes of the New Testament found this lack disturbing, and so in one place at least they inserted an explicit reference to the Trinity (1 John 5:7–8).[9] The Trinity is a later Christian invention, which was based, in the arguments of Athanasius and others, on passages of Scripture but which does not actually appear in any of the books of the New Testament.

Within three hundred years Jesus went from being a Jewish apocalyptic prophet to being God himself, a member of the Trinity. Early Christianity is nothing if not remarkable.

HEAVEN AND HELL

In some corners of Christendom today, especially the ones that I was at one time associated with, the religion is all about the afterlife. On the very personal level, people are eager to experience the joys of heaven and to avoid the fires of hell. Most Christians I meet today believe that when you die, your soul goes to one place or the other.

I've never quite figured out all the inconsistencies of this view. On the one hand, the afterlife of the soul sounds like some kind disembodied existence, since your body stays in the grave; on the other hand, people think that there will be physical pleasure or pain in the afterlife, and that you'll be able to recognize your grandparents. That would require having a body.

The earliest Christians, starting with Jesus, did not believe in that sort of heaven and hell, as a place that your soul goes when you die. This, too, is a later Christian invention.

The Early Apocalyptic Views of the Afterlife

Scholars have widely argued that Jesus and his followers were Jewish apocalypticists. The apocalyptic view started to develop, well over a century before Jesus, as a way to deal with the problem of theodicy, or "God's justice." (They didn't use that term; it was coined in the seventeenth century by the German philosopher Leibniz.) The problem of theodicy is to explain how God can be seen as just, considering the state of pain and misery in the world. Given the amount of suffering that people experience, how can one believe that a good and loving God is in charge?

The apocalyptic view of ancient Judaism did not address this problem in modern philosophical terms, but the concerns of those who adapted this view were very similar. Beginning centuries earlier there had been thinkers in Israel who maintained that the people of God had experienced such hardship as a people and individually because they had sinned against God and God was punishing them for it. This is sometimes called the prophetic view because it is the perspective found on page after page of the prophets of the Old Testament.[10]

But what happens when people do what the prophets urge, when they return to the ways of God, stop behaving in ways contrary to his laws, begin to live in the manner that he requires, and yet they continue to suffer? The prophetic view can make sense of the suffering of the wicked: they are getting what they deserve. But it cannot make sense of the suffering of the righteous. Why do the wicked prosper but the righteous suffer?

There were different responses to that question among ancient Israelites, including the response, or rather responses, found most famously in the book of Job.[11] The apocalyptic worldview takes a different tack. For apocalypticists, suffering is only a temporary state of affairs. For some mysterious reason God has relinquished control of this world to cosmic forces of evil that are wreaking havoc upon it. But soon, in the near future, God will intervene in history and make right all that is wrong. He will overthrow the forces of evil, disband the wicked kingdoms that they support, and bring in a new kingdom, here on earth, a kingdom of peace and justice. The wicked rulers of this world and all who side with them will be destroyed, and the poor and the oppressed will rule supreme.

This view is first found in the Bible in the Old Testament book of Daniel, which was the last of the Hebrew Bible books to be written, sometime in the middle of the second century BCE. It is a view found in a number of Jewish writings produced in the centuries after Daniel, including some of the Dead Sea Scrolls. And it is a view found on the lips of Jesus.

Included in this view was the notion that at the end of this age, when God finally intervened, there would be a resurrection of the dead. Belief in the resurrection was directly related to the concerns of ancient theodicy. How is it that people have sided with God and been tortured and murdered as a result? Where is God in all this?

And how is it that other people have sided with the powers of evil, grown rich and powerful as a result, and died and gotten away with it? Where is justice?

For apocalypticists there would be justice. Not in this life or this age, but in the resurrection, in the age to come. God would raise all people from the dead, bodily, to give them an eternal reward or an eternal punishment. No one would escape. Evil would not have the last word; God would have the last word. And death would not be the end of the story.

So taught the early Jewish apocalypticists, and so taught Jesus. The Kingdom of God was soon to appear with the coming of the Son of Man. People needed to prepare for it by mending their ways and siding with God, even though it meant suffering in this age. But a new age was coming in which God and his ways would rule supreme, in the Kingdom of God to come, here on this earth. All would eventually be made right with this world, and everyone would be brought back to life, bodily, to see and experience it.

This was also the teaching of the apostle Paul and, so far as we can tell, of all the earliest Christians. One key difference between Paul and Jesus is that Paul believed that Jesus himself would bring this kingdom when he returned in glory (1 Thessalonians 4–5). Moreover, for Paul the resurrection at the end of the age has already in some sense begun. That is one reason Jesus' resurrection was so significant for Paul. Since the resurrection is to occur at the end of the age, and since Jesus has already been raised, that shows we are living at the end of the age. That is why Paul speaks of living in the end times.

But what happens to a person who dies *before* the end of the age? Paul evidently came to believe that there is some kind of interim existence with Christ for those who die before the return of Jesus. That's why he told the Philippians, "For me to live is Christ, and to die is gain" (1:21). He evidently believed that believers in Jesus would have some kind of temporary body given them in heaven, but this was a purely temporary arrangement. When Christ returned in glory, the "dead in Christ will rise first," and then all those still living, Paul among them, would be gloriously transformed, so that their bodies would be made immortal (1 Thessalonians 4:13–18; 1 Corinthians 15:50–57). They would then live eternally, here on earth.

Thus, for Jesus, Paul, and the earliest Christians, eternal life was a life lived in the body, not above in heaven but down here where we are now. Paul emphasizes this point strenuously in the book of 1 Corinthians. The fact that Jesus' body was raised from the dead shows what the future resurrection would involve: bodies being raised physically from the dead and transformed into immortal bodies. Paul scoffed at his opponents in Corinth for thinking they had already experienced a spiritual resurrection, so that they were enjoying the full benefits of salvation now, in the spirit. The resurrection was physical, and since it was physical, it obviously had not happened yet. This world is still carrying on under the forces of evil, and only at the end will all be resolved and the followers of Jesus be vindicated, transformed, and given an eternal reward.

This is also the view of the Apocalypse of John. After all the catastrophes that hit this planet at the end of time—catastrophes that the author revels in telling, in chapter after gory chapter—"a new heavens and a new earth" will appear. There will be a future resurrection of all who died; there will be a new, heavenly Jerusalem that descends from the sky to replace the old, corrupt, and now destroyed Jerusalem as the City of God. It will have gates of pearl and streets of gold. And that is where the saints will live forever, here on earth (see Revelation 21).

The Transformation of the Apocalyptic Vision

What happens when this expected end doesn't happen? What happens when the apocalyptic scenario that Jesus expected to occur in "this generation" never comes? When Paul's expectation that he will be alive at the second coming of Christ is radically disconfirmed by his own death? When the resurrection of the dead is delayed interminably, making a mockery of the widespread belief that it will happen "soon"?

One thing that happens, of course, is that some people begin to mock. That is the problem addressed in the last book of the New Testament, 2 Peter, whose author insists that when God says that it will all happen very soon, he means by the divine calendar, not the human. And one needs always to remember that "with the Lord, a day is as a thousand years and a thousand years as one day" (2 Peter 3:8). Following this logic, if the end is supposed to come next Tuesday, it could be a Tuesday four thousand years from now.

When the end does not come, people who want to remain faithful to the original vision of Jesus and his disciples have to grapple seriously with the fact that an essential element of that vision appears to have been wrong. Of course the faithful would not claim that Jesus was wrong. More likely, he was misunderstood. And so there begins a long and significant process of reinterpretation, in which the original message comes to be transformed into a less tactile, less tangible, less easily disconfirmed view. Specifically, the teaching of a future resurrection of the body, in which the righteous will be rewarded and the wicked punished here on earth, gets transmuted into a message of heaven and hell, where judgment comes not at the end of the age but at the end of one's life. Your soul goes to one place or the other.

I suggested in chapter 5 that Jesus' message—like that of other apocalypticists—can be understood as a kind of horizontal dualism between this age here on earth and the age to come, also here on earth. I call it a horizontal dualism because it can be imagined as a horizontal time line divided into half. At the end of this age, which is imminent, there will be a judgment and we will enter into the new age, on the other side of the dividing line.

When the end never came, Christian thinkers reconceptualized this time line and in a sense rotated it on its axis, so that now the "end" involves not a horizontal dualism but a vertical one. Now it is not a matter of two ages, this one and the one to come, but of two spheres, this world and the world above. No longer is the physical resurrection discussed or even believed. Now what matters is this world of suffering below and a world of ecstasy in heaven above.

This duality works itself out in a doctrine of heaven and hell. Why above and why below? Because the dualism remains in place, but has become spatial rather than temporal. Above is where God dwells, and that is where your soul will go when you die if you have sided with God and believed in his Christ; below is where God decidedly does not dwell. In that place there is only evil: the Devil and his wicked demons. That is where your soul will go for eternal punishment if you have refused to side with God and rejected his Christ.

This view of the eternal and bodiless existence of the soul is not found in the earliest Christian writings, but only in writings that appeared later. For example, it is set forth in the Apocalypse of Peter (discussed in chapter 6). In that text, Peter is given a guided tour of the realms of the blessed and the damned. Souls are in ecstasy in the world above while others are in torment in the world below. The text envisions eternal life not as a bodily existence to be lived here on earth after the resurrection, but as a spiritual existence in which your soul is destined for one place or another after you die. It is an eternal spiritual existence with eternal rewards or punishments, depending on how you have lived your life and whether you have accepted the salvation of God.

In short, with the passing of time, the apocalyptic notion of the resurrection of the body becomes transformed into the doctrine of the immortality of the soul. What emerges is the belief in heaven and hell, a belief not found in the teachings of Jesus or Paul, but one invented in later times by Christians who realized that the kingdom of God never would come to this earth. This belief became a standard Christian teaching, world without end.

CONCLUSION

What we might think of as traditional Christianity did not simply drop from the sky, full grown and fully developed, soon after the ministry of Jesus. Nor did it emerge directly and simply from his teachings. In many ways, what became Christianity represents a series of rather important departures from the teachings of Jesus. Christianity, as has long been recognized by critical historians, is the religion *about* Jesus, not the religion *of* Jesus.

All of the aspects of traditional Christianity that I have considered in this chapter can be thought of as creations of the early church. When some scholars look at these developments they see strong lines of continuity with what came before in the teachings of Jesus. Christian theologians may detect the hand of God at work behind all these developments. Other scholars are more impressed by the discontinuities, and are struck by how each of these "orthodox" Christian views emerged less as necessary consequences from the teachings of Jesus and his early followers than as doctrines that developed largely because of historical and cultural factors that influenced later Christians. These later views eventually became widespread and even "commonsensical" in subsequent periods of the church (whether or not there was a God involved in the process).

Whether one stresses the continuities or the discontinuities in the development of early Christianity, it is clear that the beliefs and perspectives that emerged among Jesus' later followers were different from the religion of Jesus himself. Paul was not the only one responsible for this set of theological innovations, this invention of what we think of as Christianity. He may not even bear the greatest responsibility among those who transformed the religion of Jesus into the religion about Jesus. There were numerous Christians involved in these transformations, the vast majority of them lost in the mists of antiquity, unnamed Christians thinkers and preachers who reinterpreted the traditions of Jesus for their own

time, whose reinterpretations were guided and molded by historical and cultural forces that we, living later, can sometimes only
surmise and ponder.

Christianity as we have come to know it did not, in any event,
spring into being overnight. It emerged over a long period of time,
through a period of struggles, debates, and conflicts over competing
views, doctrines, perspectives, canons, and rules. The ultimate emergence of the Christian religion represents a human invention—in
terms of its historical and cultural significance, arguably the greatest invention in the history of Western civilization.[12]

Is Faith Possible?

On the final day of my undergraduate course on the New Testament, I give my students a writing assignment. All semester we have been taking the historical-critical approach to the New Testament, discussing its many different perspectives on key theological issues, its historical problems, its internal discrepancies, the fact that many of its books were written by people who were not who they claimed to be, and so on. My students, most of whom come from conservative Christian backgrounds, have had a range of personal reactions to this material. But for the entire semester I have kept their noses to the grindstone, teaching the historical approach to early Christianity instead of the devotional approach that most of them were raised on.

At the end of the term I want them to reflect on what they have been doing and to say what they really think about it all. And so I ask them to write a two-page response to an intentionally provocative question, drawn from a hypothetical discussion. Here are my instructions:

You're talking to someone about religion and, as sometimes happens, she turns on the steam. "Look," she says, "the New Testament is full of contradictions; we can't know what the man Jesus actually did; the apostle Paul turned Jesus' simple preaching of the coming Kingdom into a complicated theological system of sin, judgment, and redemption; and most of the NT writers actually believed that the end was coming in their own lifetime. This book is misogynist and anti-Semitic and homophobic and has been used to justify all sorts of horrendous acts of suppression over the ages: just listen to some of the televangelists! This is a dangerous book!"

How do you respond?

Our final discussion of the semester is based on what the students write. Their responses, as you might imagine, are extraordinarily broad-ranging. A few students will argue that everything this woman says is flat-out wrong: that there are no contradictions in the Bible, that Paul and Jesus were preaching exactly the same thing, and so on. Not many students will argue this (though they certainly would have done so at the beginning of the semester), because they have seen the evidence and they know that there are historical problems with the New Testament.

Other students will take just the opposite view, and argue that the woman is right up and down the line, that the Bible is so much a product of its own time that it has done more harm than good, leading people to act in hateful ways in advancing their own personal agendas and ideologies.

Other students will agree with a lot of what the woman says, but will argue that the Bible is still a book that for them is inspired and that contains important guidelines for how they should live their lives. Most of these students do not think that the Bible is inerrant or that it can be somehow taken from its first-century context and plopped down into our own context as if we shared the worldviews and perspectives of the different authors. And they will acknowledge that different parts of the Bible have different (even contradictory) things to say on important topics. Their view is that one needs to evaluate these different biblical messages and see which ones are particularly germane to their own situations, as American Christians living in the twenty-first century, not Palestinian Jews, say, living in the first.

Students are often surprised to learn that I am completely sympathetic to this final point of view. The goal of my class is not to attack the Bible or to destroy the students' faith. One of my goals is to get them to think about issues that many of them care deeply about and that ultimately matter.

Historical Criticism and Faith

So, too, with this book. Some readers will find it surprising that I do not see the material in the preceding chapters as an attack on Christianity or an agnostic's attempt to show that faith, even Christian faith, is meaningless and absurd. That is not what I think, and it is not what I have been trying to accomplish.

I have been trying, instead, to make serious scholarship on the Bible and earliest Christianity accessible and available to people who may be interested in the New Testament but who, for one reason or another, have never heard what scholars have long known and thought about it.

One of my subsidiary purposes has been to point out that none of the information presented here is news to scholars or their students, many of whom have attended top-level seminaries and divinity schools throughout North America and Western Europe. The historical-critical approach to the New Testament is taught in all these schools. To be sure, different scholars and teachers will disagree with me on one point or another—on whether a particular view of Luke stands at odds with the view of Mark, whether the Gospel of John contains a historically accurate datum at one point or another, whether Paul should be seen as the author of 2 Thessalonians or not, and so on. But the basic views that I've sketched here are widely known, widely taught, and widely accepted among New Testament scholars and their students, including the students who graduate from seminaries and go on to pastor churches. Why do these students so rarely teach their congregations this information, but insist instead on approaching the Bible devotionally rather than historical-critically, not just in the pulpit (where a devotional approach would be expected) but also in their adult education classes? That has been one of my leading questions since I started writing this book.

Some pastors, of course, do try to convey their historical-critical knowledge of the Bible to members of their congregations—often with mixed results. Some parishioners are eager to learn all they can about what scholars are saying about the Bible, and others simply don't want to hear about it, perhaps because it is too complicated or, even more likely, too threatening to their faith.

But my sense is that most pastors get the strong impression from their parishioners that examining historical-critical material is not a priority in light of other pressing concerns facing the congregation. Or, simply, pastors don't know where to begin. Possibly this is because of the way they themselves were trained in seminary, where they learned the Bible in their biblical studies courses, their theology in their theological courses, and their pastoral duties in their pastoral courses—without ever having any classes that showed how these areas should be closely related to one another. In particular, most prospective pastors never learn in seminary how the historical-critical approach taught in one course can be of any relevance to the theology they are taught in another.[1] That's a pity, because historical criticism can have serious theological payoffs, and these should be embraced and proclaimed.

Or perhaps pastors are afraid that if the person in the pew learns what scholars have said about the Bible, it will lead to a crisis of faith, or even the loss of faith. My personal view is that a historical-critical approach to the Bible does not necessarily lead to agnosticism or atheism. It can in fact lead to a more intelligent and thoughtful faith—certainly more intelligent and thoughtful than an approach to the Bible that overlooks all of the problems that historical critics have discovered over the years.

This view may come as a surprise to some of my readers, who know that I myself have gone from evangelical Christianity to agnosticism. It is true that historical criticism did more or less shatter my evangelical views of the Bible. But it did not lead me to become an agnostic. Something else was responsible for that, years after I had given up an evangelical understanding of the Bible: my inability to understand how a good and loving God could be in control of this world given the miserable lives that most people—even believers— are forced to endure here.

My views of the Bible as the inerrant Word of God changed years earlier, and for completely different reasons. As soon as I came fully to grips with the reality that we don't have the actual inspired words of God in the Bible—since we no longer have the originals, and in some places don't know what the originals said—it opened the door to the possibility that the Bible is a very human book.[2] This allowed me to study it from a historical-critical perspective. And doing so led to all the results we have seen in this book.

- I came to see that there were flat-out discrepancies among the books of the New Testament. Sometimes these discrepancies could be reconciled if one worked hard enough at it with pious imagination; other times the discrepancies could not, in my judgment, be reconciled, however fanciful the explanation (Jesus dies on different days in Mark and John).

- I further came to see that these differences related not just to small details here and there. Sometimes different authors had completely different understandings of important issues: Was Jesus in doubt and despair on the way to the cross (Mark) or calm and in control (Luke)? Did Jesus' death provide an atonement for sin (Mark and Paul) or not (Luke)? Did Jesus perform signs to prove who he was (John) or did he refuse to do so (Matthew)? Must Jesus' followers keep the law if they are to enter the Kingdom (Matthew) or absolutely not (Paul)?

- In addition, I came to see that many of the books of the New Testament were not written by the people to whom they are attributed (Matthew and John) or by the people who claimed to be writing them (2 Peter, 1 Timothy). Most of these books appeared to have been written after the apostles themselves were dead; only eight of the twenty-seven books are almost certain to have been written by the people traditionally thought to be their authors.

- The Gospels for the most part do not provide disinterested factual information about Jesus, but contain stories that had been in oral circulation for decades before being written down. This makes it very difficult to know what Jesus actually said, did, and experienced. Scholars have devised ways to get around these problems, but the reality is that the Jesus portrayed in the Gospels (for example, the divine being become human in the Gospel of John) represents a later understanding of who Jesus was, not a historical account of who he really was.

- There were lots of other Gospels available to the early Christians, as well as epistles, Acts, and apocalypses. Many of these claimed to be written by apostles, and on the surface such claims are no more or less plausible than the claims of the books that eventually came to make up the New Testament. This raises the question of who made the decisions about which books to include, and of what grounds they had for making the decisions. Is it possible that nonapostolic books were let into the canon by church leaders who simply didn't know any better? Is it possible that books that should have been included were left out?

- The creation of the Christian canon was not the only invention of the early Church. A whole range of theological perspectives came into existence, not during the life of Jesus or even through the teachings of his original apostles but later, as the Christian church grew and came to be transformed into a new

religion rather than a sect of Judaism. These include some
of the most important Christian doctrines, such as that of a
suffering Messiah, the divinity of Christ, the Trinity, and the
existence of heaven and hell.

And so, just as I came to see the Bible as a very human book, I
came to see Christianity as a very human religion.[5] It did not descend from on high. It was created, down here on earth, among the
followers of Jesus in the decades and centuries after his death. But
none of this made me an agnostic.

History and Myth

You might think that someone who came to realize that Christianity was a human creation would decide to opt out of the Christian
faith, quit the Church, and start doing something else with his
Sunday mornings. But it didn't work that way for me, and it hasn't
worked that way for lots and lots of other scholars like me, who
started out as strong evangelicals, came to realize the persuasive-
ness of the historical-critical perspectives on the New Testament,
but continued in one way or another to be people of faith. Some of
my closest friends teach in divinity schools and seminaries, training Christian pastors. And they agree up and down the line with
most of what I've said in these chapters. A number of them use my
textbook on the New Testament for their introductory courses, a
book that spells out many of the views discussed here.

In my case, when I came to realize that Christianity was a human
creation, I felt the need to evaluate what I thought about its claims.
And I came to think that they resonated with me extremely well—
with how I looked at the world and thought about my place in it.
I came to think of the Christian message about God, Christ, and
the salvation he brings as a kind of religious "myth," or group of
myths—a set of stories, views, and perspectives that are both un-
proven and unprovable, but also un-disprovable—that could, and
should, inform and guide my life and thinking.

I continued to believe in a literal God, though I was less and less sure what could actually be said about him (or her or it). And I continued to believe that Jesus himself certainly existed. But the religion built up around God and Jesus was based, I came to believe, on various myths, not historical facts. Jesus' death was not a myth, but the idea that it was a death that brought about salvation was a myth. It could not be historically proved or disproved, but it was a powerful story that I thought could and should govern the way I look at the world and live my life. The death of Jesus was, for me, an act of self-giving love. According to this myth, Jesus was willing to live, and die, for the sake of others. This was an idea that I found to be both noble and ennobling. I believed that his example of self-sacrifice made Christ a being worthy of worship, and I felt that his was an example for me to emulate. This was not because I could prove his self-sacrifice as a historical fact but because I could resonate with it personally.

The resurrection of Jesus was not a historical event that could be proved or disproved, since historians are not able, by the nature of their craft, to demonstrate the occurrence of a miracle. It was a bold mythical statement about God and the world. This world is not all there is. There is life beyond this world. And the horrible actions of humans, such as crucifying an innocent man, are not the end of the story. Evil does not have the last word; God has the last word. And death is not final. God triumphs over all, including death itself.

Salvation, for me, became less and less a question of whether I would go to heaven or hell when I die. I came to realize that these concepts were also, in a sense, myths. There is not literally a place of eternal torment where God, or the demons doing his will, will torture poor souls for 30 trillion years (as just the beginning) for sins they committed for thirty years. What kind of never-dying eternal divine Nazi would a God like that be? Heaven meant having a right standing before God and being assured that at the end, when we die, we will in some sense be united with Him. We therefore have nothing to fear in death. Hell was not a literal place of torment, but an alienation from God that kept one from ever having true peace.

God himself was a kind of myth for me. I certainly thought he existed, but his existence could not be proved or disproved. He was the force of goodness and awe and wonder in the world. He was the one who was above all else, far beyond what we could imagine, as we gaze out into the evening sky and consider the billions of stars and the billions of galaxies. He was above and beyond it all, a force of good and goodness in the world.

It would take a book to describe my theology as it developed at the time. My point here is that I came to think that the historical-critical approach to the New Testament had not destroyed my faith; it had deepened my faith and made me more sophisticated in the way I thought and talked about God, his world, his Christ, and his salvation. Yes, this way of thinking about the world was human-made. But what kind of thinking is *not* human-made? We are humans! Of course we will think like humans. No one can think any other way—not even people (some of them reading this now) who claim that they think the thoughts of God as God has revealed them. Even that notion is a human idea—an idea that people have because it was handed down by other people living before them, since the time that a person made it up.

Leaving the Faith

And so I did not leave the Christian faith because of the inherent problems of faith per se, or because I came to realize that the Bible was a human book, or that Christianity was a human religion. All that is true—but it was not what dismantled my acceptance of the Christian myth. I left the faith for what I took to be (and still take to be) an unrelated reason: the problem of suffering in the world.

There came a time in my life when I found that the myths no longer made sense to me, no longer resonated with me, no longer informed the way I looked at the world. I came to a place where I could no longer see how—even if viewed mythically—the central Christian beliefs were in any sense "true" for me, given the oppressive and powerful reality of human suffering in the world. That is the subject of another book.[4] For here it is enough to say that it was because of this particular shift in my thinking (not because of my historical-critical views of the Bible) that I left the church. Most of my friends have not done so. Almost all of these friends are academics who agree with me when it comes to the historical understanding of the Bible and the Christian faith. But for them the myths still work and resonate with them. These friends find a kind of solace and power in their faith. They appreciate the rich historical heritage given to them by the centuries of Christian thinkers and theologians. They are passionate about the Christian hymns and Christian liturgies and services of worship. They believe that truth is much deeper than what you can say, historically, about the Bible or the development of the Christian religion in the first four centuries.

Even now, as I type these words, I'm on a beach holiday with two of my closest, most intimate friends, two people whom I love dearly and who would do anything for me, and I for them. As it turns out, they are both smarter than I, better read than I, more sophisticated philosophically than I (we can't all be intellectual superstars). They both would have, and do have, no problem with the historical information I have laid out in this book. And they both unashamedly call themselves Christian. Ask them if they believe in God, they would say yes. Think Christ is God? Yes. Think he is the Lord? Yes. Faith is not a matter of smarts.

The Theological Value of Historical Criticism

It is my firmly held view that a historical understanding of the Bible does not necessarily lead to the kind of agnosticism that I myself have adopted. This will strike a lot of people as so obvious that they won't understand why I even need to say it. I feel compelled to say it is because there are a lot of other people—especially evangelical Christians—for whom this would be news.

At the same time, I would like to insist that those who continue to remain in the faith should not discount the theological importance of the historical approach to the New Testament. In fact, rather than acting as if historical criticism is irrelevant to faith, scholars, teachers, and their students should explore more fully the theological significance of historical criticism. Let me give just two examples, one obvious and the other less so.

The obvious example is a negative one: if the findings of historical criticism are right, then some kinds of theological claims are certainly to be judged as inadequate and wrong-headed. It would be impossible, I should think, to argue that the Bible is a unified whole, inerrant in all its parts, inspired by God in every way. It can't be that. There are too many divergences, discrepancies, contradictions; too many alternative ways of looking at the same issue, alternatives that often are at odds with one another. The Bible is not a unity, it is a massive plurality. God did not write the Bible, people did. Many of these people were inspired in the sense that they wrote works that can inspire others to think great and important thoughts and to do great and important deeds. But they were not inspired in the sense that God somehow guided them to write what they wrote.

The less obvious example is the positive flip side of the preceding one. There are many views in the Bible. Each of these views was written in a specific historical and cultural context and was completely shaped by the context within which it was written. None of these views can be removed from its original context, plopped down into a different context, such as twenty-first-century America, and be expected to communicate an inerrant revelation to us today. But since there are so many different messages in the Bible, often about the same subject, the reader of the Bible can evaluate the appropriateness of this message or that, and see what relevance it may have for life in the present. Some messages will be more appropriate for certain contexts than others. And readers of the Bible should not be afraid to proclaim one message instead of another.[5]

I hope that everyone will agree that Jesus' teaching as it relates to children ("Let the little children come unto me") provides a more useful guide than the teaching of Psalm 137 ("Blessed is he who takes your little ones and dashes them against the rocks"). Similarly, some biblical views of women are superior to others. And so the apostle Paul's attitude about women is that they could be and should be leaders of the Christian communities—as evidenced by the fact that in his own communities there were women who were church organizers, deacons, and even apostles (Romans 16). That attitude is much better than the one inserted by a later scribe into Paul's letter of 1 Corinthians, which claims women should always be silent in the church (1 Corinthians 14:35–36), or the one forged under Paul's name in the letter of 1 Timothy, which insists that women remain silent, submissive, and pregnant (1 Timothy 2:11–15).

In thinking about which parts of the Bible have something to say in the modern context, it is important to recall the historical view that the biblical authors were all living in a different world from ours and reflected the assumptions and beliefs of people in their world. Their world, to pick a particularly cogent example, had no concept of what we think of as homosexuality. To put it differently, homosexuality didn't exist in that world. Why? Not because men didn't have sex with men (they did) or women with women (they did), but because there was no sense of sexual orientation in that world, or any world, until the notion of sexual orientation developed among Western thinkers in the nineteenth and twentieth centuries. As a result, the very assumptions that lie behind the apostle Paul's denigration of same-sex relations are very different from the assumptions that people in the modern world have about themselves as sexual beings. You cannot very well take Paul's instructions on same-sex relations, remove them from the assumptions that Paul had about sex and gender, and transplant them onto a different set of assumptions.

This is true for everything found in the Bible. It was written in a different world, a different context. The idea that "Jesus is coming back" is built on the idea that above us, in the sky, over the clouds, is a space where God lives, and that Jesus has gone up there to live with Him. He ascended bodily and he is coming, bodily, back down. No one any longer thinks that above the clouds is a place where God and Jesus live. Above the clouds is more of the atmosphere, and above that is space, and beyond that are billions of stars—and that's just our own galaxy. If the very notion that Jesus is coming back down assumes that there is an "up"—what does one do with that idea in a universe such as ours where there is, literally, no up and down, except in relation to where you happen to be standing at the moment? You obviously need to translate the idea into some kind of modern idiom for it to make sense. Or, put another way, you need to remythologize the myth of Jesus' return. Otherwise you are forced to accept not only the idea that Jesus is coming back but the cosmology on which it is based.

So, too, with all the Bible's teachings—about women, about same-sex relations, about extra-marital sex, about capital punishment, about war, about wealth, about slavery, about disease, about . . . well, about everything.

Some people may think that it is a dangerous attitude to take toward the Bible, to pick and choose what you want to accept and throw everything else out. My view is that everyone already picks and chooses what they want to accept in the Bible.[6] The most egregious instances of this can be found among people who claim not to be picking and choosing. I have a young friend whose evangelical parents were upset because she wanted to get a tattoo, since the Bible, after all, condemns tattoos. In the same book, Leviticus, the Bible also condemns wearing clothing made of two different kinds of fabric and eating pork. And it indicates that children who disobey their parents are to be stoned to death. Why insist on the biblical teaching about tattoos but not about dress shirts, pork chops, and stoning?

In my opinion, people need to use their intelligence to evaluate what they find to be true and untrue in the Bible. This is how we need to live life generally. Everything we hear and see we need to evaluate—whether the inspiring writings of the Bible or the inspiring writings of Shakespeare, Dostoevsky, or George Eliot, of Ghandi, Desmond Tutu, or the Dalai Lama.

Then Why Study the Bible?

Probably the one question I get asked more than any other, by people who know that I am an agnostic scholar of the New Testament, is why I continue to study and teach the New Testament if I no longer believe in it?

This is a question that has never made much sense to me. The Bible is the most important book in the history of Western civilization. It is the most widely purchased, the most thoroughly studied, the most highly revered, and the most completely misunderstood book—ever! Why wouldn't I want to study it?

I have friends who teach medieval English. They don't believe in Chaucer, but they think Chaucer is important, and so they spend their lives studying and teaching and writing about Chaucer. The same is true of my friends who teach the classics—Homer, Sophocles, Euripides, Plato, Aristotle, Seneca, Livy, Martial, and Plautus. These are all important authors whose works all deserve the devotion of a scholar's life, irrespective of whatever the scholar's personal beliefs happen to be. The same goes for my friends who study and teach Shakespeare, John Donne, Charles Dickens, or T. S. Eliot.

And it's the same with scholarship devoted to the Bible. The only difference with the Bible is that so many people in our world actually believe in the Bible. I do not belittle anyone who continues to cherish the Bible as an inspired text, but in addition to reading the Bible devotionally there is a value in reading it historically. To be sure, a historical reading can show many of the shortcomings of the Bible—discrepancies, contradictions, faulty claims, impossible statements, and harmful ideologies. But a historical reading can open up entirely new vistas in our understanding of the Bible and its multifarious messages.

Furthermore, even those of us who do not believe in the Bible can still learn from it. It is a book that deserves to be read and studied, not just as a document of faith but also as a historical record of the thoughts, beliefs, experiences, activities, loves, hates, prejudices, and opinions of people who stand at the very foundation of our civilization and culture. It can help us think about the big issues of life—why we are here, what we should be doing, what will become of this world. It can inspire us—and warn us—by its examples. It can urge us to pursue truth, to fight oppression, to work for justice, to insist on peace. It can motivate us to live life more fully while yet we can. It can encourage us to live more for others and not only for ourselves. There will never be a time in the history of the human race when such lessons will have become passé, when the thoughts of important religious thinkers of the past will be irrelevant for those of us living, and thinking, in the present.

Notes

CHAPTER 1: A HISTORICAL ASSAULT ON FAITH

1. From the way John 4:54 gets translated, some readers have been confused into thinking that it refers only to the second sign performed in Galilee; a more appropriate translation is that this is Jesus' second sign, one that he performed after coming from Jerusalem to Galilee.

2. I certainly do not think that pastors should preach the results of historical criticism from the pulpit in their weekly sermons (although I think sermons should definitely be rooted and based on sound scholarship). But there are numerous opportunities in churches, outside the weekly sermon, for pastors to teach their parishioners what scholars have long said about the Bible. And in most churches this simply is never done.

CHAPTER 2: A WORLD OF CONTRADICTIONS

1. A very useful tool for students of the Bible is a Bible Synopsis, in which the stories of the Gospels are literally placed in parallel columns next to each other, for easy comparison. Many professors have a Bible Synopsis as a required textbook for their classes on the New Testament. One of the most popular is edited by Kurt Aland, *Synopsis of the Four Gospels* (Peabody, MA: Hendrickson, 2006).

2. It is the lead example that I provide in my college-level textbook on the New Testament, *The New Testament: A Historical Introduction to the Early Christian Writings*, 4th ed. (New York: Oxford University Press, 2008), pp. 262–65.

3. See the discussion on pp. 144–45.

4. In this Gospel, the Passover day coincided with the Sabbath, so that here too he is crucified on a Friday.

5. Some scholars have argued that John's account is more historically probable than Mark's, since otherwise Jesus' trial before the Jewish authorities would have had to take place on the day of the Passover festival, in violation of (later?) Jewish law. If this is right, then Mark would have changed the date, possibly in order to portray Jesus' last meal as a foreshadowing of the Christian practice of the Lord's Supper. Most scholars are not persuaded by this view, however, and think that John, writing

some thirty years after Mark, is more likely to be the one responsible for changing the date.

6. Unlike modern engagements, ancient Jewish espousals required a divorce to be terminated.

7. Some scholars have tried to resolve the contradiction by invoking the complicated rules of "levirate marriage," where a man marries his brother's wife after his brother had died. This solution does not, in fact, solve the problems of the different genealogies, as demonstrated in the authoritative account of Raymond Brown, *The Birth of the Messiah: A Commentary on the Infancy Narratives of Matthew and Luke* (Garden City, NJ: Doubleday, 1977), vol. 1, pp. 503–04.

8. If you read the 1 Chronicles passage, bear in mind that Uzziah is called Azariah in this book, as can be seen by comparing 2 Kings 14:21 with 2 Chronicles 26:1.

9. See my discussion in *Misquoting Jesus: The Story Behind Who Changed the Bible and Why* (San Francisco: HarperSanFrancisco, 2005), pp. 158–61.

10. The first three Gospels are called the Synoptic Gospels because they have so many stories in common that they can be placed in parallel columns and "seen together"— the literal meaning of "synoptic."

11. Most biblical scholars are convinced that Luke and Acts were written by the same person; read Luke 1:1–4 and Acts 1:1–5 and you'll see why.

12. The reasons for thinking that Mark himself did not write the last twelve verses are so compelling that most modern Bible translations include them in brackets with a footnote indicating that they are not the original ending. For one thing, they are not found in our oldest and best manuscripts. Also, these verses are in a writing style and use vocabulary not found elsewhere in Mark. Furthermore, the transition from verse 8 to verse 9 does not make sense when read in the Greek. For a fuller discussion, see my *Misquoting Jesus: The Story Behind Who Changed the Bible and Why* (San Francisco: HarperSanFrancisco, 2005), pp. 65–68.

13. For a discussion of some of these methods, see chapters 6–11 in my *The New Testament: A Historical Introduction to the Early Christian Writings*, 4th ed. (New York: Oxford University Press, 2008).

CHAPTER 3: A MASS OF VARIANT VIEWS

1. Of course when trying to understand these different points of view we need to engage in the work of interpretation. Contrary to what some people assume, texts don't speak for themselves. They must be interpreted. And this can never be done "objectively," as if we, the readers, were robots; texts are interpreted subjectively by humans. From a historical-critical perspective, though, each author of the New Testament should be read and interpreted on his own terms, without having some *other* author's terms imposed on him.

2. Some scribes copying Luke took out this prayer, evidently because they did not like its implication that Jesus wanted the Jews to be forgiven for having him crucified. For further discussion of this issue see pp. 188–89.

3. You can see this yourself by reading Isaiah 7 and 8: Isaiah is making the point that before a child who is soon to be conceived is born and gets very old, the enemies of the people of Israel will disperse and no longer trouble them.

4. See the discussion of the passage in the commentary by Raymond Brown, *The Gospel According to John* (Garden City, NJ: Doubleday, 1966), vol. 1.

5. See the discussion on p. 155.
6. My interpretation of Paul has been heavily influenced by E. P. Sanders; see his now classic book *Paul and Palestinian Judaism: A Comparison of Patterns of Religion* (Minneapolis: Augsburg Fortress Press, 1977). For other ways of reading Paul found among other historical critics see John Gager, *Reinventing Paul* (New York: Oxford, 2002), and Stanley Stowers, *A Rereading of Romans: Justice, Jews, and Gentiles* (New Haven: Yale University Press, 1997).
7. In Paul's view, doing good deeds will naturally occur in the wake of one's coming to be in a right standing before God (being justified); but good deeds do not contribute to attaining that right standing.
8. Some scholars have seen an exception in Acts 20:28, but I think this is a misreading of the verse. For a full discussion see my book *The Orthodox Corruption of Scripture: The Effect of Early Christological Controversies on the Text of the New Testament* (New York: Oxford University Press, 1993), p. 203. The other possible exception, Luke 22:19–20, is a scribal addition to the text, not original to Luke; see ibid., pp. 197–209.
9. On this being the original wording of the text, see ibid., pp. 62–67.

CHAPTER 4: WHO WROTE THE BIBLE?

1. Some critics of one of my earlier books, on the problem of suffering, wryly suggested that the title "God's Problem" should instead be entitled "God's Problem According to Bart Ehrman"—but obviously that's not what I myself would call the book!
2. We also have relatively full Acts of Andrew, Peter, Thomas, and Paul—these, too, are interesting for seeing what legends sprang up, but they are of little use historically. For a nice collection of these texts, see J. K. Elliott, *The Apocryphal New Testament* (New York: Oxford University Press, 1993).
3. On literacy in the ancient world, see William Harris, *Ancient Literacy* (Cambridge, MA: Harvard University Press, 1989); for literacy specifically among Palestinian Jews, see Catherine Hezser, *Jewish Literacy in Roman Palestine* (Tübingen: Mohr-Siebeck, 2001).
4. To cite one well-known example of this ignorance of Jewish customs: Mark 7:3 indicates that the Pharisees "and all the Jews" washed their hands before eating, so as to observe "the tradition of the elders." This is not true: most Jews did not engage in this ritual. If Mark had been a Jew, or even a gentile living in Palestine, he certainly would have known this.
5. The Gospels were written much earlier: Mark, possibly around 70 CE, Matthew and Luke, around 80 to 85; John, around 90 or 95.
6. The church historian Eusebius calls Papias "a man of very small intelligence" (Eusebius, *Church History* 3.39).
7. This is a consensus view among scholars today. For one thing, Matthew used Mark as a source for many of his stories, copying out the Greek word for word in some passages. If our Matthew was a Greek translation of a Hebrew original, it would not be possible to explain the verbatim agreement of Matthew with Mark in the Greek itself.
8. Depending on whether this is information that he heard directly from "the elder" or from a "companion" of one of the elders.
9. Another tradition in Papias that no one thinks is historically accurate: he writes that Judas, after the betrayal, bloated up, becoming so fat that he couldn't walk down the

street because not even his head could fit between the buildings, until eventually he more or less exploded and died. It's a terrific story, but not one that anyone believes.

10. The reason for thinking that "Luke" was Paul's traveling companion is that in four passages of Acts, the author uses the first-person plural "we." These "we passages" (e.g., Acts 16:10–16) have been taken to suggest that the author was with Paul for these particular incidents. Other scholars have noted, however, that the passages begin and end remarkably abruptly. Moreover, the author never says anything like "I then joined Paul and we did this or that." Why the abruptness? It is now widely thought that the author was not Paul's companion but that one of his sources was some kind of travel diary that he uncovered in his research and that used the first-person plural.

11. See the discussion on p. 134.

12. I earlier indicated that Revelation was one of the eight books certainly written under the name of its actual author because it doesn't claim to be by John the son of Zebedee. Many later Christians who accepted it as part of the canon thought it was by a different John, known as John the Elder. This puts the book of Revelation in a different category from the book of James, which was accepted as canonical precisely because it was thought to be written by Jesus' brother.

13. This is widely claimed among New Testament scholars writing commentaries on such books as the Pastoral Epistles; experts in ancient literary forgery have long known that the claim is bogus. See the works cited in note 14. For a very accessible discussion by a conservative scholar, see Terry L. Wilder, *Pseudonymity, the New Testament, and Deception: An Inquiry into Intention and Reception* (Lanham, MD: University Press of America, 2004).

14. The only thorough discussion of virtually all the relevant data is Wolfgang Speyer, *Die literarische Fälschung im heidnischen und christlichen Altertum* (Munich: C. H. Beck, 1971). But a fascinating account of some aspects of the problem can be found in Anthony Grafton, *Forgers and Critics: Creativity and Duplicity in Western Scholarship* (Princeton: Princeton University Press, 1990).

15. This book can be found in Elliott, *Apocryphal New Testament*, pp. 379–82.

16. A good translation, with introduction, is provided by John Collins in *The Old Testament Pseudepigrapha*, ed. James H. Charlesworth (New York: Doubleday, 1983), vol. 1, pp. 317–472.

17. Two recent refutations of the idea that the neo-Pythagoreans engaged in forgery for this reason are given by Jeremy N. Duff, "Reconsideration of Pseudepigraphy in Early Christianity" (Ph.D. dissertation, University of Oxford, 1998) and Armin Baum, *Pseudepigraphie und literarische Fälschung im frühen Christentum* (Tübingen: Mohr-Siebeck, 2001).

18. Tertullian, *On Baptism*, 17. "The Acts of Paul and Thecla" can be found in Elliott, *Apocryphal New Testament*, pp. 364–74.

19. This anecdote can be found in Diogenes Laertius, *Lives of the Philosophers* 5, 92–93.

20. The one that survives can be found in Elliott, *New Testament Apocrypha*, p. 546.

21. See Elliott, *Apocryphal New Testament*, pp. 68–83.

22. This book is also sometimes called the Gospel of Nicodemus. See Elliott, *Apocryphal New Testament*, pp. 169–85.

23. For more detailed explanations of the standard scholarly views see my textbook, *The New Testament: A Historical Introduction*, chapter 24, which also provides bibliography of other scholarly works.

24. See the discussion by Victor Paul Furnish in *Anchor Bible Dictionary*, ed. D. N. Freedman (New York: Doubleday, 1992), vol. 2, s.v. "Ephesians, Epistle to the," pp. 535–42.
25. In Philippians 1:1 Paul does mention bishops (plural) and deacons, but he does not tell us what these people did or in what sense, if any, they may have been in leadership roles in the church.

CHAPTER 5: LIAR, LUNATIC, OR LORD? FINDING THE HISTORICAL JESUS

1. It is sometimes thought that the historian Suetonius also makes reference to Jesus. When discussing the expulsion of the Jews from Rome under the reign of Claudius, some twenty years after Jesus' death, Suetonius writes that it occurred because of riots that had been "instigated by Chrestus." Some scholars have argued that this is a misspelling of the name Christ, and that Jews in Rome were in an uproar over the claims of Christians that Jesus was the Messiah. This is a possibility, but even if it is true it once again does not provide us with any concrete historical information about Jesus' life. The other possibility is that Suetonius means what he says, and that the riots were started by a man named Chrestus.
2. For a full discussion of this text and the others mentioned in this section, see John Meier, *A Marginal Jew: Rethinking the Historical Jesus* (New York: Doubleday, 1991), vol. 1.
3. See Galatians 4:4; Romans 15:7; 1 Corinthians 9:5; Galatians 1:19; 1 Corinthians 15:5; 1 Corinthians 11:22–25; 1 Corinthians 7:10–11; and 1 Corinthians 9:14.
4. For more information, see my *New Testament: A Historical Introduction*, chapter 7.
5. Some scholars think that the noncanonical Gospel of Thomas, with its 114 sayings of Jesus, most of which are not found in the New Testament, may also preserve some authentic traditions from the life of Jesus.
6. First published in 1906, it is still very much worth reading (New York: Macmillan, 1978).
7. On the meaning and nature of Jewish apocalyptic thought, see pp. 77–79.
8. This is argued persuasively by E. P. Sanders in his classic study, *Jesus and Judaism* (Philadelphia: Fortress Press, 1985).
9. Outstanding exceptions are the publications by the Jesus Seminar and several of its members, including Marcus Borg, *Meeting Jesus Again for the First Time* (San Francisco: HarperSanFrancisco, 1994), and John Dominic Crossan, *The Historical Jesus: The Life of a Mediterranean Jewish Peasant* (San Francisco: HarperSanFrancisco, 1994).
10. See Dale Allison, *Resurrecting Jesus: The Earliest Christian Tradition and Its Interpreters* (London: T. & T. Clark, 2005).

CHAPTER 6: HOW WE GOT THE BIBLE

1. Many theologians maintain that God was at work behind the entire process to ensure that it worked out in the long run. In that case it is a mystery why the process was not clearer, smoother, and faster (we are talking about God, after all).
2. See my *Misquoting Jesus: The Story Behind Who Changed the Bible and Why* (San Francisco: HarperSanFrancisco, 2005).
3. Two of the more intelligent critiques on the web are by Daniel Wallace, "The Gospel According to Bart," at http://www.bible.org/page.php?page_id=4000, and Ben

Witherington, "Misanalyzing Text Criticism—Bart Ehrman's 'Misquoting Jesus,'" at http://benwitherington.blogspot.com/2006/03/misanalyzing-text-criticism-bart. html. In addition, three books were published in response from conservative perspectives: Dillon Burroughs, *Misquotes in Misquoting Jesus: Why You Can Still Believe* (Ann Arbor: Nimble Books, 2006); Timothy Paul Jones, *Misquoting Truth: A Guide to the Fallacies in Bart Ehrman's Misquoting Jesus* (Downer's Grove, IL: Intervarsity Press, 2007); and Nicholas Perrin, *Lost in Transmission: What We Can Know About the Words of Jesus* (New York: Thomas Nelson, 2008).

4. I have never, in print or in an interview, indicated that I lost my Christian faith because of textual variants in the manuscript tradition of the New Testament. As I explain in chapter 8 (and discuss in my book *God's Problem,* HarperOne, 2008), it was the problem of suffering that eventually led me to become an agnostic.

5. Later Christian theologians found another reference to the Trinity in Matthew 28:19–20: the "name of the Father, Son, and Holy Spirit." Certainly all three members of what was to become the Trinity are mentioned there, and I do not think this is a case where scribes added the reference to the text later: it is in all of our manuscripts. But the critical relationship of the three is not indicated, and that is the key point: here there is no word of the three each being a separate divine person and the three together being the one triune God.

6. Some theologians differentiate between books that are inspired by God and books that are part of the canon; for them, the canonical books are inspired and other books may be as well.

7. The word "canon" comes from the Greek *kanon,* which means straight edge or a measuring stick. It came to refer to any recognized collection of texts.

8. Some scholars no longer see the term "Gnosticism" as informative, useful, or accurate for describing these groups; see Michael Williams, *Rethinking Gnosticism: An Argument for Dismantling a Dubious Category* (Princeton: Princeton University Press, 1996), and Karen King, *What is Gnosticism?* (Cambridge, MA: Harvard University Press, 2003).

9. Like the other Nag Hammadi documents, the Gospel of Thomas was originally written in Greek; what we have now is a later Coptic translation.

10. For a further discussion, see my book *Lost Christianities: The Battles for Scripture and the Faiths We Never Knew* (New York: Oxford University Press, 2003), chapter 3.

11. See, for example, sayings 3, 11, 22, 28, 29, 37, and 56; see also my discussion in *The New Testament: A Historical Introduction to the Early Christian Writings,* 4th ed. (New York: Oxford University Press, 2008), pp. 208–13.

12. See the discussion in Bruce M. Metzger, *The Canon of the New Testament: Its Origin, Development, and Significance* (Oxford: Clarendon Press, 1987), pp. 191–201.

13. This has been disputed by a few scholars, including Mark Hahnemann, *The Muratorian Fragment and the Development of the Canon* (Oxford: Clarendon Press, 1992), who dates the list to the fourth century.

14. Bauer chose not to include a discussion of the books of the New Testament in his analysis, in part because many of them are impossible to locate geographically.

15. See my discussion in *The Orthodox Corruption of Scripture: The Effect of Early Christological Controversies on the Text of the New Testament* (New York: Oxford University Press, 1993), chapter 1.

16. Over the past century, copies of New Testament books have been found, but there is no way of knowing whether these were proto-orthodox copies. For example, the Gnostics made extensive use of the Gospel of John, and so it is impossible to tell whether an early fragment of John discovered in Egypt was used by a proto-orthodox church or a Gnostic one.

17. For translations and discussions of all these texts, see James Robinson, *The Nag Hammadi Library in English,* 4th ed. (Leiden: E. J. Brill, 1996); Charles Hedrick and Paul Mirecki, *The Gospel of the Savior: A New Ancient Gospel* (Santa Rosa, CA: Polebridge Press, 1999); and Rodolphe Kasser, Marvin Meyer, and Gregor Wurst, *The Gospel of Judas,* 2nd ed. (Washington, DC: National Geographic Society, 2008).

18. As just one example, the head of the Christian training school in Alexandria during Athanasius's lifetime, a scholar called Didymus the Blind, had a larger, more inclusive canon than Athanasius.

CHAPTER 7: WHO INVENTED CHRISTIANITY?

1. Some expected a priest who would deliver the authoritative interpretation of God's law. Among the Jews in the Dead Sea Scrolls community there was an expectation that there would be two Messiahs, one a priest and the other, possibly, a king like David. See John Collins, *The Scepter and the Star: The Messiahs of the Dead Sea Scrolls and Other Ancient Literature* (New York: Doubleday, 1995).

2. See Justin's *Dialogue with Trypho,* translated by Thomas Falls, 2nd ed. (Washington, DC: Catholic University of America Press, 2003).

3. The authoritative source for Greek and Roman attitudes toward Jews and Judaism is Menahem Stern, *Greek and Latin Authors on Jews and Judaism,* 3 vols. (Jerusalem: Israel Academy of Sciences and Humanities, 1974–85).

4. The Roman responses to the Jewish uprisings in Palestine in 66–73 CE and 132–35 CE—the first of which led to the destruction of the Temple and the second to the expulsion of the Jews from the land—should not be seen as persecutions against the Jews for being Jewish. These were politico-military responses to political uprisings. Jews elsewhere in the empire were not targeted.

5. See especially James Carroll, *Constantine's Sword: The Church and the Jews* (Boston: Houghton Mifflin, 2001).

6. I am not saying that Christianity is to blame for the Holocaust. I am saying that if it had not been for Christianity, the history of the Jewish people would have been completely different. The hatred of the Jews that came down through the history of Western Europe and that led to the Holocaust originated in Christian circles. There are a large number of books written about the early relations of Jews and Christians; three that have become classics in the field are Marcel Simon, *Verus Israel: A Study of the Relations Between Christians and Jews in the Roman Empire, 135–425,* 2nd ed. (New York: Oxford University Press, 1986); Rosemary Ruether, *Faith and Fratricide: The Theological Roots of Anti-Semitism* (New York: Seabury Press, 1974); and John Gager, *The Origins of Anti-Semitism: Attitudes Toward Judaism in Pagan and Christian Antiquity* (New York: Oxford University Press, 1983).

7. J. Louis Martyn, *History and Theology in the Fourth Gospel* (New York: Harper & Row, 1968), and Raymond Brown, *The Community of the Beloved Disciple* (New York: Paulist Press, 1979).

8. For an accessible discussion of the Arian controversy, see Richard Rubenstein, *When Jesus Became God: The Epic Fight over Christ's Divinity in the Last Days of Rome* (New York: Harcourt Brace, 1999).

9. See my discussion in *Misquoting Jesus: The Story Behind Who Changed the Bible and Why* (San Francisco: HarperSanFrancisco, 2005), pp. 80–82.

10. See my book *God's Problem: How the Bible Fails to Answer Our Most Important Question—Why We Suffer* (San Francisco: HarperOne, 2008), chapter 2.

11. See ibid., chapter 6.

12. To call Christianity an invention is not to make a claim as to whether it should be thought of as true or not. Einstein's General Theory of Relativity was an invention (no one had come up with it before), but a theory is right or not irrespective of the person who first came up with it and the social, cultural, and intellectual processes that led him to do so.

CHAPTER 8: IS FAITH POSSIBLE?

1. See especially the recent book by Dale Martin, *Pedagogy of the Bible: An Analysis and Proposal* (Louisville: Westminster John Knox Press, 2008).

2. For years I left open the possibility that it could *also* be a very divine book.

3. See the preceding note.

4. See *God's Problem*.

5. I am not claiming that the message of any book of the Bible is self-interpreting and that its meaning is somehow obvious on a simple reading—that somehow the meaning inheres in the words of the texts. Texts don't tell us their meaning. They have to be interpreted, and they are always interpreted by living, breathing human beings with loves, hates, biases, prejudices, worldviews, fears, hopes, and everything else that makes us human. All of these factors affect how texts are interpreted, and they explain why intelligent people can have such radically different interpretations of the same text. Even so, some texts, interpreted according to standard practices that we use to interpret, are more obviously relevant and germane to our human condition today than others.

6. Even, that is, after they have engaged in the difficult act of interpretation. See the preceding note.